Entity Information Life Cycle for Big Data

D1232720

Entity Information Life Cycle for Big Data
Master Data Management and Information Integration

John R. Talburt

Yinle Zhou

AMSTERDAM • BOSTON • HEIDELBERG • LONDON
NEW YORK • OXFORD • PARIS • SAN DIEGO
SAN FRANCISCO • SINGAPORE • SYDNEY • TOKYO

Morgan Kaufmann is an imprint of Elsevier

Acquiring Editor: Steve Elliot
Editorial Project Manager: Amy Invernizzi
Project Manager: Priya Kumaraguruparan
Cover Designer: Matthew Limbert

Morgan Kaufmann is an imprint of Elsevier
225 Wyman Street, Waltham, MA 02451, USA

Copyright © 2015 Elsevier Inc. All rights reserved.

No part of this publication may be reproduced or transmitted in any form or by any means, electronic or mechanical, including photocopying, recording, or any information storage and retrieval system, without permission in writing from the publisher. Details on how to seek permission, further information about the Publisher's permissions policies and our arrangements with organizations such as the Copyright Clearance Center and the Copyright Licensing Agency, can be found at our website: www.elsevier.com/permissions.

This book and the individual contributions contained in it are protected under copyright by the Publisher (other than as may be noted herein).

Notices
Knowledge and best practice in this field are constantly changing. As new research and experience broaden our understanding, changes in research methods, professional practices, or medical treatment may become necessary.

Practitioners and researchers must always rely on their own experience and knowledge in evaluating and using any information, methods, compounds, or experiments described herein. In using such information or methods they should be mindful of their own safety and the safety of others, including parties for whom they have a professional responsibility.

To the fullest extent of the law, neither the Publisher nor the authors, contributors, or editors, assume any injury and/or damage to persons or property as a matter of products liability, negligence or otherwise, or from any use or operation of any methods, products, instructions, or ideas contained in the material herein.

ISBN: 978-0-12-800537-8

British Library Cataloguing in Publication Data
A catalogue record for this book is available from the British Library

Library of Congress Cataloging-in-Publication Data
A catalog record for this book is available from the Library of Congress

For information on all MK publications
visit our website at www.mkp.com

Working together
to grow libraries in
developing countries

www.elsevier.com • www.bookaid.org

Contents

Foreword.. xi

Preface xiii

Acknowledgements... xvii

CHAPTER 1   The Value Proposition for MDM and Big Data........... 1

Definition and Components of MDM..1

Master Data as a Category of Data 1

Master Data Management 2

Entity Resolution...3

Entity Identity Information Management 4

The Business Case for MDM..6

Customer Satisfaction and Entity-Based Data Integration 6

Better Service 8

Reducing the Cost of Poor Data Quality.............................9

MDM as Part of Data Governance.......................................9

Better Security 10

Measuring Success...11

Dimensions of MDM 11

Multi-Domain MDM...11

Hierarchical MDM..12

Multi-Channel MDM..13

Multi-Cultural MDM...13

The Challenge of Big Data..13

What Is Big Data? 13

The Value-Added Proposition of Big Data 14

Challenges of Big Data..15

MDM and Big Data — The N-Squared Problem.......................15

Concluding Remarks..16

**CHAPTER 2   Entity Identity Information and the CSRUD Life
Cycle Model 17**

Entities and Entity References 17

The Unique Reference Assumption......................................18

The Problem of Entity Reference Resolution........................19

The Fundamental Law of Entity Resolution 19

Internal vs. External View of Identity.................................19

Managing Entity Identity Information 21

Entity Identity Integrity 22

The Need for Persistent Identifiers.....................................26

Entity Identity Information Life Cycle Management Models 27
POSMAD Model 27
The Loshin Model 27
The CSRUD Model 28
Concluding Remarks 28

CHAPTER 3   A Deep Dive into the Capture Phase 31
An Overview of the Capture Phase 31
Building the Foundation 32
Understanding the Data 33
Data Preparation 33
Selecting Identity Attributes 34
Attribute Uniqueness 35
Attribute Entropy 36
Attribute Weight 36
Assessing ER Results 37
Truth Sets 38
Benchmarking 38
Problem Sets 39
The Intersection Matrix 39
Measurements of ER Outcomes 42
Talburt-Wang Index 43
Other Proposed Measures 44
Data Matching Strategies 46
Attribute-Level Matching 46
Reference-Level Matching 47
Boolean Rules 47
Scoring Rule 48
Hybrid Rules 49
Cluster-Level Matching 50
Implementing the Capture Process 50
Concluding Remarks 50

CHAPTER 4   Store and Share — Entity Identity Structures 53
Entity Identity Information Management Strategies 53
Bring-Your-Own-Identifier MDM 53
Once-and-Done MDM 54
Dedicated MDM Systems 55
The Survivor Record Strategy 55
Attribute-Based and Record-Based EIS 56
ER Algorithms and EIS 58

The Identity Knowledge Base 58
    Storing versus Sharing...59
MDM Architectures 60
    External Reference Architecture..............................60
    Registry Architecture 61
    Reconciliation Engine 63
    Transaction Hub...63
Concluding Remarks...64

**CHAPTER 5   Update and Dispose Phases — Ongoing Data
Stewardship..65**
Data Stewardship...65
The Automated Update Process..66
    Clerical Review Indicators 67
    Pair-Level Review Indicators 69
    Cluster-Level Review Indicators.............................69
The Manual Update Process 70
Asserted Resolution 71
    Correction Assertions 71
    Confirmation Assertions...74
EIS Visualization Tools 77
    Assertion Management 78
    Search Mode...80
    Negative Resolution Review Mode 81
    Positive Resolution Review Mode...........................83
Managing Entity Identifiers 84
    The Problem of Association Information Latency.................84
    Models for Identifier Change Management.........................85
Concluding Remarks...87

**CHAPTER 6   Resolve and Retrieve Phase — Identity
Resolution 89**
Identity Resolution...89
Identity Resolution Access Modes 89
    Batch Identity Resolution.......................................89
    Interactive Identity Resolution 92
    Identity Resolution API 94
Confidence Scores 96
    Depth and Degree of Match...................................97
    Match Context 99
    Confidence Score Model......................................100
Concluding Remarks...102

CHAPTER 7   Theoretical Foundations 105

The Fellegi-Sunter Theory of Record Linkage 105

The Context and Constraints of Record Linkage 105

The Fellegi-Sunter Matching Rule 106

The Fundamental Fellegi-Sunter Theorem........................... 108

Attribute Level Weights and the Scoring Rule 110

Frequency-Based Weights and the Scoring Rule.................. 112

The Stanford Entity Resolution Framework............................. 112

Abstraction of Match and Merge Operations 113

The Entity Resolution of a Set of References 114

Consistent ER 115

The R-Swoosh Algorithm... 115

Entity Identity Information Management 115

EIIM and Fellegi-Sunter 115

EIIM and the SERF 116

Concluding Remarks.. 117

CHAPTER 8   The Nuts and Bolts of Entity Resolution................ 119

The ER Checklist 119

Deterministic or Probabilistic?.. 119

Calculating the Weights 121

Cluster-to-Cluster Classification 122

The Unique Reference Assumption and Transitive Closure 125

Selecting an Appropriate Algorithm...................................... 126

The One-Pass Algorithm... 128

Concluding Remarks.. 145

CHAPTER 9   Blocking.. 147

Blocking 147

Two Causes of Accuracy Loss 148

Blocking as Prematching.. 149

Blocking by Match Key... 150

Match Key and Match Rule Alignment............................... 151

The Problem of Similarity Functions................................. 152

Dynamic Blocking versus Preresolution Blocking 153

Preresolution Blocking with Multiple Match Keys................ 154

Blocking Precision and Recall 155

Match Key Blocking for Boolean Rules................................. 157

Match Key Blocking for Scoring Rules 158

Concluding Remarks.. 160

CHAPTER 10   CSRUD for Big Data..............................**161**

Large-Scale ER for MDM..161

Large-Scale ER with Single Match Key Blocking 161

The Transitive Closure Problem 163

Distributed, Multiple-Index, Record-Based Resolution 165

Transitive Closure as a Graph Problem...........................165

References and Match Keys as a Graph...........................166

An Iterative, Nonrecursive Algorithm for Transitive Closure........167

Bootstrap Phase: Initial Closure by Match Key Values........169

Iteration Phase: Successive Closure by Reference Identifier 170

Deduplication Phase: Final Output of Components.....................171

Example of Hadoop Implementation...............................175

ER Using the Null Rule.......................................177

The Capture Phase and IKB 179

The Identity Update Problem...................................180

Persistent Entity Identifiers....................................181

The Large Component and Big Entity Problems 185

Postresolution Transitive Closure.................................186

Incremental Transitive Closure.................................187

The Big Entity Problem.......................................188

Identity Capture and Update for Attribute-Based Resolution 188

Concluding Remarks..190

CHAPTER 11   ISO Data Quality Standards for Master Data.........**191**

Background 191

Data Quality versus Information Quality...........................191

Relevance to MDM..193

Goals and Scope of the ISO 8000-110 Standard.......................193

Unambiguous and Portable Data 193

The Scope of ISO 8000-110 194

Motivational Example 194

Four Major Components of the ISO 8000-110 Standard 196

Part 1: General Requirements 196

Part 2: Syntax of the Message.......................................197

Part 3: Semantic Encoding 198

Part 4: Conformance to Data Specifications.......................199

Simple and Strong Compliance with ISO 8000-110....................202

ISO 22745 Industrial Systems and Integration 203

Beyond ISO 8000-110...203
        Part 120: Provenance..204
        Part 130: Accuracy 204
        Part 140: Completeness 204
    Concluding Remarks...205

Appendix A: Some Commonly Used ER Comparators................................207
References...219
Index...227

Foreword

In July of 2015 the Massachusetts Institute of Technology (MIT) will celebrate the 20th anniversary of the International Conference on Information Quality. My journey to information and data quality has had many twists and turns, but I have always found it interesting and rewarding. For me the most rewarding part of the journey has been the chance to meet and work with others who share my passion for this topic. I first met John Talburt in 2002 when he was working in the Data Products Division of Acxiom Corporation, a data management company with global operations. John had been tasked by leadership to answer the question, "What is our data quality?" Looking for help on the Internet he found the MIT Information Quality Program and contacted me. My book *Quality Information and Knowledge* (Huang, Lee, & Wang, 1999) had recently been published. John invited me to Acxiom headquarters, at that time in Conway, Arkansas, to give a one-day workshop on information quality to the Acxiom Leadership team.

This was the beginning of John's journey to data quality, and we have been traveling together on that journey ever since. After I helped him lead Acxiom's effort to implement a Total Data Quality Management program, he in turn helped me to realize one of my long-time goals of seeing a U.S. university start a degree program in information quality. Through the largess of Acxiom Corporation, led at that time by Charles Morgan and the academic entrepreneurship of Dr. Mary Good, Founding Dean of the Engineering and Information Technology College at the University of Arkansas at Little Rock, the world's first graduate degree program in information quality was established in 2006. John has been leading this program at UALR ever since. Initially created around a Master of Science in Information Quality (MSIQ) degree (Lee et al., 2007), it has since expanded to include a Graduate Certificate in IQ and an IQ PhD degree. As of this writing the program has graduated more than 100 students.

The second part of this story began in 2008. In that year, Yinle Zhou, an e-commerce graduate from Nanjing University in China, came to the U.S. and was admitted to the UALR MSIQ program. After finishing her MS degree, she entered the IQ PhD program with John as her research advisor. Together they developed a model for entity identity information management (EIIM) that extends entity resolution in support of master data management (MDM), the primary focus of this book. Dr. Zhou is now a Software Engineer and Data Scientist for IBM InfoSphere MDM Development in Austin, Texas, and an Adjunct Assistant Professor of Electrical and Computer Engineering at the University of Texas at Austin. And so the torch was passed and another journey began.

I have also been fascinated to see how the landscape of information technology has changed over the past 20 years. During that time IT has experienced a dramatic shift in focus. Inexpensive, large-scale storage and processors have changed the face of IT. Organizations are exploiting cloud computing, software-as-a-service, and open source software, as alternatives to building and maintaining their own data centers and developing custom solutions. All of these trends are contributing to the commoditization of technology. They are forcing companies to compete with better data instead of better technology. At the same time, more and more data are being produced and retained, from structured operational data to unstructured, user-generated data from social media. Together these factors are producing many new challenges for data management, and especially for master data management.

The complexity of the new data-driven environment can be overwhelming. How to deal with data governance and policy, data privacy and security, data quality, MDM, RDM, information risk management, regulatory compliance, and the list goes on. Just as John and Yinle started their journeys as individuals, now we see that entire organizations are embarking on journeys to data and information quality. The difference is that an organization needs a leader to set the course, and I strongly believe this leader should be the Chief Data Officer (CDO).

The CDO is a growing role in modern organizations to lead their company's journey to strategically use data for regulatory compliance, performance optimization, and competitive advantage. The MIT CDO Forum recognizes the emerging criticality of the CDO's role and has developed a series of events where leaders come for bidirectional sharing and collaboration to accelerate identification and establishment of best practices in strategic data management.

I and others have been conducting the MIT Longitudinal Study on the Chief Data Officer and hosting events for senior executives to advance CDO research and practice. We have published research results in leading academic journals, as well as the proceedings of the MIT CDO Forum, MIT CDOIQ Symposium, and the International Conference on Information Quality (ICIQ). For example, we have developed a three-dimensional cubic framework to describe the emerging role of the Chief Data Officer in the context of Big Data (Lee et al., 2014).

I believe that CDOs, MDM architects and administrators, and anyone involved with data governance and information quality will find this book useful. MDM is now considered an integral component of a data governance program. The material presented here clearly lays out the business case for MDM and a plan to improve the quality and performance of MDM systems through effective entity information life cycle management. It not only explains the technical aspects of the life cycle, it also provides guidance on the often overlooked tasks of MDM quality metrics and analytics and MDM stewardship.

Richard Wang
MIT Chief Data Officer and Information Quality Program

Preface

THE CHANGING LANDSCAPE OF INFORMATION QUALITY

Since the publication of *Entity Resolution and Information Quality* (Morgan Kaufmann, 2011), a lot has been happening in the field of information and data quality. One of the most important developments is how organizations are beginning to understand that the data they hold are among their most important assets and should be managed accordingly. As many of us know, this is by no means a new message, only that it is just now being heeded. Leading experts in information and data quality such as Rich Wang, Yang Lee, Tom Redman, Larry English, Danette McGilvray, David Loshin, Laura Sebastian-Coleman, Rajesh Jugulum, Sunil Soares, Arkady Maydanchik, and many others have been advocating this principle for many years.

Evidence of this new understanding can be found in the dramatic surge of the adoption of data governance (DG) programs by organizations of all types and sizes. Conferences, workshops, and webinars on this topic are overflowing with attendees. The primary reason is that DG provides organizations with an answer to the question, "If information is really an important organizational asset, then how can it be managed at the enterprise level?" One of the primary benefits of a DG program is that it provides a framework for implementing a central point of communication and control over all of an organization's data and information.

As DG has grown and matured, its essential components become more clearly defined. These components generally include central repositories for data definitions, business rules, metadata, data-related issue tracking, regulations and compliance, and data quality rules. Two other key components of DG are master data management (MDM) and reference data management (RDM). Consequently, the increasing adoption of DG programs has brought a commensurate increase in focus on the importance of MDM.

Certainly this is not the first book on MDM. Several excellent books include *Master Data Management and Data Governance* by Alex Berson and Larry Dubov (2011), *Master Data Management in Practice* by Dalton Cervo and Mark Allen (2011), *Master Data Management* by David Loshin (2009), *Enterprise Master Data Management* by Allen Dreibelbis, Eberhard Hechler, Ivan Milman, Martin Oberhofer, Paul van Run, and Dan Wolfson (2008), and *Customer Data Integration* by Jill Dyché and Evan Levy (2006). However, MDM is an extensive and evolving topic. No single book can explore every aspect of MDM at every level.

MOTIVATION FOR THIS BOOK

Numerous things have motivated us to contribute yet another book. However, the primary reason is this. Based on our experience in both academia and industry, we believe that many of the problems that organizations experience with MDM implementation and operation are rooted in the failure to understand and address certain critical aspects of entity identity information management (EIIM). EIIM is an extension of entity resolution (ER) with the goal of achieving and maintaining the highest level of accuracy in the MDM system. Two key terms are "achieving" and "maintaining."

Having a goal and defined requirements is the starting point for every information and data quality methodology from the MIT TDQM (Total Data Quality Management) to the Six-Sigma DMAIC (Define, Measure, Analyze, Improve, and Control). Unfortunately, when it comes to MDM, many organizations have not defined any goals. Consequently these organizations don't have a way to know if they have achieved their goal. They leave many questions unanswered. What is our accuracy? Now that a proposed programming or procedure has been implemented, is the system performing better or worse than before? Few MDM administrators can provide accurate estimates of even the most basic metrics such as false positive and false negative rates or the overall accuracy of their system. In this book we have emphasized the importance of objective and systematic measurement and provided practical guidance on how these measurements can be made.

To help organizations better address the maintaining of high levels of accuracy through EIIM, the majority of the material in the book is devoted to explaining the CSRUD five-phase entity information life cycle model. CSRUD is an acronym for capture, store and share, resolve and retrieve, update, and dispose. We believe that following this model can help any organization improve MDM accuracy and performance.

Finally, no modern day IT book can be complete without talking about Big Data. Seemingly rising up overnight, Big Data has captured everyone's attention, not just in IT, but even the man on the street. Just as DG seems to be getting up a good head of steam, it now has to deal with the Big Data phenomenon. The immediate question is whether Big Data simply fits right into the current DG model, or whether the DG model needs to be revised to account for Big Data.

Regardless of one's opinion on this topic, one thing is clear — Big Data is bad news for MDM. The reason is a simple mathematical fact: MDM relies on entity resolution, and entity resolution primarily relies on pair-wise record matching, and the number of pairs of records to match increases as the square of the number of records. For this reason, ordinary data (millions of records) is already a challenge for MDM, so Big Data (billions of records) seems almost insurmountable. Fortunately, Big Data is not just matter of more data; it is also ushering in a new paradigm for managing and processing large amounts of data. Big Data is bringing with it new tools and techniques. Perhaps the most important technique is how to exploit distributed processing. However, it is easier to talk about Big Data than to do something about it. We wanted to avoid that and include in our book some practical strategies and designs for using distributed processing to solve some of these problems.

AUDIENCE

It is our hope that both IT professionals and business professionals interested in MDM and Big Data issues will find this book helpful. Most of the material focuses on issues of design and architecture, making it a resource for anyone evaluating an installed system, comparing proposed third-party systems, or for an organization contemplating building its own system. We also believe that it is written at a level appropriate for a university textbook.

ORGANIZATION OF THE MATERIAL

Chapters 1 and 2 provide the background and context of the book. Chapter 1 provides a definition and overview of MDM. It includes the business case, dimensions, and challenges facing MDM and also starts the discussion of Big Data and its impact on MDM. Chapter 2 defines and explains the two primary technologies that support MDM — ER and EIIM. In addition, Chapter 2 introduces the CSRUD Life Cycle for entity identity information. This sets the stage for the next four chapters.

Chapters 3, 4, 5, and 6 are devoted to an in-depth discussion of the CSRUD life cycle model. Chapter 3 is an in-depth look at the Capture Phase of CSRUD. As part of the discussion, it also covers the techniques of truth set building, benchmarking, and problem sets as tools for assessing entity resolution and MDM outcomes. In addition, it discusses some of the pros and cons of the two most commonly used data matching techniques — deterministic matching and probabilistic matching.

Chapter 4 explains the Store and Share Phase of CSRUD. This chapter introduces the concept of an entity identity structure (EIS) that forms the building blocks of the identity knowledge base (IKB). In addition to discussing different styles of EIS designs, it also includes a discussion of the different types of MDM architectures.

Chapter 5 covers two closely related CSRUD phases, the Update Phase and the Dispose Phase. The Update Phase discussion covers both automated and manual update processes and the critical roles played by clerical review indicators, correction assertions, and confirmation assertions. Chapter 5 also presents an example of an identity visualization system that assists MDM data stewards with the review and assertion process.

Chapter 6 covers the Resolve and Retrieve Phase of CSRUD. It also discusses some design considerations for accessing identity information, and a simple model for a retrieved identifier confidence score.

Chapter 7 introduces two of the most important theoretical models for ER, the Fellegi-Sunter Theory of Record Linkage and the Stanford Entity Resolution Framework or SERF Model. Chapter 7 is inserted here because some of the concepts introduced in the SERF Model are used in Chapter 8, "The Nuts and Bolts of ER." The chapter concludes with a discussion of how EIIM relates to each of these models.

Chapter 8 describes a deeper level of design considerations for ER and EIIM systems. It discusses in detail the three levels of matching in an EIIM system: attribute-level, reference-level, and cluster-level matching.

Chapter 9 covers the technique of blocking as a way to increase the performance of ER and MDM systems. It focuses on match key blocking, the definition of match-key-to-match-rule alignment, and the precision and recall of match keys. Preresolution blocking and transitive closure of match keys are discussed as a prelude to Chapter 10.

Chapter 10 discusses the problems in implementing the CSRUD Life Cycle for Big Data. It gives examples of how the Hadoop Map/Reduce framework can be used to address many of these problems using a distributed computing environment.

Chapter 11 covers the new ISO 8000-110 data quality standard for master data. This standard is not well understood outside of a few industry verticals, but it has potential implications for all industries. This chapter covers the basic requirements of the standard and how organizations can become ISO 8000 compliant, and perhaps more importantly, why organizations would want to be compliant.

Finally, to reduce ER discussions in Chapters 3 and 8, Appendix A goes into more detail on some of the more common data comparison algorithms.

This book also includes a website with exercises, tips and free downloads of demonstrations that use a trial version of the HiPER EIM system for hands-on learning. The website includes control scripts and synthetic input data to illustrate how the system handles various aspects of the CSRUD life cycle such as identity capture, identity update, and assertions. You can access the website here: http://www.BlackOakAnalytics.com/develop/HiPER/trial.

Acknowledgements

This book would not have been possible without the help of many people and organizations. First of all, Yinle and I would like to thank Dr. Rich Wang, Director of the MIT Information Quality Program, for starting us on our journey to data quality and for writing the foreword for our book, and Dr. Scott Schumacher, Distinguished Engineer at IBM, for his support of our research and collaboration. We would also like to thank our employers, IBM Corporation, University of Arkansas at Little Rock, and Black Oak Analytics, Inc., for their support and encouragement during its writing.

It has been a privilege to be a part of the UALR Information Quality Program and to work with so many talented students and gifted faculty members. I would especially like to acknowledge several of my current students for their contributions to this work. These include Fumiko Kobayashi, identity resolution models and confidence scores in Chapter 6; Cheng Chen, EIS visualization tools and confirmation assertions in Chapter 5 and Hadoop map/reduce in Chapter 10; Daniel Pullen, clerical review indicators in Chapter 5 and Hadoop map/reduce in Chapter 10; Pei Wang, blocking for scoring rules in Chapter 9, Hadoop map/reduce in Chapter 10, and the demonstration data, scripts, and exercises on the book's website; Debanjan Mahata, EIIM for unstructured data in Chapter 1; Melody Penning, entity-based data integration in Chapter 1; and Reed Petty, IKB structure for HDFS in Chapter 10. In addition I would like to thank my former student Dr. Eric Nelson for introducing the null rule concept and for sharing his expertise in Hadoop map/reduce in Chapter 10. Special thanks go to Dr. Laura Sebastian-Coleman, Data Quality Leader at Cigna, and Joshua Johnson, UALR Technical Writing Program, for their help in editing and proofreading. Finally I want to thank my teaching assistants, Fumiko Kobayashi, Khizer Syed, Michael Greer, Pei Wang, and Daniel Pullen, and my administrative assistant, Nihal Erian, for giving me the extra time I needed to complete this work.

I would also like to take this opportunity to acknowledge several organizations that have supported my work for many years. Acxiom Corporation under Charles Morgan was one of the founders of the UALR IQ program and continues to support the program under Scott Howe, the current CEO, and Allison Nicholas, Director of College Recruiting and University Relations. I am grateful for my experience at Acxiom and the opportunity to learn about Big Data entity resolution in a distributed computing environment from Dr. Terry Talley and the many other world-class data experts who work there.

The Arkansas Research Center under the direction of Dr. Neal Gibson and Dr. Greg Holland were the first to support my work on the OYSTER open source entity resolution system. The Arkansas Department of Education — in particular former Assistant Commissioner Jim Boardman and his successor, Dr. Cody Decker, along with Arijit Sarkar in the IT Services Division — gave me the opportunity to build a student MDM system that implements the full CSRUD life cycle as described in this book.

The Translational Research Institute (TRI) at the University of Arkansas for Medical Sciences has given me and several of my students the opportunity for hands-on experience with MDM systems in the healthcare environment. I would like to thank Dr. William Hogan, the former Director of TRI for teaching me about referent tracking, and also Dr. Umit Topaloglu the current Director of Informatics at TRI who along with Dr. Mathias Brochhausen continues this collaboration.

Last but not least are my business partners at Black Oak Analytics. Our CEO, Rick McGraw, has been a trusted friend and business advisor for many years. Because of Rick and our COO, Jonathan Askins, what was only a vision has become a reality.

John R. Talburt & Yinle Zhou

The Value Proposition for MDM and Big Data

DEFINITION AND COMPONENTS OF MDM
MASTER DATA AS A CATEGORY OF DATA

Modern information systems use four broad categories of data including master data, transaction data, metadata, and reference data. Master data are data held by an organization that describe the entities both independent and fundamental to the organization's operations. In some sense, master data are the "nouns" in the grammar of data and information. They describe the persons, places, and things that are critical to the operation of an organization, such as its customers, products, employees, materials, suppliers, services, shareholders, facilities, equipment, and rules and regulations. The determination of exactly what is considered master data depends on the viewpoint of the organization.

If master data are the nouns of data and information, then transaction data can be thought of as the "verbs." They describe the actions that take place in the day-to-day operation of the organization, such as the sale of a product in a business or the admission of a patient to a hospital. Transactions relate master data in a meaningful way. For example, a credit card transaction relates two entities that are represented by master data. The first is the issuing bank's credit card account that is identified by the credit card number, where the master data contains information required by the issuing bank about that specific account. The second is the accepting bank's merchant account that is identified by the merchant number, where the master data contains information required by the accepting bank about that specific merchant.

Master data management (MDM) and reference data management (RDM) systems are both systems of record (SOR). A SOR is "a system that is charged with keeping the most complete or trustworthy representation of a set of entities" (Sebastian-Coleman, 2013). The records in an SOR are sometimes called "golden records" or "certified records" because they provide a single point of reference for a particular type of information. In the context of MDM, the objective is to provide a single point of reference for each entity under management. In the case of master data, the intent is to have only one information structure and identifier for each entity under management. In this example, each entity would be a credit card account.

Metadata are simply data about data. Metadata are critical to understanding the meaning of both master and transactional data. They provide the definitions, specifications, and other descriptive information about the operational data. Data standards, data definitions, data requirements, data quality information, data provenance, and business rules are all forms of metadata.

Reference data share characteristics with both master data and metadata. Reference data are standard, agreed-upon codes that help to make transactional data interoperable within an organization and sometimes between collaborating organizations. Reference data, like master data, should have only one system of record. Although reference data are important, they are not necessarily associated with real-world entities in the same way as master data. RDM is intended to standardize the codes used across the enterprise to promote data interoperability.

Reference codes may be internally developed, such as standard department or building codes or may adopt external standards, such as standard postal codes and abbreviations for use in addresses. Reference data are often used in defining metadata. For example, the field "BuildingLocation" in (or referenced by) an employee master record may require that the value be one of a standard set of codes (system of reference) for buildings as established by the organization. The policies and procedures for RDM are similar to those for MDM.

MASTER DATA MANAGEMENT

In a more formal context, MDM seems to suffer from lengthy definitions. Loshin (2009) defines master data management as "a collection of best data management practices that orchestrate key stakeholders, participants, and business clients in incorporating the business applications, information management methods, and data management tools to implement the policies, procedures, services, and infrastructure to support the capture, integration, and shared use of accurate, timely, consistent, and complete master data." Berson and Dubov (2011) define MDM as the "framework of processes and technologies aimed at creating and maintaining an authoritative, reliable, sustainable, accurate, and secure environment that represents a single and holistic version of the truth for master data and its relationships…"

These definitions highlight two major components of MDM as shown in Figure 1.1. One component comprises the policies that represent the data governance aspect of MDM, while the other includes the technologies that support MDM. Policies define the roles and responsibilities in the MDM process. For example, if a company introduces a new product, the policies define who is responsible for creating the new entry in the master product registry, the standards for creating the product identifier, what persons or department should be notified, and which other data systems should be updated. Compliance to regulation along with the privacy and security of information are also important policy issues (Decker, Liu, Talburt, Wang, & Wu, 2013).

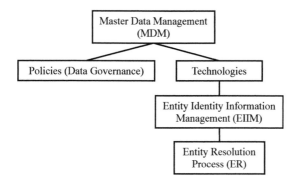

FIGURE 1.1

Components of MDM.

The technology component of MDM can be further divided into two major sub-components, the entity resolution (ER) process and entity identity information management (EIIM).

ENTITY RESOLUTION

The base technology is entity resolution (ER), which is sometimes called record linking, data matching, or de-duplication. ER is the process of determining when two information system references to a real-world entity are referring to the same, or to different, entities (Talburt, 2011). ER represents the "sorting out" process when there are multiple sources of information that are referring to the same set of entities. For example, the same patient may be admitted to a hospital at different times or through different departments such as inpatient and outpatient admissions. ER is the process of comparing the admission information for each encounter and deciding which admission records are for the same patient and which ones are for different patients.

ER has long been recognized as a key data cleansing process for removing dupli-cate records in database systems (Naumann & Herschel, 2010) and promoting data and information quality in general (Talburt, 2013). It is also essential in the two-step process of entity-based data integration. The first step is to use ER to determine if two records are referencing the same entity. This step relies on comparing the iden-tity information in the two records. Only after it has been determined that the records carry information for the same entity can the second step in the process be executed, in which other information in the records is merged and reconciled.

Most de-duplication applications start with an ER process that uses a set of matching rules to link together into clusters those records determined to be dupli-cates (equivalent references). This is followed by a process to select one best example, called a survivor record, from each cluster of equivalent records. After the survivor record is selected, the presumed duplicate records in the cluster are discarded with only the single surviving records passing into the next process. In record de-duplication, ER directly addresses the data quality problem of redundant and duplicate data prior to data integration. In this role, ER is fundamentally a data cleansing tool (Herzog, Scheuren & Winkler, 2007). However, ER is increasingly being used in a broader context for two important reasons.

The first reason is that information quality has matured. As part of that, many organizations are beginning to apply a product model to their information management as a way of achieving and sustaining high levels of information quality over time (Wang, 1998). This is evidenced by several important developments of recent years, including the recognition of Sustaining Information Quality as one of the six domains in the framework of information quality developed by the International Association for Information and Data Quality (Yonke, Walenta & Talburt, 2012) as the basis for the Information Quality Certified Professional (IQCP) credential.

Another reason is the relatively recent approval of the ISO 8000-110:2009 standard for master data quality prompted by the growing interest by organizations in adopting and investing in master data management (MDM). The ISO 8000 standard is discussed in more detail in Chapter 11.

ENTITY IDENTITY INFORMATION MANAGEMENT

Entity Identity Information Management (EIIM) is the collection and management of identity information with the goal of sustaining entity identity integrity over time (Zhou & Talburt, 2011a). Entity identity integrity requires that each entity must be represented in the system one, and only one, time, and distinct entities must have distinct representations in the system (Maydanchik, 2007). Entity identity integrity is a fundamental requirement for MDM systems.

EIIM is an ongoing process that combines ER and data structures representing the identity of an entity into specific operational configurations (EIIM configurations). When these configurations are all executed together, they work in concert to maintain the entity identity integrity of master data over time. EIIM is not limited to MDM. It can be applied to other types of systems and data as diverse as RDM systems, referent tracking systems (Chen et al., 2013a), and social media (Mahata & Talburt, 2014).

Identity information is a collection of attribute-value pairs that describe the characteristics of the entity — characteristics that serve to distinguish one entity from another. For example, a student name attribute with a value such as "Mary Doe" would be identity information. However, because there may be other students with the same name, additional identity information such as date-of-birth or home address may be required to fully disambiguate one student from another.

Although ER is necessary for effective MDM, it is not, in itself, sufficient to manage the life cycle of identity information. EIIM is an extension of ER in two dimensions, knowledge management and time. The knowledge management aspect of EIIM relates to the need to create, store, and maintain identity information. The knowledge structure created to represent a master data object is called an entity identity structure (EIS).

The time aspect of EIIM is to assure that an entity under management in the MDM system is consistently labeled with the same, unique identifier from process to process. This is only possible through an EIS that stores the identity information of the entity along with its identifier so both are available to future processes. Persistent entity identifiers are not inherently part of ER. At any given point in time, the only goal of an ER process is to correctly classify a set of entity references into clusters where all of the references in a given cluster reference the same entity. If these clusters are labeled, then the cluster label can serve as the identifier of the entity. Without also storing and carrying forward the identity information, the cluster identifiers assigned in a future process may be different.

The problem of changes in labeling by ER processes is illustrated in Figure 1.2. It shows three records, Records 1, 2, and 3, where Records 1 and 2 are equivalent references to one entity and Record 3 is a reference to a different entity. In the first ER run, Records 1, 2, and 3 are in a file with other records. In the second run, the same Records 1, 2, and 3 occur in context with a different set of records, or perhaps the same records that were in Run 1, but simply in a different order. In both runs the ER process consistently classifies Records 1 and 2 as equivalent and places Record 3 in a cluster by itself. The problem from an MDM standpoint is that the ER processes are not required to consistently label these clusters. In the first run, the cluster comprising Records 1 and 2 is identified as Cluster 543 whereas in the second run the same cluster is identified as Cluster 76.

ER that is used only to classify records into groups or clusters representing the same entity is sometimes called a "merge-purge" operation. In a merge-purge process the objective is simply to eliminate duplicate records. Here the term "duplicate" does not mean that the records are identical, but that they are duplicate representations of the same entity. To avoid the confusion in the use of the term duplicate, the term "equivalent" is preferred (Talburt, 2011) — i.e. records referencing the same entity are said to be equivalent.

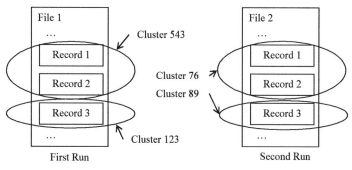

FIGURE 1.2

ER with consistent classification but inconsistent labeling.

The designation of equivalent records also avoids the confusion arising from use of the term "matching" records. Records referencing the same entity do not necessarily have matching information. For example, two records for the same customer may have different names and different addresses. At the same time, it can be true that matching records do not reference the same entity. This can occur when important discriminating information is missing, such as a generational suffix or age. For example, the records for a John Doe, Jr. and a John Doe, Sr. may be deemed as matching records if one or both records omit the Jr. or Sr. generation suffix element of the name field.

Unfortunately, many authors use the term "matching" for both of these concepts, i.e. to mean that the records are similar and reference the same entity. This can often be confusing for the reader. Reference matching and reference equivalence are different concepts, and should be described by different terms.

The ability to assign each cluster the same identifier when an ER process is repeated at a later time requires that identity information be carried forward from process to process. The carrying forward of identity information is accomplished by persisting (storing) the EIS that represents the entity. The storage and management of identity information and the persistence of entity identifiers is the added value that EIIM brings to ER.

A distinguishing feature of the EIIM model is the entity identity structure (EIS), a data structure that represents the identity of a specific entity and persists from process to process. In the model presented here, the EIS is an explicitly defined structure that exists and is maintained independently of the references being processed by the system. Although all ER systems address the issue of identity representation in some way, it is often done implicitly rather than being an explicit component of the system. Figure 1.3 shows the persistent (output) form of an EIS as implemented in the open source ER system called OYSTER (Talburt & Zhou, 2013; Zhou, Talburt, Su & Yin, 2010).

During processing, the OYSTER EIS exists as in-memory Java objects. However, at the end of processing, the EIS is written as XML documents that reflect the hierarchical structure of the memory objects. The XML format also serves as a way to serialize the EIS objects so that they can be reloaded into memory at the start of a later ER process.

THE BUSINESS CASE FOR MDM

Aside from the technologies and policies that support MDM, why is it important? And why are so many organizations investing in it? There are several reasons.

CUSTOMER SATISFACTION AND ENTITY-BASED DATA INTEGRATION

MDM has its roots in the customer relationship management (CRM) industry. The CRM movement started at about the same time as the data warehousing (DW)

```
<root>
  <Metadata>
    <Modifications)
      <Modification ID="1" OysterVersion="3.2" Date="2013-03-29 04.51.07" RunScript="Run001" />
    </Modifications>
    <Attributes>
      <Attribute Name="@RefID" Tag="A" />
      <Attribute Name="Phone" Tag="B" />
      <Attribute Name="FirstName" Tag="C" />
      <Attribute Name="StrNbr" Tag="D" />
      <Attribute Name="LastName" Tag="E" />
      <Attribute Name="SSN" Tag="F" />
    </Attributes>
  </Metadata>
  <Identities>
    <Identity Identifier="X9KTZ5GOQ5RVHOWV" CDate="2012-03-29">
      <References>
        <Reference>
          <Value>A^ListA.A953698|C^ANTONIOV|D^247H|E^CARDONA|F^196369947</Value>
          <Traces>
            <Trace> OID="X9KTZ5GOQ5RVHOWV" RunID="1" Rule="@"/>
          </Traces>
        </Reference
        <Reference>
          <Value>A^ListA.A989582|C^ANTONIOV|D^5221|E^CARDONA|F^196369974</Value>
          <Traces>
            <Trace> OID="X9KTZ5GOQ5RVHOWV" RunID="1" Rule="@"/>
          </Traces>
        </Reference
      </References>
    <Identity Identifier= ...
    ...
  </Identities>
</root>
```

FIGURE 1.3

Example of an EIS in XML format created by the OYSTER ER system.

movement in the 1980s. The primary goal of CRM was to understand all of the interactions that a customer has with the organization so that the organization could improve the customer's experience and consequently increase customer satisfaction. The business motivation for CRM was that higher customer satisfaction would result in more customer interactions (sales), higher customer retention rates and a lower customer "churn rate," and additional customers would be gained through social networking and referrals from more satisfied customers.

If there is one number most businesses understand, it is the differential between the higher cost of acquiring a new customer versus the lower cost of retaining an existing customer. Depending upon the type of business, small increases in customer retention can have a dramatic effect on net revenues. Loyal customers often provide a higher profit margin because they tend to continue purchasing from the same company without the need for extensive marketing and advertising. In highly competitive markets such as airlines and grocery retailers, loyalty programs have a high priority.

The underpinning of CRM is a technology called customer data integration (CDI) (Dyché & Levy, 2006), which is basically MDM for customer entities. Certainly customer information and product information qualify as master data for any organization selling a product. Typically both customers and products are under MDM in these organizations. CDI technology is the EIIM for CRM. CDI enables the business to recognize the interactions with the same customer across different sales channels and over time by using the principles of EIIM.

CDI is only one example of a broader class of data management processes affecting data integration (Doan, Halevy & Ives, 2012). For most applications, data integration is a two-step process called entity-based data integration (Talburt & Hashemi, 2008). When integrating entity information from multiple sources, the first step is to determine whether the information is for the same entity. Once it has been determined the information is for the same entity, the second step is to reconcile possibly conflicting or incomplete information associated with a particular entity coming from different sources (Holland & Talburt, 2008, 2010a; Zhou, Kooshesh & Talburt, 2012). MDM plays a critical role in successful entity-based data integration by providing an EIIM process consistently identifying references to the same entity.

Entity-based data integration has a broad range of applications in areas such as law enforcement (Nelson & Talburt, 2008), education (Nelson & Talburt, 2011; Penning & Talburt, 2012), and healthcare (Christen, 2008; Lawley, 2010).

BETTER SERVICE

Many organizations' basic value proposition is not primarily based on money. For example, in healthcare, although there is clearly a monetary component, the primary objective is to improve the quality of people's lives through better drugs and medical treatments. This also holds true for many government and nonprofit agencies where the primary mission is service to a particular constituency. MDM systems bring value to these organizations as well.

As another example, law enforcement has a mission to protect and serve the public. Traditionally, criminal and law enforcement information has been fragmented across many agencies and legal jurisdictions at the city, county, district, state, and federal levels. However, law enforcement as a whole is starting to take advantage of MDM. The tragic events of September 11, 2001 brought into focus the need to "connect the dots" across these agencies and jurisdictions in terms of linking records referencing the same persons of interest and the same events. This is also a good example of Big Data, because a single federal law enforcement agency may be managing information on billions of entities. The primary entities are persons of interest identified through demographic characteristics and biometric data such as fingerprints and DNA profiles. In addition, they also manage many nonperson entities such as locations, events, motor vehicles, boats, aircrafts, phones, and other electronic devices. Linking law enforcement information for the same entities across jurisdictions with the ability to derive additional information from patterns of linkage have made criminal investigation both more efficient and more effective.

REDUCING THE COST OF POOR DATA QUALITY

Each year United States businesses lose billions of dollars due to poor data quality (Redman, 1998). Of the top ten root conditions of data quality problems (Lee, Pipino, Funk, & Wang, 2006), the number one cause listed is "multiple source of the same information produces different values for this information." Quite often this problem is due to missing or ineffective MDM practices. Without maintenance of a system or record that includes every master entity with a unique and persistent identifier, then data quality problems will inevitably arise.

For example, if the same product is given a different identifier in different sales transactions, then sales reports summarized by product will be incorrect and misleading. Inventory counts and inventory projections will be off. These problems can in turn lead to the loss of orders and customers, unnecessary inventory purchases, miscalculated sales commissions, and many other types of losses to the company. Following the principle of Taguchi's Loss Function (Taguchi, 2005), the cost of poor data quality must be considered not only in the effort to correct the immediate problem but also must include all of the costs from its downstream effects. Tracking each master entity with precision is considered fundamental to the data quality program of almost every enterprise.

MDM AS PART OF DATA GOVERNANCE

MDM and RDM are generally considered key components of a complete data governance (DG) program. In recent years, DG has been one of the fastest growing trends in information and data quality and is enjoying widespread adoption. As enterprises recognize information as a key asset and resource (Redman, 2008), they understand the need for better communication and control of that asset. This recognition has also created new management roles devoted to data and information, most notably the emergence of the CDO, the Chief Data Officer (Lee, Madnick, Wang, Wang, & Zhang, 2014). DG brings to information the same kind of discipline governing software for many years. Any company developing or using third-party software would not think of letting a junior programmer make even the smallest ad hoc change to a piece of production code. The potential for adverse consequences to the company from inadvertently introducing a software bug, or worse from an intentional malicious action, could be enormous. Therefore, in almost every company all production software changes are strictly controlled through a closely monitored and documented change process. A production software change begins with a proposal seeking broad stakeholder approval, then moves through a lengthy testing process in a safe environment, and finally to implementation.

Until recently this same discipline has not been applied to the data architecture of the enterprise. In fact, in many organizations a junior database administrator (DBA) may actually have the authority to make an ad hoc change to a database schema or to a record layout without going through any type of formal change process. Data management in an enterprise has traditionally followed the model of local "ownership." This means divisions, departments, or even individuals have seen themselves as the "owners" of the data in their possession with the unilateral right to make changes as suits the needs of their particular unit without consulting other stakeholders.

An important goal of the DG model is to move the culture and practice of data management to a data stewardship model in which the data and data architecture are seen as assets controlled by the enterprise rather than individual units. In the data stewardship model of DG, the term "ownership" reflects the concept of accountability for data rather than the traditional meaning of control of the data. Although accountability is the preferred term, many organizations still use the term ownership. A critical element of the DG model is a formal framework for making decisions on changes to the enterprise's data architecture. Simply put, data management is the decisions made about data, while DG is the rules for making those decisions.

The adoption of DG has largely been driven by the fact that software is rapidly becoming a commodity available to everyone. More and more, companies are relying on free, open source systems, software-as-a-service (SaaS), cloud computing services, and outsourcing of IT functions as an alternative to software development. As it becomes more difficult to differentiate on the basis of software and systems, companies are realizing that they must derive their competitive advantage from better data and information (Jugulum, 2014).

DG programs serve two primary purposes. One is to provide a mechanism for controlling changes related to the data, data processes, and data architecture of the enterprise. DG control is generally exercised by means of a DG council with senior membership from all major units of the enterprise having a stake in the data architecture. Membership includes both business units as well as IT units and, depending upon the nature of the business, will include risk and compliance officers or their representatives. Furthermore, the DG council must have a written charter that describes in detail the governance of the change process. In the DG model, all changes to the data architecture must first be approved by the DG council before moving into development and implementation. The purpose of first bringing change proposals to the DG council for discussion and approval is to try to avoid the problem of unilateral change. Unilateral change occurs when one unit makes a change to the data architecture without notification or consultation with other units who might be adversely affected by the change.

The second purpose of a DG program is to provide a central point of communication about all things related to the data, data processes, and data architecture of the enterprise. This often includes an enterprise-wide data dictionary, a centralized tracking system for data issues, a repository of business rules, the data compliance requirements from regulatory agencies, and data quality metrics. Because of the critical nature of MDM and RDM, and the benefits of managing this data from an enterprise perspective, they are usually brought under the umbrella of a DG governance program.

BETTER SECURITY

Another important area where MDM plays a major role is in enterprise security. Seemingly each day there is word of yet another data breach, leakage of confidential information, or identity theft. One of the most notable attempts to address these problems is the Center for Identity at the University of Texas, Austin, taking an inter-disciplinary approach to the development of a model for identity threat assessment and prediction (Center for Identity, 2014). Identity and the management of identity information (EIIM) both play a key role in systems that attempt to address security issues through user authentication. Here again, MDM provides the support needed for these kinds of systems.

MEASURING SUCCESS

No matter what the motivations are for adopting MDM, there should always be an underlying business case. The business case should clearly establish the goals of the implementation and metrics for how to measure goal attainment. Power and Hunt (2013) list "No Metrics for Measuring Success" as one of the eight worst practices in MDM. Best practice for MDM is to measure both the system performance, such as false positive and negative rates, and also business performance, such as return-on-investment (ROI).

DIMENSIONS OF MDM

Many styles of MDM implementation address particular issues. Capabilities and features of MDM systems vary widely from vendor to vendor and industry to indus-try. However, some common themes do emerge.

MULTI-DOMAIN MDM

In general, master data are references to key operational entities of the enterprise. The definition for entities in the context of master data is somewhat different from the general definition of entities such as in the entity-relation (E-R) database model. Whereas the general definition of entity allows both real-world objects and abstract concepts to be an entity, MDM is concerned with real-world objects having distinct identities.

In keeping with the paradigm of master data representing the nouns of data, major master data entities are typically classified into domains. Sørensen (2011) classifies entities into four domains: parties, products, places, and periods of time. The party domain includes entities that are persons, legal entities, and house-holds of persons. These include parties such as customers, prospects, suppliers, and customer households. Even within these categories of party, an entity may have more than one role. For example, a person may be a patient of a hospital and at the same time a nurse (employee) at the hospital.

Products more generally represent assets, not just items for sale. Products can also include other entities, such as equipment owned and used by a construction company. The place domain includes those entities associated with a geographic location — for example, a customer address. Period entities are generally associated with events with a defined start and end date such as fiscal year, marketing campaign, or conference.

As technology has evolved, more vendors are providing multi-domain solutions. Power and Lyngsø (2013) cite four main benefits for the use of multi-domain MDM including cost-effectiveness, ease of maintenance, enabling proactive management of operational information, and prevention of MDM failure.

HIERARCHICAL MDM

Hierarchies in MDM are the connections among entities taking the form of parent–child relationships where some or all of the entities are master data. Conceptually these form a tree structure with a root and branches that end with leaf nodes. One entity may participate in multiple relations or hierarchies (Berson & Dubov, 2011).

Many organizations run independent MDM systems for their domains: for example, one system for customers and a separate system for products. In these situations, any relationships between these domains are managed externally in the application systems referencing the MDM systems. However, many MDM software vendors have developed architectures with the capability to manage multiple master data domains within one system. This facilitates the ability to create hierarchical relationships among MDM entities.

Depending on the type of hierarchy, these relationships are often implemented in two different ways. One implementation style is as an "entity of entities." This often happens in specific MDM domains where the entities are bound in a structural way. For example, in many CDI implementations of MDM, a hierarchy of household entities is made up of customer (person) entities containing location (address) entities. In direct-mail marketing systems, the address information is almost always an element of a customer reference. For this reason, both customer entities and address entities are tightly bound and managed concurrently.

However, most systems supporting hierarchical MDM relationships define the relationships virtually. Each set of entities has a separately managed structure and the relationships are expressed as links between the entities. In CDI, a customer entity and address entity may have a "part of" relationship (i.e. a customer entity "contains" an address entity), whereas the household to customer may be a virtual relationship (i.e. a household entity "has" customer entities). The difference is the customers in a household are included by an external link (by reference).

The advantage of the virtual relationship is that changes to the definition of the relationship are less disruptive than when both entities are part of the same data structure. If the definition of the household entity changes, then it is easier to change just that definition than to change the data schema of the system. Moreover, the same entity can participate in more than one virtual relationship. For example, the CDI system may want to maintain two different household definitions for two different types of marketing applications. The virtual relationship allows the same customer entity to be a part of two different household entities.

MULTI-CHANNEL MDM

Increasingly, MDM systems must deal with multiple sources of data arriving through different channels with varying velocity, such as source data coming through network connections from other systems (e.g. e-commerce or online inquiry/update). Multi-channel data sources are both a cause and effect of Big Data. Large volumes of network data can overwhelm traditional MDM systems. This problem is particularly acute for product MDM in companies with large volumes of online sales.

Another channel that has become increasingly important, especially for CDI, is social media. Because it is user-generated content, it can provide direct insight into a customer's attitude toward products and services or readiness to buy or sell (Oberhofer, Hechler, Milman, Schumacher & Wolfson, 2014). The challenge is that it is largely unstructured, and MDM systems have traditionally been designed around the processing of structured data.

MULTI-CULTURAL MDM

As commerce becomes global, more companies are facing the challenges of operating in more than one country. From an MDM perspective, even though an entity domain may remain the same — e.g. customer, employee, product, etc. — all aspects of their management can be different. Different countries may use different character sets, different reference layouts, and different reference data to manage information related to the same entities. This creates many challenges for MDM systems assuming traditional data to be uniform. For example, much of the body of knowledge around data matching has evolved around U.S. language and culture. Fuzzy matching techniques such as Levenshtein Edit Distance and SOUNDEX phonetic matching do not apply to master data in China and other Asian countries.

Culture is not only manifested in language, but in the representation of master data as well, especially for party data. The U.S. style of first, middle, and last name attributes for persons is not always a good fit in other cultures. The situation for address fields can be even more complicated. Another complicating factor is countries often having different regulations and compliance standards around certain data typically included in MDM systems.

THE CHALLENGE OF BIG DATA
WHAT IS BIG DATA?

Big Data has many definitions. Initially Big Data was just the recognition that, as systems produced and stored more data, the volume had increased to the point that it could no longer be processed on traditional system platforms. The traditional definition of Big Data simply referred to volumes of data requiring new, large-scale systems/software to process the data in a reasonable time frame.

Later the definition was revised when people recognized the problem was not just the volume of data being produced, but also the velocity (transactional speed) at which it was produced and variety (structured and unstructured) of data. This is the origin of the so-called "Three Vs" definition, which sometimes has been extended to four Vs by including the "veracity" (quality) of the data.

THE VALUE-ADDED PROPOSITION OF BIG DATA

At first organizations were just focused on developing tools allowing them to continue their current processing for larger data volumes. However, as organizations were more driven to compete based on data and data quality, they began to look at Big Data as a new opportunity to gain an advantage. This is based largely on the premise that large volumes of data contain more potential insight than smaller volumes. The thinking was that, instead of building predictive models based on small datasets, it is now feasible to analyze the entire dataset without the need for model development.

Google™ has been the leader in the Big Data revolution, demonstrating the value of the thick-data-thin-model approach to problem solving. An excellent example is the Google Translate product. Previously most attempts to translate sentences and phrases from one language to another consisted of building sophisticated models of the source and target and implementing them as natural language processing (NLP) applications. The Google approach was to build a large corpus of translated documents; when a request to translate text is received, the system searches the corpus to see if the same or similar translation was already available in the corpus. The same method has been applied to replace or supplement other NLP applications such as named entity recognition in unstructured text (Osesina & Talburt, 2012; Chiang et al., 2008).

For example, given a large volume of stock trading history and indicator values, which of the indicators, if any, are highly predictive leading indicators of the stock price? A traditional approach might be to undertake a statistical factor analysis on some sample of the data. However, with current technologies it might be feasible to actually compute all of the possible correlations between the combinations of indicators at varying lead times.

In addition to allowing companies to answer the same directed questions as before for much larger datasets (supervised learning), Big Data is now giving companies the ability to conduct much broader undirected searches for insights not previously known (unsupervised learning) (Provost & Fawcett, 2013).

Data analysis has added a second dimension to the Big Data concept. "Data science" is the new term combining the large volume, or 3V, aspect of Big Data with the analytics piece. Even though the term should refer to both, sometimes data science only refers to one or the other, i.e. the tools and technology for processing Big Data (the engineering side) or the tools and techniques for analyzing Big Data (the data analytics side).

CHALLENGES OF BIG DATA

Along with the added value and opportunities it brings, Big Data also brings a number of challenges. The obvious challenge is storage and process performance. Fortunately, technology has stepped up to the challenge with cheaper and larger storage systems, distributed and parallel computing platforms, and cloud computing. However, using these new technologies requires changes in ways of thinking about data processing/management and the adoption of new tools and methodologies. Unfortunately, many organizations tend to be complacent and lack the sense of urgency required to undergo successful change and transformation (Kotter, 1996).

Big Data is more than simply a performance issue to be solved by scaling up technology; it has also brought with it a paradigm shift in data processing and data management practices. For example, Big Data has had a big impact on data governance programs (Soares, 2013a, 2013b, 2014). For example, the traditional system design is to move data to a program or process, but in many Big Data applications it can be more efficient to move processes to data. Another is the trend toward denormalized data stores. Normalization of relational databases has been a best practice for decades as a way to remove as much data redundancy as possible from the system. In the world of Big Data tools, there is a growing trend toward allowing, or even deliberately creating, data redundancy in order to gain performance.

The Big Data paradigm shift has also changed traditional approaches to programming and development. Developers already in the workforce are having to stop and learn new knowledge and skills in order to use Big Data tools, and colleges and universities require time to change their curricula to teach these tools. Currently, there is a significant gap between industry—education supply and demand. The people training in Big Data tools and analysis are typically referred to as data scientists, and many schools are rebranding their programs as data science.

MDM AND BIG DATA — THE N-SQUARED PROBLEM

Although many traditional data processes can easily scale to take advantage of Big Data tools and techniques, MDM is not one of them. MDM has a Big Data problem with Small Data. Because MDM is based on ER, it is subject to the $O(n^2)$ problem. $O(n^2)$ denotes the effort and resources needed to complete an algorithm or data process growing in proportion to the square of the number of records being processed. In other words, the effort required to perform ER on 100 records is 4 times more than the effort to perform the same ER process on 50 records because $100^2 = 10,000$ and $50^2 = 2,500$ and $10,000/2,500 = 4$. More simply stated, it takes 4 times more effort to scale from 50 records to 100 records because $(100/50)^2 = 4$.

Big Data not only brings challenging performance issues to ER and MDM, it also exacerbates all of the dimensions of MDM previously discussed. Multi-domain, multi-channel, hierarchical, and multi-cultural MDM are impacted by the growing volume of data that enterprises must deal with. Although the problems are formidable, ER and MDM can still be effective for Big Data. Chapters 9 and 10 focus on Big Data MDM.

CONCLUDING REMARKS

Although MDM requires addressing a number of technical issues, overall it is a business issue implemented for business reasons. The primary goal of MDM is to achieve and maintain entity identity integrity for a domain of master entities managed by the organization. The MDM system itself comprises two components — a policy and governance component, and an IT component. The primary IT component is EIIM which is, in turn, supported by ER. EIIM extends the cross-sectional, one-time matching process of ER with a longitudinal management component of persistent EIS and entity identifiers.

Except for External Reference Architecture, the other principal MDM architectures share the common feature of a central hub. Most of the discussion in the remaining chapters will focus on the operation of the hub, and its identity knowledge base (IKB).

Big Data and data science have seemingly emerged overnight with great promise for added value. At the same time, they have created a paradigm shift in IT in a short time. The impacts are being felt in all aspects of the organization, and everyone is struggling to understand both the technology and how best to extract business value. The impact of Big Data is particularly dramatic for MDM and the implementation of MDM, because Big Data pushes the envelope of current computing technology.

Entity Identity Information and the CSRUD Life Cycle Model

ENTITIES AND ENTITY REFERENCES

For the purposes of this book, *entities* are defined to be distinguishable real-world objects such as people, products, or places. This definition does not include concepts or types as is often the case in defining entities in other contexts. So for this discussion, person as a concept or type is not an entity, whereas a particular person, i.e. an instance of the person type, is an entity. This approach is consistent with the object-oriented programming distinction between a class and an object as a specific instance of a class. At the same time, being an object or instance of a concept or type should not be confused with being intangible or nontactile. For example, events, though not tactile objects, are often considered entities. The key point is that each entity is distinct and distinguishable from every other entity of the same type.

Having said that, the distinction between *entity* and *entity type* is not always so clear. What is considered an entity really depends upon the viewpoint of the organization defining the entity and the design of its information system. For example, consider the case of product information. A particular product line, such as a Model XYZ Television, might be considered an entity as distinct from a Model ABC Toaster. At the same time, there are actually many instances of each product, i.e. many XYZ television sets and ABC toasters each labeled with a unique serial number. Each television and each toaster can also be considered an entity. However, most organization's MDM system would treat each product line as an entity rather than each product instance, although other systems supported by the MDM system, such as inventory, may be concerned with tracking products at the instance level.

Understanding which attributes are most important for any given application is a key step in any data management process (Heien, Wu, & Talburt, 2010). In the context of MDM, each entity type has a set of attributes taking on different values that describe the entities' characteristics. For student entities these might be the student's name, date-of-birth, height, or weight. Entity attributes with the combination of values most useful for distinguishing one entity from another are called identity attributes.

From an information systems perspective it is important to make a clear distinction between an entity and a reference to an entity. Information systems do not manipulate physical entities; rather, they model the real world by creating and storing data that describe or reference entities in the real world.

An entity reference in an information system is a set of attribute-value pairs intended to describe a particular real-world entity in a particular context. An entity may have zero or more identities within a given domain. For example, a person may have two identities in a school system because he or she is both a student and an employee at the school. An entity may of course have different identities in different domains. For example, a person is a customer in Macy's and has another identity being an employee at IBM (Josang & Pope, 2005). An entity identity expressed in a certain domain is referred to as a surrogate identity.

In a school information system a student walking around on the campus is the entity, and the various records in the school administration software system describing the student are the entity references. This usage of the term *entity* is at odds with the typical database modeling terminology in which each row of a student table would be called an entity rather than an entity reference.

THE UNIQUE REFERENCE ASSUMPTION

An important assumption in the discussion of entity resolution (ER) is the "unique reference assumption." This assumption states:

> *"In an information system, every entity reference is always created to refer to one, and only one, entity."*

The reason for this assumption is that, in practice, an information system reference may appear to be ambiguous, i.e. it could refer to more than one real-world entity or possibly not to any entity. A salesperson could write a product description on a sales order, but because the description is incomplete, a data-entry operator might enter the correct description, but enter the wrong product identifier. Now it is no longer clear whether the newly created reference in the information system refers to the product according to its description or according to its product identifier. Despite this problem, it was the intent of the salesperson to record the description of a specific product.

Sebastian-Coleman (2013) describes this same concept in terms of Shannon's Schematic for Communication in which both the transmitter or creator of information and the receiver of the information make interpretations introducing noise into the communication channel. Similarly, Wang and Strong (1996) have recognized interpretability and understandability as key dimensions of their data quality framework. The degree of completeness, accuracy, timeliness, believability, consistency, accessibility, and many other aspects of reference data can dramatically affect the outcome of an ER process. This is one of the many reasons why ER is so integral to the field of information quality.

THE PROBLEM OF ENTITY REFERENCE RESOLUTION

As defined in the previous chapter, ER is the process of determining whether two information system references to real-world objects are referring to the same object or to different objects. The term *entity* is used because of the references to real-world objects —persons, places, or things — and *resolution* because ER is fundamentally a decision process. Technically it would be better to describe it as *entity reference resolution*, but the current term is well-established. Jonas (2007) prefers the term "semantic reconciliation."

Although ER is defined as a decision regarding a pair of references, these decisions can be systematically applied to a larger set of references in such a way that each reference is ultimately classified into a cluster of references, all of which are deemed to reference the same entity. These clusters will form a partition of the set of references so each reference will be classified into one and only one cluster. Viewed in this larger context, ER is also defined as "the process of identifying and merging records judged to represent the same real-world entity" (Benjelloun et al., 2009). This will be discussed in more detail in Chapter 3.

THE FUNDAMENTAL LAW OF ENTITY RESOLUTION

The fundamental law of entity resolution recasts the data quality principle of entity identity integrity into the vocabulary of ER. When an ER process decides two references are equivalent, the decision is instantiated in the system through a special attribute added to each reference called a "link" attribute. The absolute value of the link attribute is not important; in ER what is important is its relative value, i.e. records determined to be equivalent by the ER process are given the same link values and records determined not to be equivalent are given different link values. The process of assigning these values is called "linking" and two references sharing the same link value are said to be "linked." Therefore, the fundamental law of ER can be stated as

> *"An entity resolution system should link two references if and only if the references are equivalent."*

Failure to obey this law is manifest in two types of errors, false positive and false negative errors. As noted earlier, a false negative error occurs when the ER process fails to link two references that are equivalent, and a false positive error occurs when the ER process links two references that are not equivalent. The evaluation of ER process outcomes is essentially a matter of counting false positive and false negative errors.

INTERNAL VS. EXTERNAL VIEW OF IDENTITY

Entities are described in terms of their characteristics called *attributes*. The values of these attributes provide information about a specific entity. Identity attributes, when taken together, distinguish one entity from another. Identity attributes for people are things like name, address, date-of-birth, and fingerprints; the questions often asked in order to identify a person requesting a driver's license or hospital admission provide good examples of identity attributes. For a product, the identity attributes might be model number, size, manufacturer, or Universal Product Code (UPC).

Fundamentally, the problem of ER is identity management, but from the outside looking in. Take the example of someone being admitted to the hospital. When that person provides the admitting information about identity, they are mapping or projecting some small portion of their overall identity into the information system. Once the information is in the system together with other references to this same patient and to other patients, an ER process tries to infer which references are equivalent and which are not equivalent based on these identity clues.

One way to describe this situation is in terms of an internal view versus an external view of identity (Talburt, Zhou, & Shivaiah, 2009). Figure 2.1 illustrates the basic elements of name and address contact history for a woman born "Mary Smith." Because these are records of where this woman was living, it is also called an occupancy history. Figure 2.1 shows three occupancy records, each with a name, an address, and a period of time that the occupancy was valid. Also note the change in name between Occupancy 1 and Occupancy 2.

There are two ways to view the issue of identity shown in Figure 2.1. One is to start with the identity based on biographical information, e.g. Mary Smith, a female born on December 3, 1980, in Anytown, NY, to parents Robert and Susan Smith, and to follow the identity through its various representations of name and address. This internal view of identity as shown in Figure 2.1 is the view of Mary Smith herself and might well be the view of a sibling or other close relative, someone with first-hand knowledge about her occupancy history.

The internal view of identity represents a closed universe model in which, for a given set of identity attributes, all of the attribute values are known to the internal viewer, and any unknown value for one of these attributes must belong to a different identity. An ER system possessing this information could always correctly resolve whether any given name and address reference was part of a particular identity or not.

On the other hand, an external view of identity is one in which some number of attribute values for an identity have been collected, but it is not certain if it is a complete collection of values or even if all of the values are correct. When a system

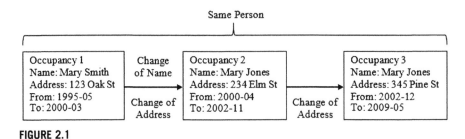

FIGURE 2.1

An occupancy history.

working from an external view is presented with a reference, the system must always decide whether the reference should be linked to an existing identity, or if it represents a new identity in the system. An external view of identity represents an open universe model because, unlike the internal view, the system cannot assume it has complete and correct knowledge of all identity values.

As an example, suppose a system has only Occupancy Records 1 and 2 of the identity in Figure 2.1. In that case the system's knowledge of this identity is incomplete. It may be incomplete because Occupancy Record 3 has not been acquired or because it is in the system but has not been linked to Records 1 and 2. In the latter case, the system would treat Record 3 as part of a different identity. Even though an internal viewer would know that the Occupancy Record 3 should also be part of the identity in Figure 2.1, the system does not have sufficient information to make that decision.

In addition to the problem of creating an incomplete view of an identity, the system may assemble an inaccurate view of an identity. When presented with a new occupancy record, the system may erroneously link it with an existing identity to which it does not belong. Again, this speaks to the close ties between ER and IQ. In particular, it points out that the accuracy of data integration has two important components. First is the accuracy of the individual records, but the second is the correct aggregation of the records related to the same entity.

In an external view of identity, the collection of attribute values that have been linked together by the system comprises its view of the identity of the entity. In other words, an ER system based on an external view builds its knowledge about entity identities piece-by-piece. The external view of identity resembles how a business or a government agency would use ER tools in an effort to link their records into a single view of a customer or agency client.

All ER systems use identity at some level in order to resolve references, but not all ER systems implement identity management functions. For example, the simplest form of ER is the merge-purge process. It uses identity by assuming references with certain closely matching attribute values are equivalent and assigns these matching references the same link identifier. At the end of the merge-purge process, the system forms an external view of the identity of each entity represented in the file. This view comprises the information in the references linked together in the same cluster. However, after the merge-purge process has ended, the identity information in each cluster is lost. Merge-purge systems by their nature do not retain and manage entity identities for future processing. Each merge-purge process starts from scratch and the identity knowledge it assembles is transient, existing only during the processing of the current file.

MANAGING ENTITY IDENTITY INFORMATION

As discussed in Chapter 1, Entity Identity Information Management (EIIM) is the extension of ER that focuses on storing and maintaining information relating to the identity of the entities under management. In EIIM, each entity is represented by a single knowledge structure called an entity identity structure (EIS). When an EIS is created, it is assigned a unique identifier which becomes the information system's identifier for the real-world object corresponding to the EIS.

The goal of EIIM is two-fold. First is to achieve a state in which each EIS represents one, and only one, real-world entity, and different real-world entities are represented by different EIS. This is the goal of entity identity integrity as stated earlier. The second goal is to assure that when an EIS that is created to represent a given real-world entity is assigned a unique identifier, the EIS will continue to have that same identifier in the future. This is the goal of persistent identifiers. Despite best efforts, achieving these goals in all cases is almost impossible, especially for large numbers of entities and entity references. Due to differences in source data, timing, age of references, and other factors affecting the ability to correctly link references, some level of false positive and false negative errors will inevitably occur in any automated MDM system.

A false positive error occurs when an EIS has identity information for more than one real-world entity. A false positive violates the goal of entity identity integrity because a single EIS represents more than one real-world entity. It may also cause the system to violate the goal of maintaining persistent identifiers. When the information in the EIS is separated to correctly represent the identities of both entities, it may require creating a new EIS for each entity. The entity represented by the new EIS will have a new identifier creating a situation where the identifier for an identity has changed. Entities "split out" from the original EIS will require new identifiers. First, they were represented by the over-merged EIS, and then after the correction, they are represented by a new EIS with a different identifier.

The false negative error occurs when two or more EIS represent the same real-world entity. Clearly this violates entity identity integrity. The correction for this problem is to merge the EIS representing the same entity. Because each EIS should have only one identifier, only one of the original identifiers can survive after the merger, and the other identifiers must be retired. Again this creates a situation where the identifier for an identity has changed.

ENTITY IDENTITY INTEGRITY

A fundamental constraint of any database system is that different rows should not have the same identity. However, in most database models, identity is defined as the primary key value, i.e. no two rows should have the same primary key value. In the case where a table is intended to represent master data, this simple approach to identity does not take into consideration the question of reference. As anyone with any experience with database systems understands, just because two rows in a table have different primary key values, it does not necessarily follow that they are references to different entities.

In a master data table each entity should be represented by one, and only one, row. The most common failure of a master data table stems from more than one reference to the same object. This "over representation" of entities is often the root cause of many data quality issues in database systems. This kind of data redundancy in customer, student, patient, product, account, or other master data can cascade through the entire system, producing many other problems.

In most database tables, the primary key value is an arbitrarily assigned value, only there to guarantee the value is unique but unrelated to the values of the entity's identity attributes. Assigning a primary key without regard for the represented identity may obey the letter of the primary key constraint, but it violates the spirit of entity identity integrity. Entity identity integrity is at the heart of MDM processing.

Entity identity integrity requires

- Each entity in a domain has one and only one representation in the system
- Distinct entities have distinct representations in the system

Figure 2.2 illustrates the state of entity identity integrity in which each real-world object has only one reference in the information system, and different objects have different references.

Entity identity integrity can be represented as a one-to-one, onto (in mathematical terminology, injective and surjective) function from the information system references to the real-world objects.

Huang, Lee, and Wang (1999) describe a concept similar to entity identity integrity called "proper representation." Proper representation, shown in Figure 2.3, is

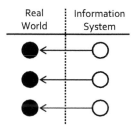

FIGURE 2.2

Entity identity integrity.

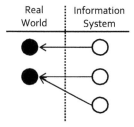

FIGURE 2.3

Redundant representation (proper representation).

less stringent than entity identity integrity because it only requires that different objects have different references but does not require each object to have only one reference.

In proper representation, the mapping from the information systems references to the real-world objects is only required to be what is called a *surjective function*. A surjective function is one in which every element in the range of the function (in this case the real-world objects) has at least one element in the domain of the function (in this case the system references) mapped to it. Proper representation still allows for multiple references to the same object. Huang et al. (1999) use the term *proper representation* because in general there are cases where it is desirable to have many references to the same object in an information system. For example, when a table is holding sales transactions for a product, one would expect that there would be many different sales of the same product.

However, when the references are to master data, then proper representation really means redundant representation and signals the occurrence of a false negative error. A false negative occurs in an MDM system when there are two distinct references to the same entity.

Huang et al. (1999) also describe a state called "ambiguous representation" shown in Figure 2.4. Ambiguous representation occurs when two or more distinct objects have only one reference in the information system. From an MDM perspective ambiguous representation represents a false positive error in which one reference refers to two distinct objects.

As noted earlier, every MDM system of any size will have some level of false negative and false positive errors. Moreover, these errors tend to be inversely related because the decisions are largely based on matching or similarity. When the match criteria are relaxed in order to correct false negatives in the data, it may create a situation in which previously true negative references match and are clustered together to create false positives. Similarly, imposing more stringent match conditions will tend to reduce false positives, but may in turn prevent true positive links, thereby increasing false negatives. Given a choice, most organizations prefer to make false negative errors over making positive errors.

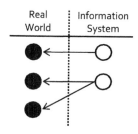

FIGURE 2.4

Ambiguous representation.

There are several reasons for this tendency. In many customer-based applications, a false negative often has less business risk than a false positive. For example, a bank would rather fail to recognize that two accounts are owned by the same customer than to have two different customers assigned to and making transactions in the same account. The same example also illustrates a second reason. In general, it is easier to merge transactions for the same entity once separated by different identifiers than it is to sort out transactions belonging to different entities merged together by the same entity identifier.

A third reason is simply a matter of culture and expectation. Unfortunately, most people, including system managers, are somewhat accustomed to poor data quality. No one seems to be surprised when a system fails to bring together master records that are dissimilar. In some sense it is easier to explain, and perhaps there is more forgiveness for, why two master records for the same entity were not brought together than to explain why two master records were incorrectly merged.

A meaningless state (Huang et al., 1999) occurs when the SOR contains a reference unresolvable to any real-world object (Figure 2.5). Meaningless states can occur for different reasons. One is a lack of synchronization over time. A valid reference in the SOR may later become invalid — for example, a reference to a network circuit remaining in the system even though the circuit has been removed and no longer exists. In this case, the decision to keep the reference may be warranted for historical or archival reasons. However, most meaningless states arise due to data quality errors when identifiers and identity attribute values are corrupted by people and processes.

An incomplete state (Huang et al., 1999) exists when objects in the domain of interest do not have corresponding references in the information system (Figure 2.6). Incompleteness can manifest in an MDM system for different reasons. It can be during the initial implementation of the system when the existence and attribute values of the entities have yet to be established and registered. It can also occur when a new entity entering a system has delayed or failed system registration.

The process for establishing MDM registry entries often takes two forms, a formal registration and discovery by transaction. For the patient example, a formal

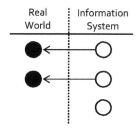

FIGURE 2.5

Meaningless state.

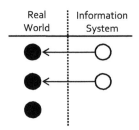

FIGURE 2.6

Incomplete representation.

process of admission gathers and enters registration information in detail. In a system with formal registration, no transaction can be recorded for an entity until that entity has been registered and has an identifier.

However, other MDM system designs are more dynamic and allow entities to be discovered through transactions. Discovery is often used for customer entities in businesses with no formal registration process. A person or company becomes a customer by simply making a purchase. As purchase transactions are processed, the system tries to determine if the purchaser is already registered as a customer entity. If not, the system establishes a new entry and identifier for the customer. Because a transaction will tend to have less identifying information than a full registration record, a system registering entities "on the fly" in this way typically requires more stewardship and adjustment than one in which entities are preregistered. Systems with dynamic registration have a higher probability of creating false negatives. As more information is accumulated in subsequent processes, what appeared initially to be a new entity is later determined to be a previously registered entity with somewhat different identifying information, such as the same customer with a new address.

THE NEED FOR PERSISTENT IDENTIFIERS

By definition, ER attempts to achieve entity identity integrity at a particular point in time; that is, given a set of entity references, an ER process successively compares and sorts entity references into groups representing the same real-world entity. This sorting is typically followed by a purging process through which duplicate references are removed, leaving only one reference for each entity. ER used in this way is often referred to as a "merge-purge" process in which various files are reformatted into a common layout, merged into a single file, and the duplicate or redundant (equivalent) references are removed.

However, achieving entity identity integrity at a single point in time is not sufficient to support MDM. Another important requirement of MDM is that once an identifier for an entity is established in the information system, it will continue to have the same identifier over time, i.e. master data objects are given "persistent identifiers." Although some operational processes can operate without persistent entity identifiers, the lack of persistence is a major problem for data warehouses that store historical data. If transactions for the same customer or patient are given different identifiers at different times, then it becomes extremely problematic to analyze the information and make effective decisions. Lee et al. (2006) list multiple sources of the same information as the first of the top ten root causes of data quality problems.

In order to create and maintain a persistent identifier, an ER process must also store and manage the identity information of the entity object so the same object can be recognized and given the same identifier in subsequent processes. Thus, MDM requires the application of ER processes to maintain entity identity integrity and also requires entity identity information management (EIIM) to maintain persistent identifiers.

ENTITY IDENTITY INFORMATION LIFE CYCLE MANAGEMENT MODELS

As has long been recognized in the field of information management, information has a life cycle. Information is not static; it changes over time. Several models of information life cycle management have been developed and a few of these are discussed here.

POSMAD MODEL

English (1999) formulated a five-phase information life cycle model of plan, acquire, maintain, dispose, and apply, adapted from a generalized resource management model. McGilvray (2008) later extended the model by adding a "store and share" phase and naming it the POSMAD life cycle model, an acronym for

- Plan for information
- Obtain the information
- Store and Share the information
- Maintain and manage the information
- Apply the information to accomplish your goals
- Dispose of the information as it is no longer needed

POSMAD is similar to the CRUD model long used by database modelers as primarily a process model for the basic database operations of creating rows (C), reading rows (R), updating rows (U), and deleting rows (D).

THE LOSHIN MODEL

Entity information also has a life cycle, and understanding it is critical to successful EIIM. For example, Loshin (2009) has described a five-phase life cycle for master data objects similar to the POSMAD life cycle but cast in MDM and EIIM terminology. The five phases are

- Establishment
- Distribution
- Access and Use
- Deactivation and Retire
- Maintain and Update

THE CSRUD MODEL

Following the lead of the CRUD model, another five-phase MDM life cycle model is proposed here that has a similar operational focus. The five phases of CSRUD are

- Capture — the initial creation of EIS for the system. Capture occurs when an MDM system is first installed. However, there is almost always some form of MDM, either in a dedicated system or an internal ad hoc system that must be migrated into the new system.
- Store and Share — the saving of EIS in a persistent format such as a database or flat-file format.
- Resolution and Retrieve — the actual use of the MDM information in which transactions with master data identifying information are compared (resolved) against the EIS in order to determine their identity. When an entity reference in a transaction is determined to be associated with a particular EIS, the EIS identifier is added to the transaction. For this reason, the process is sometimes called "link append" because the EIS identifier added to the transaction is used to link together transactions for the same entity.
- Update — the adding of new EIS related to new entities and updating previously created EIS with new information. The update process can be either automated or manual. Manual updates are often used to correct false positive and false negative errors introduced by the automated update process.
- Dispose — the retiring of EIS from the system. EIS are retired for two reasons. The first is the case where the EIS is correct, but is no longer active or relevant. The second is in the correction of false negative errors where two or more EIS are merged into a single EIS.

CONCLUDING REMARKS

The key take-away from Chapter 2 is MDM is an ongoing process, not a one-time event. Entity identity information will change, and the MDM system needs to have enough functionality to take these changes into account. The MDM system should be able to address all five phases of the CSRUD Life Cycle including the initial design and capture of the entity identity information, storing and sharing identity information, resolving inquiries for entity identity, updating entity identity information as it changes, and retirement of entities and entity identifiers. Each of the five phases will be discussed at length in the next chapters, as follows:

- Chapter 3, Capture Phase
- Chapter 4, Store and Share Phase
- Chapter 5, Update Phase and Dispose Phase
- Chapter 6, Resolve and Retrieve Phase.

A Deep Dive into the Capture Phase

AN OVERVIEW OF THE CAPTURE PHASE

Figure 3.1 shows the overall flow of the capture phase of the CSRUD life cycle model. Entity references are placed into a staging area where they undergo data cleansing and data standardization based. Next they are processed by the ER engine implementing an ER algorithm and matching rule.

Each cluster of references the system determines are for the same entity is assigned a unique identifier. At the end of the process the cluster and its identifier are stored as an entity identity structure (EIS) in an identity knowledge base (IKB).

In addition to the IKB, the capture process has two other important outputs. One is the link index, and the other consists of the clerical review indicators. The link index is simply a two-column list. The items in the first column are the identifiers of the input, and the items in the second column are the EIS identifiers created during the capture process. Each row corresponds to one input reference where the first

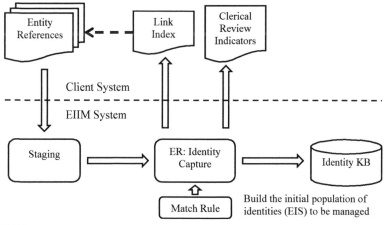

FIGURE 3.1

Schematic of the capture phase.

entry in the row is the unique identifier of the reference (from the client system), and the second entry is the identifier of the EIS to which the reference was assigned by the capture process. The link index is produced so that the client can append the entity identifiers to the original references for further processing within the client system.

For example, if the input references are enrollment records for students in a large school district, the link index would show which student (entity) identifier was assigned by the ER process to each enrollment record. If each record represents a different student, then all of the student identifiers would be different unless the ER process has made a false positive error. On the other hand, if two references have the same identifier, they may be positives because they represent the same transfer student between schools within the district.

The second output shown in Figure 3.1 is a list of review indicators. Review indicators are conditions or events that occurred during the ER process and alerted a data steward to the possibility of a linking error. As the name implies, review indicators should be manually reviewed by a data steward or other domain expert to determine whether or not an error was actually made or not. Just as important, if the person determines an error was made, then the system should provide some mechanism to help the person correct the error.

Review indicators represent an important aspect of ER and MDM data stewardship. They provide an important input into the update phase of the CSRUD life cycle. Unfortunately, review indicators along with formal ER results assessment are the two most neglected aspects of MDM implementations. The design and use of review indicators will be discussed in more detail as part of the update phase of the CSRUD life cycle in Chapter 5.

BUILDING THE FOUNDATION

The CSRUD life cycle starts with the initial capture of entity identity information from entity references. Although the capture phase is a one-time process, it involves a number of activities that, if not done correctly, will hinder the future performance of the MDM system. The capture phase is similar to the design phase of a software development project: a critical first step laying the foundation for the entire system.

The key activities and steps for the capture phase are:

1. Assess the quality of the data
2. Plan the data cleansing process
3. Select candidates for both primary and supporting identity attributes
4. Select and set up the method or methods for assessing the entity identity integrity of the results
5. Decide on the matching strategy
6. Craft an initial data-matching rule

7. Run the capture with the rule and assess the results
8. Analyze the false positive and false negative errors and determine their causes
9. Improve the matching rule
10. Repeat Steps 6 through 9 until an acceptable level of error has been obtained.

UNDERSTANDING THE DATA

The capture phase starts with a data quality assessment of each source. The assessment includes profiling the sources with a data quality profiling tool to understand the structure and general condition of the data and also visually inspecting the records in order to find specific conditions that may become obstacles to the ER process. The assessment will

- Identify which attributes are present in each source. Some attributes may be present in some sources, but not others. Even when the same attributes or types of attributes appear in two different sources, they may be in different formats or structured differently. For example, one source may have the entire customer name in a single unstructured field, whereas another source has the customer name elements (given name, family name, etc.) in separate fields.
- Generate statistics, such as uniqueness and missing value counts, that will help to decide which attributes will have the highest value as identity attributes. These are candidates for use in the matching rule.
- Assess the extent of data quality problems in each source, such as:
  - Missing values, including null values, empty strings, blank values, and place-holder values, e.g. "LNU" for Last Name Unknown.
  - Inconsistent representation (variation) of values whether due to inconsistent coding, such as "Ark" and "AR" as codes for "Arkansas" in the state address field, or due to inconsistent formatting, such as coding some telephone numbers as "(501) 555-1234" and others as "501.555.1234". Here the most useful profiling outputs are value frequency tables, pattern frequency tables, and maximum and minimum values (outliers).
  - Misfielding, such as a person's given name in the surname field, or an email address in a telephone field.

DATA PREPARATION

The next step is to decide on which data cleansing and standardization processes can be applied to address the issues found by the assessment. In the case where some files have combined related attribute values into a single unstructured field and others have the same information decomposed into separate fields, the first decision is whether to have a cleansing step attempting to parse (separate) elements in the unstructured field or combine the separate fields into a single field. The decision to parse unstructured fields will depend upon the complexity of the field and the availability of a parsing tool to accurately identify and separate the components. The decision to combine separate fields into one will depend upon the availability of a comparator algorithm able to effectively determine the similarity of compound, multi-valued fields.

The choice about combined versus parsed fields also ties to the larger issues of how much data preparation should be done prior to ER and how much should be handled by the ER process itself. Separating the data cleansing and transformation processes and making them external to the ER process may be simpler, but it also creates a dependency. If for some reason the data cleansing and transformation processes are not applied, or if they are applied differently at different times, an ER process running the same input data using the same match rule could produce dramatically different results. That said, moving data cleansing and transformation responsibility into the ER process tends to increases the complexity of matching rules, and if matching functions have more steps to perform, program execution times could increase. With the advent of faster and cheaper processors the trend has been to move more of the data cleansing and transformation processes into the ER matching process itself, thereby reducing the dependency on external data preparation processes.

SELECTING IDENTITY ATTRIBUTES

One of the keys to success in any data quality project is an analysis to determine the critical data elements (CDEs) (Jugulum, 2014). For ER the CDEs are the identity attributes. Identity attributes are those attributes of an entity reference whose values are most helpful in distinguishing one entity from another. The values of some attributes provide the system with more power to discriminate among entities than other attributes. For customer references, name and address information, especially in combination, are often the primary basis for identification. However, other attributes can help confirm good matches or prevent unwise matches. For example, reliable gender information may prevent matching "J Smith (Male)" with "J Smith (Female)" for customers John and Jan Smith at the same address. In contrast, reliable telephone information might reinforce the decision to accept "John Smith, 123 Main St, 555-1234" with "John Smith, 345 Oak St, 555-1234" as the same customer even though the two references have different street addresses.

Primary identity attributes are those identity attributes whose values have the most uniqueness and completeness. For example, in the U.S. one of the most powerful discriminators for persons is the federally assigned unique social security number (SSN) for each individual. However, if a SSN is not present in the source, then it cannot be used in an ER process. Even in those cases where SSN might be present, such as school enrollment records, they do not always provide a perfect matching solution. Often SSN are erroneously reported or entered incorrectly into the system. Invalid values are sometimes deliberately entered when the data capture system requires a SSN value to be present, but the real value is not provided. Because it is rare that the values of one attribute will reliably identify all entities, in almost all cases, matching rules for entity references use a combination of identity attributes.

Supporting identity attributes are those identity attributes, such as gender or age, with values having less uniqueness or completeness. Supporting identity attributes are used in combination with primary identity attributes to confirm or deny matches. For example, in product master data the product supplier code is an attribute with possibly low uniqueness if many of the products under management come from the same supplier. In this case, the supplier code by itself would have limited discriminating power, but could still help to confirm or deny a match on other attribute values.

Three commonly used measures providing insight into the capability of an identity attribute to distinguish between entities include:

- Uniqueness
- Entropy
- Weight

ATTRIBUTE UNIQUENESS

The uniqueness of an attribute in a given table or dataset is the ratio of the count of unique values to the count of all non-null values the attribute takes on. Most profiling tools automatically give uniqueness as a column statistic. If an attribute takes on a different value for every row or record of the dataset, then its uniqueness will be 100%. On the other hand, an attribute like student gender, which only takes on a few distinct values, will have an extremely low uniqueness value.

When assessing a set of references for primary and secondary attributes, it is important to remember the most desirable measure is not the uniqueness of the attribute's values across all of the references, but the uniqueness of its values with respect to the entities the references represent. Assuming some redundancy in references, i.e. cases where different references in the set are referring to the same entity, then in those cases it is better if the attribute takes on the same value for equivalent references. In other words, if two references are for the same student, then having the same first name value in both references is a good thing even though it lowers the uniqueness of the first name attribute across the complete set of references. The most desirable feature of an identity attribute is the degree to which it has the same value for equivalent records and different values for nonequivalent references. The point is the level of uniqueness should be commensurate with the expected level of entity reference redundancy in the set of references. The actual measure for this is called the attribute weight as defined later in this section.

ATTRIBUTE ENTROPY

Another measure often used to evaluate identity attributes is entropy as defined by Shannon (1948). Although similar to uniqueness, entropy takes into account the relative frequency of the unique values of an attribute.

$$Entropy = -\sum_{j=1}^{n}\{prob(v_j)\cdot\log_2(prob(v_j))\}$$

In this formulation, the probability of a value (v_j) is its relative frequency in the dataset. In some ways, entropy is to uniqueness what standard deviation is to the mean in statistics. The more diverse the set of values an attribute takes on, the higher its entropy will be. In the case of an attribute having a constant value, the probability of that value will be 1, and because the $\log_2(1) = 0$, the entropy of a constant value attribute will be 0.

Unlike uniqueness, the entropy value will vary with the distribution of values. For example, consider the gender attribute for a dataset comprising 100 references to students. If every reference has a non-null gender value of "M" or "F", then the uniqueness measure will be 0.02 (2/100). However, the entropy measure will vary depending upon the distribution of values. For example, if there are an equal number of male and female students then the probability of "M" and "F" are both 0.5 (or 50%). In this case, the entropy of the gender attribute will be

$$-(0.5\cdot\log_2(0.5) + 0.5\cdot\log_2(0.5)) = -(0.5\cdot(-1) + 0.5\cdot(-1)) = 1$$

On the other hand, if 70% of the students are female and 30% are male, then the entropy will be

$$-(0.7\cdot\log_2(0.7) + 0.3\cdot\log_2(0.3)) = -(0.7\cdot(-0.515) + 0.3\cdot(-1.737)) = 0.882$$

ATTRIBUTE WEIGHT

Fellegi and Sunter (1969) provided a formal measure of the power of an identity attribute to predict equivalence, i.e. to discriminate between equivalent and nonequivalent pairs, in the specific context of entity resolution. Unlike uniqueness or entropy, the attribute weight takes into account the variation of an attribute's values vis-à-vis reference equivalence.

To see how this works, suppose R is a large set of references having an identity attribute x. Further suppose S is a representative sample from R for which the equivalence or nonequivalence of each pair of references in S is already known. A sample set like S is sometimes called a Truth Set, Training Set, or Certified Record Set, for the larger set R.

If D represents all of the possible distinct pairs of references in S, then $D = E \cup N$ where E is the set of equivalent pairs in D, and N is the set of nonequivalent pairs in D. According to Fellegi and Sunter (1969), the discriminating power of x is given by

$$\log_2 \left(\frac{probability(x\ values\ agree\ in\ pair\ t | t \in E)}{probability(x\ values\ agree\ in\ pair\ t | t \in N)} \right)$$

The numerator of this fraction is the probability equivalent pairs of references will agree on the value of attribute x, whereas the denominator is the probability nonequivalent pairs will agree on x. This fraction and its logarithmic value produce large positive numbers when the denominator is small, meaning agreement on x is a good indicator for equivalent pairs. In the case of equal probability, the ratio is 1 and the logarithmic value is 0. If agreement on x is more likely to indicate the pairs of references are nonequivalent, then the ratio is less than one and the logarithmic value is negative. The computation of the weight of an identity attribute is fundamental to a data-matching technique often referred to as "probabilistic" matching, a topic discussed in more detail later.

ASSESSING ER RESULTS

If the goal of EIIM is to attain and maintain entity identity integrity (obey the Fundamental Law of ER), then it is important to be able to measure attainment of the goal. In ER this measurement is somewhat of a conundrum. In order to measure the degree of entity identity integrity attainment, it is necessary to know which references are equivalent and which are not equivalent. Of course if one already knew this for all references, then ER would be unnecessary in the first place.

Unfortunately, in many organizations the assessment of ER and EIIM results is done poorly if at all. ER and MDM managers often rely entirely on inspection of the match groups to see if the references brought together have a reasonable degree of similarity. However, as an approach to assessment, inspecting clusters for quality of match is inadequate in two fundamental ways. First, not all matching references are equivalent, and second, equivalent references do not always match.

Just inspecting clusters of matching references does not actually verify that the references are equivalent. Verification of equivalence is not the role of a matching expert; it should be done by a domain expert who is in a position to know if the references really are for the same real-world object. Furthermore, cluster inspection leaves out entirely the consideration of equivalent references not in the matching group under inspection, but that should be (Schumacher, 2010). These are references erroneously placed in clusters other than the one being inspected. In order to have a realistic assessment of ER results, the visual inspection of clusters should be replaced by, or at least supplemented with, other more comprehensive and systematic methods. Two commonly used approaches to this issue often used together are truth set development and benchmarking (Syed et al., 2012).

TRUTH SETS

A truth set is a sample of the reference for which entity identity integrity is known to be 100%. For a large set of references R, a truth set T is a representative sample of references in R for which the true equivalence or nonequivalence of each pair of references has been verified. This verification allows the references to be correctly linked with a "True Link." In other words, two references in T have the same true link if and only if they refer to the same real-world entity. The true link identifier must be assigned and verified manually to make sure each cluster of references with the same true link value reference the same entity and that clusters with different true link values reference different entities.

Assessment using the truth set is simply a matter of performing ER on the truth set, then comparing the cluster created by the ER matching process to the True Link clusters. If the ER link clusters coincide exactly with the True Link clusters, then the ER process has attained entity identity integrity for the references in the truth set. If a cluster created by the ER process overlaps with two or more truth set clusters, then the ER process has produced some level of linking errors. Measuring the degree of error will be discussed in more detail later.

BENCHMARKING

Benchmarking, on the other hand, is the process of comparing one ER outcome to another ER outcome acting on the same set of references. Even though benchmarking is a relative measure, it is useful because most organizations trying to develop a new MDM system rarely start from scratch. Usually, they start with the known performance of a legacy system. Benchmarking is similar to the truth set approach because some previous ER result (set of clusters) is a surrogate for the truth set. The difference is, when a new ER grouping is compared to the benchmark grouping and overlaps are found, it is not immediately clear if the new grouping is more or less correct than the benchmark grouping, just that they are different.

Benchmarking is based on the following assumption: when both systems agree, those links are the most likely to be correct. This assumption allows the evaluation process to focus on references linked differently in the benchmark than in the new process. These differences must still be verified, but this method considerably reduces the review and verification burden. Where there are a large number of differences, a random sample of the differences of manageable size can be taken to estimate whether the differences indicate that the new process is making better or worse linking decisions than the benchmark.

Benchmarking and truth set evaluation are often used together because neither is an ideal solution. It is difficult to build a large truth set because of the need to actually verify the correctness and completeness of the links. An accurate truth set cannot be built by the visual inspection method. It requires verification by data experts who have direct knowledge of the real-world entities. For example, when managing student identities for a school system, the final determination whether the enrollment records are for the same student should be made by the teachers or administrators at the school the student attends.

Because truth sets tend to be relatively small, they may not include relatively infrequent data anomalies or reference configurations particularly problematic for the ER matching rule. The obvious advantage of the benchmark is that it can include all of the references in production at any given time. The disadvantage of the benchmark approach is its lack of precision. Even though links made by both systems are assumed to be correct, they may not be. Both ER processes may simply be making the same mistakes.

PROBLEM SETS

Though not a method for overall assessment of ER results, collecting and setting aside problem references is another analysis technique commonly used to supplement both truth set and benchmark evaluation. Maydanchik (2007) and others advocate for the systematic collection of problem records violating particular data quality rules. In the case of ER, these are pairs of references posing particular challenges for the matching rule. These pairs of references are often collected during the creation of a truth set, when making a benchmark assessment, or from matching errors reported by clients of the system.

Even though the correct linking for problem reference pairs is known, it is usually not a good idea to incorporate them into the truth set. Ideally, the truth set should be representative of the overall population of the references being evaluated. If it is representative, then the accuracy of the ER process acting on the truth set is more likely to reflect the overall accuracy of the ER process. Even though it may be tempting to place the references in the problem set into the truth set to make the truth set larger, adding them can diminish the usefulness of the truth set for estimating the accuracy of the ER process. Adding problem records into the truth set will tend to skew estimates of the ER accuracy lower than they should be.

THE INTERSECTION MATRIX

Whether using the truth set or the benchmarking approach, the final step of the ER assessment is to compare clusters created by the two processes running against the same set of references. Table 3.1 shows 10 customer references in a truth set referencing 4 entities (customers). These are the references having the True Link values "Cust1", "Cust2", "Cust3", and "Cust4". At the same time these records have been linked by an ER process with six link values of "5", "36", "43", "56", "66", and "74".

Applying links to a set of references always generates a natural partition of the references into a subset of references sharing the same link value. A partition of the set S is a set of nonempty, nonoverlapping subsets of S that cover S, i.e. the union of the subsets is equal to S.

Table 3.1 References with Two Sets of Links

	First Name	Last Name	Address	True Link	ER Link
R1	Mary	Smith	123 Oak St	Cust1	56
R2	Maria	Smith	456 Elm St	Cust1	56
R3	M	Smith	123 Oak Ct	Cust2	36
R4	Marilyn	Smith	765 Pine Rd	Cust2	36
R5	Mary Lynn	Smythe	873 Cedar Ln	Cust3	74
R6	M L	Smithe	237 Cherry St	Cust2	36
R7	Marie	Smith	45 Elm	Cust4	66
R8	Lynn	Smith	873 Cedar St	Cust3	74
R9	Mary	Smith	132 Oak	Cust1	43
R10	M	Smythe	237 Cherry	Cust2	5

Using the example in Table 3.1, the True Link creates a partition T of S into 4 subsets where each subset corresponds to a unique link value

$$T = \{\{R1, R2, R9\}, \{R3, R4, R6, R10\}, \{R5, R8\}, \{R7\}\}$$

Similarly, the ER process creates a partition P of S having six subsets

$$P = \{\{R1, R2\}, \{R3, R4, R6\}, \{R5, R8\}, \{R7\}, \{R9\}, \{R10\}\}$$

Therefore, the comparison of ER outcomes is essentially a problem in comparing the similarity between partitions of the same set. One way to organize the comparison between two partitions of the same set is to create an intersection matrix as shown in Table 3.2.

The rows of Table 3.2 correspond to the partition classes (subsets) of the P partition of the S created by the ER process. The columns correspond to the partition classes of the T partition created by the Truth Links. At the intersection of each row and column in Table 3.2 are two numbers. The first number is the size of the intersection between the partition classes in the case where there is a

Table 3.2 The Intersection Matrix of T and P

P\T	{R1,R2,R9}		{R3,R4, R6,R10}		{R5,R8}		{R7}		L	
{R1,R2}	2	1							2	1
{R3,R4,R6}			3	3					3	3
{R5,R8}					2	1			2	1
{R7}							1	0	1	0
{R9}	1	0							1	0
{R10}			1	0					1	0
E	3	3	4	6	2	1	1	0	10	45

nonempty intersection. The second number is the count of distinct pairs of references that can be formed using the references in the intersection. This is given by the formula

$$Pair\ Count = \frac{(N)(N-1)}{2}$$

where N is the number of references in the intersection.

The last row of the matrix is labeled E because it summarizes the counts of equivalent references and distinct pairs of equivalent references. For example, the second column has 4 equivalent references {R3, R4, R6, R10} that can form 6 pairs ($4 \times 3/2$). Similarly, the last column is labeled L because it summarizes the counts of references linked by the ER process and possible pairs of distinct linked references. For example, the second row has 3 linked records {R3, R4, R6}, which can form 3 distinct pairs. The last number in the matrix is the total number of references (10) and the total number of distinct pairs that can be formed from all references (45).

The intersection matrix in Table 3.2 can also be used to understand the distribution of true and false positives and true and false negatives. Let R be a set of entity references, and let D represent the set of all possible distinct pairs of references in R. In the example of Table 3.2, R has 10 elements and D has 45 elements. Following the Fundamental Law of Entity Resolution, the set D can be decomposed into four nonoverlapping subsets TP, TN, FP, and FN where

- TP is the set of True Positive resolutions. A pair of references belongs in TP if the references are equivalent and the ER process has linked them together.
- TN is the set of True Negative resolutions. A pair of references belongs in TN if the references are not equivalent and the ER process has not linked them together.
- FP is the set of False Positive resolutions. A pair of references belongs in FP if the references are not equivalent and the ER process has linked them together.
- FN is the set of False Negative resolutions. A pair of references belongs in FN if the references are equivalent and the ER process has not linked them together.

The Fundamental Law of ER holds when FP and FN are empty. Figure 3.2 illustrates the concepts represented as a Venn diagram.

The counts for each of these sets can be derived from the intersection matrix shown in Table 3.2. The pair counts at the nonempty cell intersections represent TP pairs because they are pairs of equivalent records now linked together. Table 3.2 shows the 5 true positive pairs in D.

$$|TP| = 1 + 3 + 1 + 0 + 0 = 5$$

The number of equivalent pairs (E) can be found by adding the pair counts in the last row.

$$|E| = 3 + 6 + 1 + 0 = 10$$

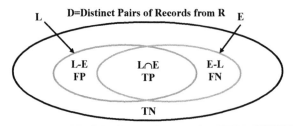

References (R)	Linked Pairs (L)	Not-Linked
Equivalent Pairs E	**True Positive** $L \cap E$	**False Negative** $E - L$
Not Equivalent D − E	**False Positive** $L - E$	**True Negative** $D - (L \cup E)$

FIGURE 3.2

The decomposition of D into FP, TP, FN, and TN.

Similarly, the number of linked pairs (L) can be found by adding the pair counts in the last column.

$$|L| = 1 + 3 + 1 + 0 + 0 + 0 = 5$$

From these, all of the remaining counts can now be calculated as

$$|FP| = |L| - |TP| = 5 - 5 = 0$$

$$|FN| = |E| - |TP| = 10 - 5 = 5$$

$$|TN| = |D| - |TP| - |FP| - |FN| = 45 - 5 - 0 - 5 = 35$$

MEASUREMENTS OF ER OUTCOMES

The TP, TN, FP, and FN counts provide the input for several ER measurements. The first is linking (ER) accuracy.

$$Linking\ Accuracy = \frac{|TP| + |TN|}{|TP| + |TN| + |FP| + |FN|} = \frac{5 + 35}{5 + 35 + 0 + 5} = 88.9\%$$

The accuracy measurement is a rating that takes on values in the (0,1) interval. When FP = FN = Ø, the accuracy value will be 1.0. If either FP ≠ Ø or FN ≠ Ø, the value will be less than 1.0. The accuracy calculation coincides with the Rand Index (Rand, 1971), which is also used in statistics to compare two clustering results.

The accuracy measurement incorporates the effects of both FP errors and FN errors in the same calculation. Often ER requirements put limits on each type of error independently and call for independent measurements. These typically are measured in terms of "rates."

$$\textit{False Negative Rate} = \frac{|FN|}{|TP| + |FN|} = \frac{5}{5+5} = 50\%$$

$$\textit{False Positive Rate} = \frac{|FP|}{|TN| + |FP|} = \frac{0}{35+0} = 0\%$$

The false negative rate is the ratio of the actual number of false negatives (FN) to the total number possible. An ER process can only create a false negative error when it fails to link equivalent pairs of references. Therefore, the basis for the ratio is the total number of equivalent records $E = TP \cup FN$ (see Figure 3.2).

Similarly, the false positive rate is the ratio of the actual number of false positives (FP) to the total number possible. An ER process can only create a false positive error when it links nonequivalent pairs of references. Therefore, the basis for the ratio is the total number of nonequivalent records $\sim E = TN \cup FP$ (see Figure 3.2).

Three other commonly used measurements borrowed from the field of data mining are precision, recall, and F-measure.

$$\textit{Linking Precision} = \frac{|TP|}{|TP| + |FP|} = \frac{5}{5+0} = 100\%$$

$$\textit{Linking Recall} = \frac{|TP|}{|TP| + |FN|} = \frac{5}{5+5} = 50\%$$

$$\textit{Linking F} - \textit{Measure} = \frac{2(\textit{Precision} \cdot \textit{Recall})}{\textit{Precision} + \textit{Recall}} = \frac{2 \cdot 1.0 \cdot 0.5}{1.0 + 0.5} = 66.7\%$$

These measurements think of linking as a classification operation in data mining. Linking precision looks only at reference pairs linked by the ER process, then asks what percentage of those were correct links. Precision is not affected by failure to link equivalent records (FN), focusing only on the correctness of the links that were made.

Conversely, recall is the measure of how many pairs of references that should have been linked (E) were actually linked by the process. Recall ignores improperly linking nonequivalent records (FP), focusing only on how many correct links were made. The F-Measure combines both precision and recall into a single measure by computing their harmonic mean.

TALBURT-WANG INDEX

The Talburt-Wang Index or TWi is another measurement combining both FP and FN errors into one number (Hashemi, Talburt, & Wang, 2006; Talburt, Kuo, Wang, & Hess, 2004; Talburt, Wang et al., 2007). However, its computation is much simpler and does not require the actual calculation of the TP, TN, FP, PN counts. Instead it measures the number of overlaps between two partitions formed by different linking operations. In the TWi the size of the overlap is not taken into account, only the number of overlaps. If S is a set of references, and A and B represent two partitions of S created by separate ER processes, then define V, the set of overlaps between A and B as

$$V = \{A_i \cap B_j | A_i \cap B_j \neq \emptyset\}$$

Then the Talburt-Wang Index is defined as

$$TWi(A, B) = \frac{\sqrt{|A| \cdot |B|}}{|V|}$$

Applying this to the truth set evaluation between sets T and P as shown in Table 3.2 gives

$$TWi(T, P) = \frac{\sqrt{|T| \cdot |P|}}{|V|} = \frac{\sqrt{4 \cdot 6}}{6} = 81.6\%$$

Two important characteristics of the TWi are

$$0 < TWi(A, B) \leq 1.0$$

$$TWi(A, B) = 1.0 \text{ if and only if } A = B$$

In the case A represents the partition formed by a truth set, then the TWi(A, B) is an alternative measure of linking accuracy.

The utility of the TWi is its simplicity of calculation, even for large data sets. Suppose that S is a set of references and that S has been partitioned by two linking processes, i.e. each reference in S has two link identifiers. If S is sorted in primary order by the first link identifier and secondary by the second link identifier, then the three values for the TWi can be calculated in one pass through the records. The overlaps are those sequences of references where both link identifiers are the same.

Table 3.3 shows the references from Table 3.1 sorted in primary order by True Link and secondary by ER Link. The alternate shading of the rows where both identifiers are the same indicates the 6 overlaps between the two partitions. If the number of unique True Links is known and the number of unique ER links is known from previous processing, then the TWi can be easily calculated by counting the overlap groups in the sorted file.

OTHER PROPOSED MEASURES

Two other proposed measures of ER outcomes are Pairwise Comparison and Cluster Comparison. These can best be explained by a simple example. Let

$$R = \{a, b, c, d, e, f, g, h\}$$

Table 3.3 Table 3.1 Sorted by True Link Then ER Link

	True Link	ER Link
R9	Cust1	43
R1	Cust1	56
R2	Cust1	56
R10	Cust2	5
R3	Cust2	36
R4	Cust2	36
R6	Cust2	36
R5	Cust3	74
R8	Cust3	74
R7	Cust4	66

represent a set of 8 entity references. Furthermore suppose that the references in R have been resolved by two different ER processes, and that A and B are the resulting partitions of R formed by each process

$$A = \{\{a, c\}, \{b, e, f\}, \{d, g\}, \{h\}\}$$

$$B = \{\{a\}, \{b, c, e\}, \{f, d\}, \{g\}, \{h\}\}$$

Menestrina, Whang, and Garcia-Molina (2010) proposed a pairwise method where "Pairs(A)" is the set of all distinct pairs within the partition classes. In this example

$$\text{Pairs}(A) = \{(a, c), (b, e), (b, f), (e, f), (d, g)\}$$

$$\text{Pairs}(B) = \{(b, c), (c, e), (b, e), (f, d)\}$$

Then the pairwise measures are defined as

$$\text{PairPrecision}(A, B) = \frac{|\text{Pairs}(A) \cap \text{Pairs}(B)|}{|\text{Pairs}(A)|} = \frac{1}{5}$$

$$\text{PairRecall}(A, B) = \frac{|\text{Pairs}(A) \cap \text{Pairs}(B)|}{|\text{Pairs}(B)|} = \frac{1}{4}$$

$$\text{pF}(A, B) = \frac{2 \cdot \text{PairPrecision}(A, B) \cdot \text{PairRecall}(A, B)}{\text{PairPrecision}(A, B) + \text{PairRecall}(A, B)} = \frac{2}{9} = 0.222$$

Menestrina et al. (2010) also proposed a Cluster Comparison method that is similar to Pairwise Comparison, but instead of using the Pairs() operator, it uses the intersection of the partitions, i.e. the partition classes A and B have in common. In the example given, the two partitions A and B only share the partition class {h}. Therefore

$$A \cap B = \{\{h\}\}$$

The Cluster Comparison measures are

$$\text{ClusterPrecision}(A, B) = \frac{|A \cap B|}{|A|} = \frac{1}{4}$$

$$\text{PairRecall}(A, B) = \frac{|A \cap B|}{|B|} = \frac{1}{5}$$

$$cF(A, B) = \frac{2 \cdot \text{ClusterPrecision}(A, B) \cdot \text{ClusterRecall}(A, B)}{\text{ClusterPrecision}(A, B) + \text{ClusterRecall}(A, B)} = \frac{2}{9} = 0.222$$

DATA MATCHING STRATEGIES

Data matching is at the heart of ER. ER systems are driven by the Similarity Assumption stating:

"Given two entity references, the more similar the values for their corresponding identity attributes, the more likely the references will be equivalent."

For this reason, the terms "data matching" or "record matching" are sometimes used interchangeably with "entity resolution." Although there is usually a strong correlation between similarity and equivalence, it is not a certainty, only an increasing likelihood. As noted earlier, not all equivalent references match, and not all matching references are equivalent.

In order to really grasp the inner workings of MDM, it is important to understand that data matching takes place at three levels in an ER system:

1. The Attribute level
2. The Reference level
3. The Cluster level (or Structure level)

ATTRIBUTE-LEVEL MATCHING

At its lowest level, data matching is used to judge the similarity between two identity attribute values. A comparator is an algorithm that takes two attribute values as input and determines if they meet a required level of similarity. The simplest comparator determines "exact" match. If the two values are numeric, say age, then the two numeric values must be equal. If the two values are strings, say a person's given name, then the two strings must be identical character-for-character. The problem with exact match is values encoded as character strings are prone to variation such as mistyping and misspelling. In exact match, even differences in letter casing (upper versus lower case) and spacing will not be an exact match.

In general, comparators are designed to overcome variation in representations of the same value. Therefore, in addition to exact match, other types of comparators provide either some level of standardization or some level of approximate match, sometimes referred to as a "fuzzy" match. This is especially true for comparators for values typically represented by character strings such as names or addresses.

What constitutes similarity between two character strings depends on the nature of the data and the cause of the variation. For example, person names may vary because names sounding the same may be spelled differently. The names "Philip" and "Phillip" have identical pronunciations and can easily be confused by someone entering the name on a keyboard during a telephone encounter such as a telemarketing sale. To address the variation caused by names sounding alike but spelled differently, a number of "phonetic" comparators have been developed such as the Soundex algorithm.

In this particular example, the Soundex algorithm will convert both the strings "Philip" and "Phillip" into the same value "P410." This is done by first removing all of the vowels, then systematically replacing each character except the first character with a digit that stands for a group of letters having a similar sound.

Variation in string values caused by mistyping or other types of data quality errors are addressed by another family of comparators performing what is known as "approximate string matching" or ASM algorithms. One of the most famous is the Levenshtein Edit Distance comparator. It measures the similarity between two character strings as the minimum number of character delete, insert, or substitution operations that will transform one string into the other. For example, the edit distance between the strings "KLAUSS" and "KRAUS" is 2 because only 2 edit operations, the substitution of "R" for "L" in the first string and the deletion of the second "S", are necessary to transform "KLAUSS" into "KRAUS".

A more complete description of commonly used ER and MDM comparators can be found in Appendix A.

REFERENCE-LEVEL MATCHING

Most ER systems use one of two types of matching rules: Boolean rules or scoring rules. These are sometimes referred to as "deterministic" and "probabilistic," respectively. However, these terms are somewhat of a misnomer because all ER rules are both deterministic and probabilistic. A process is said to be deterministic if, whenever given the same input, it always produces the same output. This is certainly true for all ER rules implemented as computer code because computer programs are, by nature, deterministic. In addition, all ER matching rules are probabilistic because the increasing similarity of two references only increases the probability they are equivalent. No matter how similar they are, there is still some probability they are not equivalent. Conversely, no matter how dissimilar two references, there is still a probability they may be equivalent. For this reason, they are referred to here as Boolean and scoring rules to make a clear distinction.

BOOLEAN RULES

As the name implies, Boolean rules are logical propositions connected by the logical operators AND and OR (Figure 3.3). In the context of ER the logical propositions are that two values of an attribute meet a prescribed level of similarity.

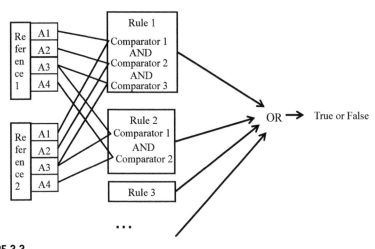

FIGURE 3.3

Schematic of Boolean rule structure.

The two rules shown here are examples of a simple Boolean rule set potentially used in managing student enrollment data.

Rule 1:
(First: Soundex) AND (Last: Exact) AND (School_ID: Exact)
Rule 2:
(First: Exact) AND (Last: Exact) AND (Street_Nbr: Exact)

In Rule 1, the term "First" is the attribute of the student's first name (given name), and the first name values are required to agree by the Soundex phonetic similarity algorithm. The term "Last" is the attribute representing the student's last name (family name) and the "School_ID", is an identifier for the student's current school. In Rule 1, both "Last" and "School_ID" must be the same. Because each term is connected by an AND operator, all three conditions must hold in order for Rule 1 to be true, i.e. signal a match.

In Rule 2, "First", "Last", and the street number of the student's address ("Street_Nbr") must all be the same. However, the logical operation between rules is an implied "OR". Therefore, if two references satisfy either Rule 1 or Rule 2 or both, the two references will be considered a match.

SCORING RULE

While Boolean rule sets can contain multiple rules comparing the same identity attributes in different ways, a scoring rule is a single rule that compares all the identity attributes at one time. Each comparison contributes a "weight" or score depending upon whether the similarity was satisfied (values agree) or not satisfied (values disagree).

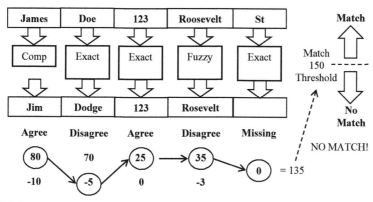

FIGURE 3.4

Schematic of scoring rule structure.

The diagram in Figure 3.4 shows an example of a scoring rule that compares five identity attributes of two customer references. The first name comparator is an alias or nickname match. The last name, street number, and street suffix require exact match, and the street name is a fuzzy match, such as Levenshtein edit distance. In this example, the first names agree by alias, the last names disagree by exact, the street numbers agree by exact, the street names agree by fuzzy match (e.g. Levenshtein edit distance <2), and one of the street suffix values is missing.

The score is calculated by summing the agreement and disagreement weights for each attribute plus the missing value weight for the street suffix, set at zero in this example. In this case, the total score for the match is 135. However, for this system the match threshold score has been set at 150. Therefore, the two references in this example are not considered a match.

The calculation of agreement and disagreement weights typically follows the Fellegi-Sunter (1969) model as discussed in the previous section on *Attribute Weight*. A more detailed description of weight calculation is covered later in the discussion in Chapter 8, "The Nuts and Bolts of Entity Resolution" and the Fellegi-Sunter Model is discussed in Chapter 7, "Theoretical Foundations."

HYBRID RULES

Some systems implement matching rules that combine some characteristics of Boolean and scoring. One example is the use of an affinity scoring rule to supplement a set of Boolean rules (Kobayashi, Nelson & Talburt, 2011; Kobayashi & Talburt, 2013). The affinity scoring rule serves as a tie-breaker when a reference matches more than one EIS, but the EIS have been asserted (flagged) as true negatives to prevent them from being merged.

For example, two EIS are associated with twins in school that have similar information including same date-of-birth, same last name, same parent's name, and same address. New references coming into the system often match both EIS by the base set of Boolean rules because they have such similar characteristics. Ordinarily when a reference matches two EIS, the system merges the two EIS due to transitive close. However, in the case where the EIS are known to be for different students, the EIS are marked as "do not merge" through a true assertion process discussed in more detail in Chapter 5.

The problem is due to the input reference referring to one of the twins, but the Boolean rules do not offer any help as to which one. When this specific situation arises, some systems then invoke a more granular scoring rule to determine which of the two EIS is a better match for input reference and should be merged with (Kobayashi & Talburt, 2014b).

CLUSTER-LEVEL MATCHING

Beyond reference-to-reference matching, there is the issue of how to match a reference to a cluster or a cluster to another cluster. In general, the answer is the cluster is "projected" as one or more references or records, and the projected references are compared using a pairwise Boolean or scoring rule. The two most common projections of clusters are record-based projection and attribute-based projection.

A more detailed description of cluster projection and cluster-level matching is covered later in Chapter 8, "The Nuts and Bolts of Entity Resolution."

IMPLEMENTING THE CAPTURE PROCESS

The actual implementation of the capture process starts by deciding on an initial Boolean or scoring match rule. In the case of a Boolean, it can be relatively simple and based on understanding and experience using the data. In the case of the scoring rule, the weights can be best guesses. The reason is because rule design is an iterative refinement process (Pullen, Wang, Wu, & Talburt, 2013b).

Starting with the initial rule and subsequent refinements, the results of using the rule must be assessed using either the truth set or benchmark methods discussed earlier to get an objective measure of false positive and false negative rates (Syed et al., 2012). Based on an analysis of these errors, the rule should be revised, run again, and assessed again. This process should continue until acceptable error rates are achieved. Once these levels are achieved, the residual errors can be addressed through a manual update process driven by the review indicators. The manual update process is discussed in more detail in Chapter 5.

CONCLUDING REMARKS

The CSRUD MDM Life Cycle starts with the capture phase. It is in this step that the match rules are iteratively developed and refined based on complete assessment of the reference data and careful measurement of entity identity integrity attainment at each iteration. Regardless of whether the system implements Boolean, scoring, or hybrid rules, ongoing ER assessment and analytics is critical. The investment in time to acquire or build proper ER assessment tools will be repaid many times, not only in the capture phase, but also for monitoring during the update phase.

Store and Share – Entity Identity Structures

ENTITY IDENTITY INFORMATION MANAGEMENT STRATEGIES

A characteristic distinguishing entity identity information management (EIIM) from entity resolution (ER) is the persistence of entity identity information, including entity identifiers, from process to process. As noted in Chapter 1 and shown in Figure 1.2, the focus of basic ER or record linking is to properly classify entity references into clusters where all references in the same cluster are equivalent, i.e. refer to the same real-world entity, and are not equivalent to references in other clusters. The focus of ER is on the correct aggregation of references into clusters and the avoidance of false positive and false negative errors.

In MDM it is important to consistently identify (label) each master data entity under management over time. This requires every MDM system to implement a strategy for storing enough entity identity information so that the same master data object can be recognized and labeled with the same identifier over time. These storage structures are called entity identity structures (EIS).

Every information system of any size will have master data. Organizations using this master data must undertake some form of MDM, either implicitly or explicitly. The MDM capability and maturity of organizations varies widely from ad hoc, manually mediated MDM to sophisticated programs with dedicated MDM software and well-executed master data governance.

BRING-YOUR-OWN-IDENTIFIER MDM

One of the earliest and perhaps still the most prevalent forms of MDM for party entities is Bring-Your-Own-Identifier (BYOI). In BYOI it is the party's responsibility to manage their own identifier. A classic example is a company payroll system. When a new employee is hired, a master employee record (EIS) with a unique employee identifier is created and recorded in the system, typically as a row in a database table. At the time it becomes the employee's responsibility to provide his or her employee identifier when conducting any employee-related transactions. For example, the employees may be required to clock-in and clock-out with a time card bearing their employee number in order to be properly paid.

Many colleges and universities use the same BYOI strategy by assigning each student a unique identifier upon admission. From that point on, all transactions with the school's systems, such as course registration, computer access, and meal plans, require the student to present his or her school-assigned identifier.

BYOI MDM is most effective in a closed system where entry and exit points from the system are well-controlled and the party's engagement occurs over a relatively long period of time. Hopefully students and employees will be engaged with the organization over a period of months and years. Although BYOI is not as practical for nonparty entities such as product entities, which can less reliably self-identify, it is not impossible. Barcode scanning and radio frequency tag identification (RFID) can allow nonparty entities to self-identify in certain situations.

It is interesting to note somewhat of a return to BYOI in recent years. This is reflected in the widespread use of customer loyalty programs where customers garner rewards for self-identifying with a card or other token. For example, most large grocery chains, clothing stores, airlines, and many other companies have extensive customer loyalty programs primarily so that customers will self-identity, thus simplifying CDI, the CRM version of MDM.

ONCE-AND-DONE MDM

In a more open system, such as a hospital or a small business, where party engagements are more frequent, a Once-and-Done (O&D) type of MDM is often employed. Here the party entities are not expected to know their own identifier. Instead, clerks or other agents of the organization make a decision at the point of entry as to whether the party already has an assigned identifier (is already under management) or whether a new identifier and identity record should be created.

This decision authority is often distributed across many different agents staffing different points of engagement with the parties. The agent's decision is often aided by some type of "look-up" system that allows the agent to search the central registry of entities by identity attributes such as name, address, or date-of-birth. Using whatever tools are at hand, the agent makes a one-time decision on an identifier for the party at the point of engagement. This identifier, either selected by the agent from previously assigned identifiers or a newly created one, goes into the system as the identifier of record for all further processing of information related to the engagement.

Although some error correction may be done manually if discovered at a later point, O&D MDM does not use automated ER systems to do system-wide reconciliations of identifiers used by the system. The accuracy of O&D MDM depends heavily on the training and diligence of the agents. Errors in O&D MDM will accumulate over time. False positive and negative errors often accumulate to the point that a large-scale intervention is required to clean up the system. These interventions often result in a large number of entity identifier changes, a situation which works against the goal of maintaining persistent identifiers.

DEDICATED MDM SYSTEMS

The movement to develop dedicated MDM software systems and master data governance began in earnest in the 1990s with the introduction of customer relationship management (CRM). Companies began to recognize customer information as master data and wanted to manage it more effectively. However, for many types of businesses, it was impractical to require customers to self-identify and, for many engagements, an agent was not always present to select an identifier. Hence, neither the BYOI nor the O&D model for MDM would be effective. Out of this dilemma was born a new kind of MDM called *customer data integration* (CDI). The application of ER to build customer recognition systems is the precursor of EIIM and MDM as we know them today (Dyché & Levy, 2006).

THE SURVIVOR RECORD STRATEGY

The most common EIIM strategy is simply to add one additional step to the ER merge-purge process that selects a single reference from each cluster to represent the entity. In this case the EIS is essentially the structure of the reference. The selected reference is called the survivor record because the other references are discarded after the single reference has been selected.

The survivor record typically has two versions, a "best record" survivor or an "exemplar record" survivor. Figure 4.1 shows an example of these two versions of the survivor record strategy.

In the best record version of the survivor strategy, user-defined rules are designed to select one reference from the cluster that is considered the best representative. What is considered a best reference will vary by application. In the example in Figure 4.1, the record R3 was selected because it has the most complete name (a full middle name instead of an initial). The problem with selecting the best record is that not all the most desirable features for a given application are always found in one reference. As in this example, even though "Liz" is the predominant (most frequent) first name value, the longer version "Elizabeth" might be preferred. In addition, the reference with the most complete name has the least frequently occurring address.

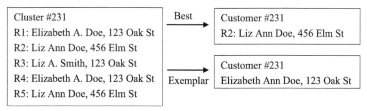

FIGURE 4.1

Best and exemplar versions of the survivor record strategy.

An alternate version of the survivor record strategy is to create an exemplar record. In this form the user defines a set of rules that create a single reference by assembling what are considered to be the best features from various references in the cluster. In the example given in Figure 4.1, the first name "Elizabeth" was selected because it is a full name rather than a nickname. The middle name "Ann" was selected again because it is the most complete. The last name "Doe" was selected because it is the most predominant as is the address "123 Oak St."

The rules for both best and exemplar record strategies will vary. For example, it could be argued the value selected for the exemplar should always be based on frequency of occurrence rather than completeness. In any case, the final choice should be based on what gives the most accurate ER results.

ATTRIBUTE-BASED AND RECORD-BASED EIS

The problem with the survivor record strategy for EIIM is due to useful information being lost. As in the example shown in Figure 4.1, the customer has two different addresses and two different last names, but only one can be carried forward into the survivor record. To solve this problem more elaborate EIS are required to go beyond the simple survivor record strategy. Sørensen (2012) calls this "going beyond true positives in deduplication." These generally fall into two categories: attributed-based EIS and record-based EIS.

In an attribute-based EIS, the goal is to preserve the variety of values occurring for each identity attribute. In its simplest form, the EIS maintains a list of unique values for each identity attribute. Figure 4.2 illustrates the principle of the attribute-based EIS.

The attribute-based EIS is the extreme of the exemplar record because it preserves every combination of values. Because two choices of values exist for each of the four attributes, this structure provides $2^4 = 16$ match combinations. One issue with the attribute-based EIS is that it can produce combinations of values possibly invalid for the entity. For example, it could produce a combination of a name at an address even though in reality the name was never associated with the address. Whether this presents a problem for the ER process will depend upon the nature of the data. The risk it represents is another reason why ER analytics are important to obtaining high-quality MDM results.

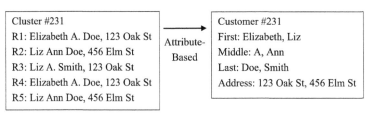

FIGURE 4.2

Attribute-based EIS strategy.

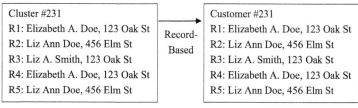

FIGURE 4.3

Record-based EIS strategy.

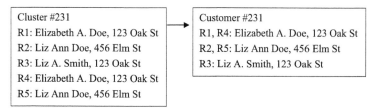

FIGURE 4.4

Record-based EIS with duplicate record filter.

In a record-based EIS, the goal is to preserve the references comprising each entity. As the name implies, a record-based EIS preserves not only reference values, but also the record structure of the references. Figure 4.3 illustrates the principle of the record-based EIS using the same cluster as shown previously in Figure 4.1.

The record-based EIS can be thought of as the extreme of the best record version of the survivor record strategy because every record is kept intact. One issue with the record-based EIS is it often carries a lot of redundant information. For example, in Figure 4.3, only two different address values exist across all five of the references.

Figure 4.4 shows one method for handling record redundancy called the duplicate record filter.

With the duplicate record filter, only one copy of each unique reference is kept with either a counter or list of record identifiers to show its multiplicity. This can save storage in applications where the references with the same information are processed frequently, and it would be burdensome to keep a complete copy of every duplicate reference.

Yet another approach is the hybrid between the record-based EIS and the exemplar version of the survivor record strategy. This is illustrated in Figure 4.5.

The EIS shown in Figure 4.5 has an exemplar record built from the predominant values for each of the identity attributes and also a copy of each reference. However, for those identity attributes where the value in the reference is the same as in the exemplar record, an asterisk (*) is used instead of the actual value. Only when the attribute value in the reference differs from the corresponding value in the exemplar record is the actual value of the attribute used in the reference.

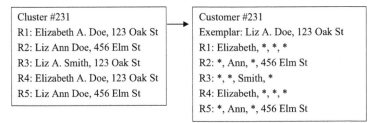

FIGURE 4.5

Record-based EIS with exemplar record.

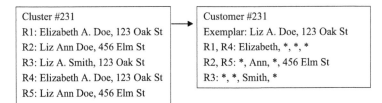

FIGURE 4.6

Record-based EIS with record filter and exemplar record.

As the structures grow more complex, to save storage there is a corresponding increase in time to manipulate the structures. For example, when a new reference is added to the EIS shown in Figure 4.5, the values in the new reference may cause a change in the predominant value for one or more attributes. If this occurs, then the exemplar and the references with that value must be adjusted appropriately.

Finally, Figure 4.6 shows a record-based EIS using both the record filter and the exemplar record.

ER ALGORITHMS AND EIS

Before leaving the topic of EIS it is important to note that the choice of EIS must be taken into consideration with other components of the MDM system. In particular, the EIS must be selected so that it will properly support the way in which match rules are applied to EIS, and support the ER algorithm that will be used for systematically comparing EIS. The interaction of EIS, matching rules, and ER algorithms is discussed in more detail in Chapter 8.

THE IDENTITY KNOWLEDGE BASE

Regardless of the EIS strategy, the collection of all EIS comprises the identity knowledge base (IKB) that is the primary repository of identity information and provides a central point of management. The IKB is sometimes referred to as the *central registry* or the *system hub*. The EIIM strategies and their associated EIS, as described in the introductory portion of this chapter, represent conceptual models. The actual implementation of these models in an information system will vary widely depending upon the characteristics of the actual MDM application including its size, the type of source data, the volatility of the information, and timeliness of access.

For example, an MDM system using survivor record EIS might reside on a single database server in which the IKB is a single master table of entities. The updates and access to the information in the master table may simply be handled with SQL statements and queries. On the other hand, expansive interactive applications using record-based EIS typically reside on large-scale distributed processor architectures. In these systems, the EIS are often virtual structures in which the references reside in different tables or distributed storage folders joined on demand in order to create a complete EIS.

STORING VERSUS SHARING

For many large-scale MDM systems, the storing and maintenance of the IKB and access to the IKB are distinct operations and sometimes use different copies of the master data (Kobayashi & Talburt, 2014a). Typically, updates happen in large batch operations in a database or distributed data architecture often not well-suited for interactive or on-demand batch access. Systems such as these typically utilize two concurrent operations: a background operation in which the information is updated, and a foreground operation that provides continuous, and often real-time, access to the information.

The illustration in Figure 4.7 shows the relation between these processes. In the background, periodic batch updates are made to IKB stored in a very large database

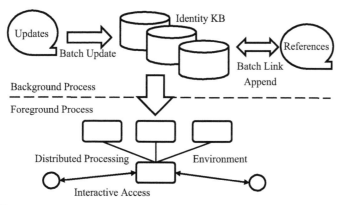

FIGURE 4.7

MDM system using background and foreground operations.

system (VLDBS). Batch access may be provided in the background as shown here, or it may be a service provided in the foreground along with interactive access. The arrow crossing the boundary is to indicate a periodic transfer of identity information from the VLDB system to refresh the information in the distributed environment. In most systems, the foreground process is a read-only system not allowing updates to flow back to the identity knowledge base.

In other cases, the two operations operate within the same system, and rather than operating concurrently, they operate alternately, i.e. time share. For example, the background updates may occur during an overnight operation and then give way to interactive operations during the business day.

MDM ARCHITECTURES

Storing and sharing strategies are closely related to the style of architecture used to implement MDM systems. MDM architectures can be described by the relationships among three principal MDM components. These components are the IKB, "source records," and "client systems." The IKB is the central repository or hub of the MDM system containing a single representation of each master entity under management. A source record is any record in the information system specifically referencing one of the master entities. Because these source records usually reside in various application-specific subsystems of the enterprise system, source records comprise two types of attributes: identity attributes and application-specific attributes. If the identifiers for the entities referenced by the source records in the application specific subsystem are managed by the IKB, then these subsystems are the MDM system's clients.

MDM architectures can be classified many ways. Berson and Dubov (2011) have classified MDM architectures into four categories based on two factors. The first factor is how the attributes in the source records are partitioned between the IKB and the client systems. The second factor is the level of interaction and control the IKB exercises over its client systems. They define four types of MDM architectures: external reference style, registry style, reconciliation engine, and transaction hub.

EXTERNAL REFERENCE ARCHITECTURE

In the external reference architecture, the IKB is a large cross-reference table connecting equivalent references located in the various client systems. The EIS in the IKB are entirely virtual, only containing pointers to the references to a particular entity. None of the actual entity identity information for a particular entity is stored in the IKB.

Both the identity attribute values and the application-specific attribute values of the source record reside in the client system as shown in Figure 4.8. The advantage of external reference architecture is that changes to an entity identifier taking place in one system can be more easily propagated to all other client systems where the same entity is referenced.

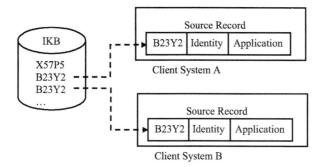

FIGURE 4.8

External reference schematic.

The external reference architecture works best when the governance policy allows for distributed authority to make master data changes in several different client systems. It does not work as well in systems where a large number of new source records must be ingested and identified on a regular basis. In systems implementing external reference architecture, the identity information needed for matching must be marshaled on demand from the client systems where it resides.

REGISTRY ARCHITECTURE

A more common architecture for MDM applications ingesting and managing large volumes of input data is registry architecture. In registry architecture each EIS in the IKB contains a collection of identity attribute values representing the entity under management. Each EIS has an identifier serving as the master identifier for the entity across all client systems. The amount of identity information retained in the EIS will vary from system to system and on the choice of EIS strategy as discussed earlier, e.g. survivor record, attribute-based, record-based, etc.

In registry architecture, each reference is divided into two parts, as shown in Figure 4.9. The value for the identity attributes are kept in the IKB. The IKB

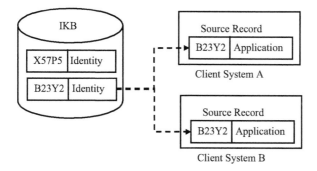

FIGURE 4.9

Registry architecture schema.

must retain sufficient identity information so that when a new source record is introduced, the system can correctly determine if it references a previously registered entity already having established entity identifiers, or if it references a new entity which must be registered in the IKB with a new entity identifier.

A third possibility is if a new source record carries additional identity information providing evidence that two EIS initially thought to represent distinct entities are actually references to the same entity. For example, a source record having both a current and previous address for a customer connects an EIS created for that customer at the previous address, and another EIS created for the same customer at the current address. As a result, one of the entity identifiers is retired, usually the most recently assigned, and the identity information in the two EIS are merged.

In registry architecture, the values for client-specific attributes are retained in the source records residing in the client systems. The two halves of the source record — the identity values and the client-specific values — are linked together by the entity identifier. The shared link identifier also does away with the need to store the identity values of the reference in the client system. The replacement of entity identity values with a unique identifier for the entity is called *semantic encoding*. Semantic encoding is one of the fundamental principles of the ISO 8000-110:2009 Standard for Master Data Quality discussed in Chapter 11.

In registry architecture, the IKB and the systems are loosely coupled. It is usually the responsibility of each client system to synchronize its entity identifiers with the identifiers in the registry through periodic batch or interactive inquiries to the registry. The registry architecture is typical for most CDI systems primarily providing an identity management service, i.e. appends link identifiers to source records on demand.

Registry architecture is sometimes used to provide anonymous entity resolution to several external clients in a trusted broker configuration (Talburt, Morgan, Talley, & Archer, 2005). Trusted broker architecture can be useful when each external client holds some information for entities also known to other clients, but also manages information for some entities unique to the client organization. The clients want to collaborate and share information about common entities, but do not want their exclusive entity information shared or exposed to other clients. This situation often arises in law enforcement, healthcare, and information sharing among government agencies.

The name comes from the fact that all of the clients must trust one neutral organization to host the hub of the registry. In addition, even though the hub internally maintains only one set of entity identifiers, it issues a different set of entity identifiers to each client. This means even though two different clients hold information about the same entity, the hub will give each client a different identifier for that same entity. The hub mediates the translation between client identifiers. In this way, the trusted broker also incorporates some features of the external reference architecture.

If a Client A wants to know whether Client B is holding information about an entity of interest, Client A sends an inquiry to the hub organization. The hub organization can then translate the Client A identifier into its internal identifier and determine if Client B has information on the entity. The hub organization can also mediate policies or regulations on access. If, according to policy, Client A's inquiry is valid, then the hub can send the information from Client B to Client A using the entity identifier of Client A.

RECONCILIATION ENGINE

One extension of the registry architecture is the reconciliation engine. A reconciliation engine essentially has the same partitioning of identity and application attributes between the IKB and the client systems. However, a reconciliation engine has additional functionality that synchronizes changes in entity identifiers with its client systems. Instead of the pull model where client systems must periodically send source records to the IKB to obtain fresh entity identifiers, the reconciliation engine, using the push model, notifies the client systems when changes are made (Kobayashi, Nelson, & Talburt, 2011).

The reconciliation engine is essentially a hybrid architecture made by combining external reference and registry architectures. In order to actively maintain synchronization of entity identifiers, a reconciliation engine must maintain pointers to each source record in each client system by entity identifier as in the external reference architecture and illustrated in Figure 4.8. At the same time, the reconciliation engine maintains the separation of identity and application-specific attribute values as in the registry architecture illustrated in Figure 4.9.

The reconciliation engine has the obvious advantage of keeping client systems synchronized, so client systems always have the most recent entity identifier. The disadvantage is the additional layer of code required to maintain synchronization, which adds more complexity to the reconciliation engine.

TRANSACTION HUB

The transaction hub architecture is also a hybrid. It attempts to solve both the attribute partitioning problem and the synchronization problem at the same time. In this case, the hybridization is between the IKB and its client systems. In a transaction hub, the IKB stores the complete source record, both identity attributes, and application-specific attributes.

By incorporating the source records into the IKB, the transaction hub is simultaneously an MDM system and an application system. The transaction hub can be a good solution for situations where the system must process large volumes of new source references while at the same time servicing high volumes of inquiries for application-specific information because the application information is immediately at hand. There is no need to fetch the application information from a client system in order to service the inquiry. However, this is only feasible if only one or two applications are integrated with the hub; otherwise the maintenance of the system becomes too complex to manage. Many financial systems incorporate the transaction hub architecture for MDM.

For example, on a daily basis a large credit reporting agency must process millions of updates to consumer account information daily received from a wide range of credit providers. At the same time the system must provide real-time responses to hundreds of thousands of online inquiries for consumer credit information from lenders. In order to meet expected levels of performance, these kinds of systems often use a transaction hub architecture to manage both identity and application-specific information within the same system.

CONCLUDING REMARKS

EIIM is a key component of MDM because it acts as the "memory" for the entities under management. The memory elements are the EIS storing the identity information for these entities. The EIIM process tries to create EIS to represent each of the entities under management in such a way that each entity is represented by one and only one EIS, and different entities are represented by different EIS. This is the goal of entity identity integrity. Several metrics for measuring goal achievement include false positive and false negative rates, accuracy, recall, precision, and the T-W Index.

The second goal of EIIM is to maintain persistent entity identifiers, i.e. the EIS representing an entity under management should always have the same identifier. Assigning and maintaining persistent identifiers is not possible without implementing some type of EIIM strategy that creates and saves identity information in an EIS. The most popular EIIM strategies are survivor record, exemplar record, attribute-based, or record-based EIS.

There are several styles of MDM architecture to choose from including external reference, registry, reconciliation engine, and transaction hub. The selection of an architecture should be carefully considered and depends on a number of factors. These factors include the volume of identities to be managed, the degree of integration between the MDM and the client systems, the volatility of the entity identity, and the requirements for time-to-update and inquiry response time.

Update and Dispose Phases – Ongoing Data Stewardship

DATA STEWARDSHIP

Data stewardship emerged as a concept along with data governance. Both data stewardship and data governance underpin the growing trend to recognize information as an enterprise asset. Whereas data governance speaks to elevating data management decisions to an enterprise business function, data stewardship speaks more to the cultural issue of caring for data on behalf of the enterprise. Data stewardship is antithetical to the concept of data ownership, at least to ownership understood as ownership conveying total and complete control.

Historically the root cause of many information quality issues can be traced to the fact that certain individuals or departments believed the data in their care actually belonged to them — and only to them. From this ownership-as-control perspective they often felt empowered to unilaterally make changes to the data or its underlying data architecture solely for their own benefit without consulting or even notifying other stakeholders. At the same time, these other stakeholders often had dependencies on the data in its unaltered form. The result was critical business processes were broken, often with dire results. The fact that such changes could happen unexpectedly then prompted organizational units to make duplicate copies of the data in order to assure it would not be altered by others. These data silos then led to the problem of redundant and unsynchronized data sets across the enterprise, one of the problems MDM seeks to address.

Still, many authors continue to refer to the ownership of data when they really mean accountability for data. In the domain of data governance, persons responsible for data are the ones who carry out the data management tasks, whereas persons accountable for data are charged with making sure that the proper data management tasks are assigned and completed.

The update phase of the CSRUD life cycle represents proper stewardship of master data. The update phase begins immediately after the initial capture phase. Although taking the time to lay the proper foundation in the capture phase is critical to future success, overall it occupies a relatively short interval of time in the total life of an MDM system. The long-term success of an MDM system will depend upon careful attention to master data stewardship and the ongoing care and management of the entity identity information.

The need to continually update identity information comes from two primary sources. The first is to keep in synchronization with the real-world entities as they change over time. Customers change addresses, new products are added, and obsolete products are removed. The rate of change will depend upon the type of entities under management and the application requirements, but without question, identity information will change.

For large systems, updates related to change in entity identity information flow through the system in a manner similar to the capture process. Just as in the capture process, information needed to update the identity knowledge base comes in the form of entity references. However, in the case of the update process, the input references must not only be compared to each other, but also to the information in the EIS that has already been built.

The second reason is that every MDM system should implement two distinct types of update, automated and manual. The automated update process is one governed by the matching rule that was developed and refined during the initial capture phase. The manual update process introduces the human-in-the-loop to the MDM process. In the manual update process the matching rule is replaced with expert knowledge. Unfortunately, many organizations do not recognize and implement the manual update and in not doing so lose the ability to implement effective continuous improvement in their MDM system.

THE AUTOMATED UPDATE PROCESS

Figure 5.1 shows the data flow in the automated update process. It closely resembles the capture process shown in Figure 3.1. The only essential difference is the current identity knowledge base (IKB) is an input into the ER process along with the new entity references.

New entity references are first staged for data cleansing and standardization. Prior to the new references entering the ER process, the EIS from the current IKB are loaded into the system. Both the new references and previous EIS participate in the ER matching process to build the new IKB.

The update process is driven by resolving the new input references. As each input reference is processed, one of three things will happen.

1. The input reference fails to match any of the existing EIS up to that point in the process. This includes the initial set of EIS from the current IKB along with any newly formed EIS from processing previous input references. If no matches are found for the input reference, the system creates a new EIS comprising only that reference.
2. The input reference matches exactly one of the EIS in the system. In this case, the reference is integrated into the EIS it matches.
3. The input reference matches two or more EIS in the system. By the transitive closure principle of reference equivalence (more on this in Chapter 8), the

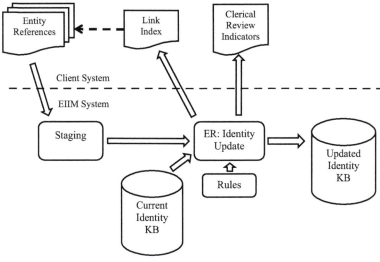

FIGURE 5.1

Update phase (automated).

reference and all of the EIS the reference matches are merged into a single EIS. References causing EIS to merge are sometimes called glue records.

From the perspective of the output IKB, each EIS in the updated IKB is either

- An EIS already in the current IKB and unaffected by the update process, i.e. no new references matched the EIS
- A new EIS created entirely from one or more new input references
- An EIS already in the current IKB, but was updated by matching one or more of the new input references. In addition to being updated by new input references, the EIS may have absorbed one or more of the original EIS if a new input reference caused them to merge, i.e. acted as a glue record.

At the end of every update, the system should generate statistics for all of these occurrences.

CLERICAL REVIEW INDICATORS

A component common to both the capture and automated update process are clerical review indicators as shown in both Figures 3.1 and 5.1. Clerical review indicators are simply warnings produced by the ER process that a linking error may have occurred. These indicators are produced by code detecting particular events or conditions correlated with linking errors.

The concept of review indicators has been a part of entity resolution and record linking since its beginning with the Fellegi-Sunter Theory of Record Linking (Fellegi & Sunter, 1969). An essential element of their proof was that, in order for a match rule to meet a given constraint on the maximum allowable false positive and false negative rates, some minimal number of reference pairs would have to be manually reviewed by a data expert who could correctly classify them as being equivalent or not equivalent. In the case of the Fellegi-Sunter model, the review indication occurs when a pair of references satisfied a particular agreement pattern. For example, in matching student enrollment records, the pattern of disagreement on first name, but agreement of last name, date-of-birth, and house number might fall into this review category. The pattern strongly suggests the records may be referencing the same student but also the possibility the records satisfying this match pattern are twin siblings. Sometimes these are called soft rules or weak rules. Instead of signaling a match, the firing of these rules signals the need for clerical review.

Similar to the conundrum posed by ER assessment one might ask, if the system knows that an error condition leading to a linking error has occurred, why not program the system to avoid the condition and avoid the error? Again the answer lies with probabilities. A review indication is produced by the system when the condition or event is associated with a higher probability a linking error has occurred, not a certainty. Review indicators are not perfect. A review indication may be a false alarm, and conversely, linking errors may occur that do not produce a review indicator.

Review indicators also play a critical role in continuous improvement. If a reviewer determines the system made an error, then correcting these errors will clearly improve the accuracy of the IKB. But more so, a careful root cause analysis of errors over time can inform refinements and improvements to the matching logic preventing these errors from happening. Clerical review indicators together with ER outcome analysis and root cause analysis form a continuous improvement cycle for ER and MDM.

Again, it is hard to overemphasize the need for these components to be in place in order to have a highly effective and efficient MDM system. While many users rely primarily on initial quality assurance validation processes applied to the reference sources, the ones most often neglected are

- Systematic evaluation of ER accuracy using truth sets, benchmarking, and problem sets.
- Review indicator logic signaling possible errors in EIS caused by matching. This is essentially a second level of quality assurance examining the coherence of references vis-à-vis other references for the same entity (same EIS), as opposed to the validation of each source examining the coherence of references vis-à-vis other references from the same source.
- Actual human review of each exception signaled by a review indicator resulting in either a correction or confirmation action.

Even the analysis of cases where the reviewer finds the indicator was wrong and the ER decision was actually correct (a false alarm) can contribute to performance improvements by leading to refinements in the review indicator logic. In addition, if a system allows reviewer decisions to be captured in the metadata of the IKB, the system can suppress review indications on EIS that have previously been reviewed and found correct. These confirmation assertions can significantly decrease the time and effort required for clerical review. The transactions causing indicator logic to be suppressed on combinations of EIS already reviewed as correct are called true assertions or confirmation assertions. In contrast, transactions used to correct errors are called correction assertions.

PAIR-LEVEL REVIEW INDICATORS

Review indicators are typically designed to work at one of two levels: at the reference matching pair level and the cluster level. The previous example of a Fellegi-Sunter agreement pattern falls into the category of pair-level indication. In other words, the review signal is associated with a pair of references satisfying a certain match condition, in this case, that the two references follow a specific agreement pattern.

Scoring rules discussed in Chapter 3 provide natural pair-level review indicator logic. By setting a second threshold score just below the match score threshold, the system can give an indication on every pair of references scoring below the match threshold and above the second threshold, called a review threshold. These represent pairs with scores close to being a match but just falling short, i.e. near matches.

Even though a Boolean rule set does not generate a score, some systems allow for some sub-rules (AND clauses) to be designated as a soft rule or weak rule. A weak rule allows for more fuzziness or looseness in the match. The weak rule can be treated either as a match or a no-match, but in either case, the pairs of references satisfying a weak rule are called out for clerical review.

CLUSTER-LEVEL REVIEW INDICATORS

Even for experts in a given data domain, decisions on clerical reviews can sometimes be difficult. In making these decisions it often helps to have the complete context. Cluster-level review indicators can provide this much-needed context by showing the contents of the EIS associated with a pair of references. Another advantage of cluster-level indicators is they can be applied at two different times: at run-time while the EIS is in main memory and matching is taking place, or they can be applied to the EIS in off-line storage after the ER process is complete.

As an example, Pullen, Wang, Talburt, and Wu (2013a) developed review indicator logic for ER systems using Shannon's entropy formulation. The entropy calculation is done by looking at the frequency of distinct values of identity attributes of the references within a cluster. For example, suppose a cluster representing a student has 10 references and one of the identity attributes is the student's first name. If 7 of the references have the first name value of "JAMES" and 3 of the references have the first name value of "JIM" then the probability of the first name "JAMES" would be 0.7 and the probability of "JIM" would be 0.3. From this the entropy of the first name values would be given by

$$E = -\sum_{i=1}^{n} p_i \cdot log_2(p_i) = -0.7 \cdot log_2(0.7) - 0.3 \cdot log_2(0.3) = 0.88129$$

A similar calculation for each identity attribute contributes to a total entropy score for the entire cluster. Their work shows that, for certain types of data, a high entropy value for a cluster is a high-precision indicator of a potential false positive error, i.e. more than one entity is represented in the cluster.

Conversely, they have also shown that low entropy can be a good indicator of false negative EIS. To be used as a false negative indicator, closely related EIS must first be brought together by a loose match key. For an example using student data, the false negative key might be a combination of last name and date-of-birth. If two EIS that have the same last name and data of birth are brought together, and if the entropy of the EIS created by combining the references from both EIS is low, then this may indicate the two EIS are false negatives of each other. If two EIS are found to be false negatives, i.e. both reference the same entity, then by transitive closure of equivalence, they should be combined into one EIS.

THE MANUAL UPDATE PROCESS

The manual update process is driven by the clerical review indicators. As shown in Figure 5.2, the manual update process begins with a data expert and a set of clerical review indications produced by a capture process or by an automated update process. For a system of any size, the reviewer will need two things. The first is a tool to assist in reviewing the EIS in order to make a review decision, and the second is a mechanism for making adjustments to the IKB based on the decision.

Adjustments made to the IKB by human (knowledge-based) decision are called assertions. If the decision is an error was made, then the action is to correct the EIS

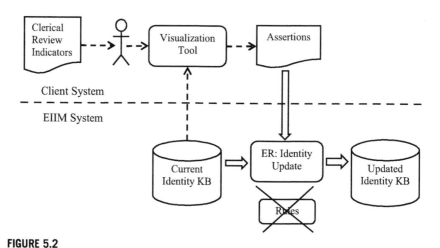

FIGURE 5.2

Update phase (manual).

in error. If the decision is no error was made, then the action is to confirm the EIS are correct. The assertion process will be discussed first. Once assertions are understood, the functions of the visualization tool will be clearer.

ASSERTED RESOLUTION

Asserted resolution, sometimes called informed linking or knowledge-based linking, is simply the reconfiguration of the EIS in the IKB based on expert knowledge. Assertions are effected by creating assertion transactions applied to the IKB through the EIIM system. Because asserted resolution is a manual process, the number of assertions applied to the IKB will always be small when compared to the large volume of updates applied through the automated update process. However, assertions are important to reduce the accumulations of false positive and false negative errors, which build up over time in an unreviewed EIIM system. Assertion complements the automated ER process and provides a mechanism for continuous improvement of the EIIM system.

Direct manipulation of the IKB through an editing tool or other ad hoc processes is never a good idea and should be prohibited by MDM governance policy. All update transactions to the IKB including assertion transaction actions should always be mediated through thoroughly tested application software logging transaction events to facilitate process auditability and to maintain IKB integrity.

CORRECTION ASSERTIONS

Assertions generally fall into three categories — correction assertions, confirmation assertions, and convenience assertions. Correction assertions are designed to alter EIS in a way that corrects malformation caused by the false positive and false negative errors inevitably occurring in the automated ER process. Confirmation assertions do not alter EIS other than to insert metadata flagging the EIS as being correct. The presence of the confirmation metadata is detected by the review indicator logic to prevent it from calling out for review EIS already confirmed as correct. In addition, the metadata inserted into EIS when correcting a false positive (structure-split-assertion) or confirming a true negative prevents the rules in the automated ER process from merging (or re-merging) EIS that should remain separated.

Structure-to-Structure Assertion

A structure-to-structure assertion is used to correct a false negative error in which two EIS are found to be equivalent, i.e. reference the same entity. Although some false negatives are self-correcting when new references connect the EIS during the identity update process, this is not always the case, and manual intervention may be required. Figure 5.3 shows the schematic of a structure-to-structure assertion.

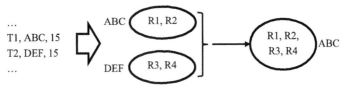

FIGURE 5.3

Structure-to-structure assertion.

In Figure 5.3, ABC and DEF are forced to merge into a single cluster. To minimize entity identifier changes, the identifier for one EIS is retained, in this case ABC. Only entity identifier DEF will have to be retired. Although Figure 5.3 only shows two EIS being merged, some systems support merging several equivalent EIS in the same assertion.

However, the retirement of DEF from the IKB will orphan any source records residing in the IKB client systems referencing DEF. These records should now reference ABC. The mechanism making this adjustment (synchronization) will depend upon the MDM architecture of the system as discussed previously. For example in a registry architecture, the client systems will have to push their records to the IKB in order to refresh its identifiers, whereas in a reconciliation engine, the IKB will notify client systems with references to DEF that it should be replaced by ABC and the IKB will notify client systems.

A structure-to-structure assertion is effected by a set of assertion transactions shown on the left side of Figure 5.3. In systems that support asserting multiple EIS, if N is the number of EIS to be merged, then N transactions are required, one for each EIS. The structure-to-structure assertion transaction has three fields — a transaction identifier, an entity identifier, and a group identifier.

In Figure 5.3 two EIS are being merged by two structure-to-structure assertion transactions. The transaction identifiers are T1 and T2. Transaction T1 references entity identifier ABC, and transaction T2 references entity identifier DEF. Both transactions have a group identifier value of 15. All EIS sharing the same group identifier value will merge, in this case ABC and DEF. If a third EIS were to be merged in this assertion, there would only need to be a third transaction with the entity identifier of the third EIS and with the same group identifier value of 15.

Structure-Split Assertion

The structure-split assertion is designed to correct false positive errors, i.e. EIS containing references to more than one entity. Unlike false negative errors, false positive errors are never self-correcting through the automated update process. ER processes are driven by matching engines only making decisions to merge EIS, never to split them. Once a false positive EIS is created, it will remain in the system until there is a manual intervention to correct it.

A schematic for the structure-split assertion is shown in Figure 5.4. In this example the EIS ABC contains five references R1, R2, R3, R4, and R5. A clerical review shows references R1 and R2 reference one entity, references R3 and R4

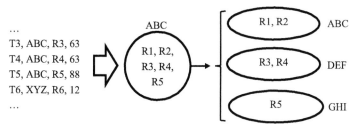

FIGURE 5.4

Structure-split assertion.

reference a second entity, and reference R5 references yet a third entity. Correcting this problem requires a set of structure-split assertion transactions. Again, to minimize the amount of effort needed to synchronize the client systems, the MDM system will not allow all of the references to be split away from the original EIS. In other words, the system requires that the original EIS must survive the structure-split assertion operation, so the original entity identifier ABC is retained in the system. The structure-split assertion transactions only need to call out the references needing to be moved out of EIS.

The transactions needed to effect a structure-split assertion are similar to those for structure-to-structure assertion, but they require one additional field. Each structure-split assertion transaction has four fields — a transaction identifier, an entity identifier, a reference identifier, and a group identifier. In Figure 5.4 there are three transactions with identifiers T3, T4, and T5. All of the transactions have entity identifier ABC; however, transaction T3 has the identifier for reference R3, transaction T4 for reference R4, and T5 for reference R5.

In a set of structure-split assertion transactions are two levels of grouping. The first level is by EIS and the second level is by split group using a group identifier. In Figure 5.4, the group of transactions applying to ABC is shown with group identifiers 63 and 88. Within the ABC group are two subgroups — subgroup 63 and subgroup 88. Subgroup 63 indicates references R3 and R4 should move together into a new EIS after being removed from ABC. For R3 and R4 the new EIS identifier is DEF. Subgroup 88 indicates that reference R5 should be in a new EIS, but different EIS than the new EIS created for R3 and R4. For R5 the new identifier is GHI.

The synchronization of identifiers in a client system for structure-split assertions is more difficult than for the structure-to-structure previously discussed. The problem now is clients' systems may contain many source records referencing identifier ABC, but after the assertion, some of these perhaps should reference the new identifier GHI. Even if the system has kept track of which source records were appended with identifier ABC, it is not obvious which of these should be changed to GHI without having to rematch the records against the identity information. This is another reason why ER systems are usually tuned to prefer false negative errors over false positive errors. Not only do the corrections to false negative errors stay corrected without special logic, the identifier retirement is simpler to manage.

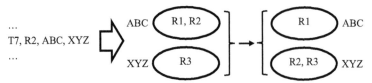

FIGURE 5.5

Reference-transfer assertion.

Reference-Transfer Assertion

The reference-transfer assertion is designed to correct both a false positive and false negative in one process. Figure 5.4 shows a situation in which the reference R2 has been clustered in ABC with R1, but should have been clustered with R3 in XYZ. In this case, R2 is a false positive with respect to R1 and a false negative with respect to R3. The solution is to move the reference R2 from ABC to XYZ.

No new EIS are created in the reference-transfer assertion process. One reference-transfer assertion transaction exists for each reference needing to be moved. Each reference-transfer assertion transaction has four fields — a transaction identifier, a reference identifier, a source entity identifier, and a target entity identifier. In the example of Figure 5.5, transaction T7 indicates a move of reference R2 from ABC to XYZ as shown in the diagram.

CONFIRMATION ASSERTIONS

Confirmation assertions are designed to label EIS as having been reviewed and confirmed as correct in order to prevent their continued review. The algorithms producing clerical review exceptions are not perfect. Some EIS called out for clerical review as potential false positives often turn out to be true positives, i.e. correctly clustered. Similarly, some groups of EIS called out for clerical review as false negatives are in fact true negatives. Without confirmation assertions, these EIS can be repeatedly called out for review by the clerical review indicator logic even though they have previously been manually reviewed and found to be correct.

However, it is important to note EIS reviewed as correct should only be excluded from subsequent reviews as long as they maintain the state they had at the time of the review. Any changes to the EIS could change their status from correct to incorrect. The implementation of confirmation assertions also requires new functionality in the ER update logic that will remove confirmation labels from the EIS metadata whenever the ER process modifies the EIS.

True Positive Assertion

The true positive confirmation assertion pertains to a single EIS. If an EIS is called out for clerical review, and if the reviewer finds all references in the EIS are for same entity, the EIS is a true positive and should be asserted as such. The true positive assertion of an EIS will add a metadata label showing the EIS is true positive.

FIGURE 5.6

True positive assertion.

The case shown in Figure 5.6 is where the EIS with entity identifier ABC was called out for clerical review as a false positive, but after inspection it was found to be correct. The true positive assertion transaction requires only two fields — a transaction identifier and the entity identifier of the true positive EIS. The action of the true positive assertion is to add a metadata tag (shown as <TP> in Figure 5.6) to the EIS. True positive assertion transaction T8 asserts ABC as a true positive EIS. The true positive tag inserted into ABC will prevent the clerical review indicator logic from calling out ABC for review as long as the tag is present.

However, if a later update process results in new references being added to ABC, then the true positive tag will be removed, and ABC may again be called out for clerical review in later processing. The metadata added to the true positive EIS may also include other information for auditing and traceability such as an identifier for the person making the review decision, the date of review, and other relevant information. These additional metadata are important for good master data governance.

True Negative Assertion

The true negative assertion confirms two or more EIS were called out for review as potential false negatives have been confirmed as correct by an expert reviewer. Just as with the true positive assertion, the true negative assertion inserts metadata tags into the reviewed EIS. In the case of true negative, additional metadata is required because a true negative state always exists between two (or more) EIS. Just labeling an EIS as a true negative does not make sense by itself. A true negative assertion of an EIS must be expressed in relation to another EIS. In addition to a true negative label, a true negative assertion must also insert the identifier of the EIS to which it is a true negative. These metadata must be inserted into all of the EIS the review process determines to be true negatives of each other.

The example in Figure 5.7 is for two EIS with identifiers ABC and DEF. The true negative assertion transactions require three fields — a transaction identifier, an entity identifier of one of the true negative EIS, and a grouping identifier. The grouping identifier is simply a provided value identifying the EIS comprising the true negative group. The value of the grouping identifier is not as important while it is the same in all transactions relating to the same true negative group and different from the identifier for any other true negative group. In this example, the group identifier is 76 for transactions T9 and T10. Because transaction T11 has a different group identifier, it relates to some other true negative group not shown.

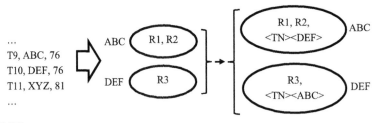

FIGURE 5.7

True negative assertion.

As shown in Figure 5.7, the true negative assertion of the EIS with identifiers ABC and DEF creates metadata cross-referencing these EIS. The EIS with identifier ABC references the EIS with identifier DEF as a true negative, and conversely, the EIS with identifier DEF references the EIS with identifier ABC as a true negative. These tags will prevent the clerical review logic from calling out the EIS identified as ABC and DEF as false negatives in future processes as long as they maintain the original state. Just as with the true positive assertion, the metadata tags suppressing subsequent true negative review must be removed if and when a later update process adds new references to any one of the EIS in a true negative group.

Reference-to-Reference Assertion

Two special types of confirmation assertions are used to move external references into correctly configured EIS. They belong to the category of convenience assertions. Convenience assertions allow the user to directly create and manipulate EIS without using matching rules.

The first convenience assertion is a reference-to-reference assertion used to create a new EIS containing a specific set of source references. The reference-to-reference assertion bypasses the matching rules and in some ways represents a special type of identity capture configuration. Reference-to-reference assertions are often used to migrate intact clusters of references from a legacy MDM system into a new MDM system.

Reference-to-reference assertion transactions require three fields — a transaction identifier, a reference, and a group identifier. As with the true negative assertion, the group identifier serves to show which references are to create the same EIS. In the case of migration from a legacy system, these group identifiers will simply be the entity identifier assigned to the references by the legacy system.

In Figure 5.8, the reference-to-reference assertion transactions T12 and T13 are grouped by identifier 35 indicating references R1 and R2 are to form a new cluster. Depending upon the system, the identifier ABC of the new EIS can be a value automatically generated by the system, or it can be a value specified by the user, and again in the case of legacy migration, could be the group identifier. In the case where identifiers are provided, the MDM system should prevent the user from inadvertently creating duplicate identifiers.

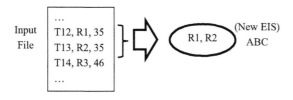

FIGURE 5.8

Reference-to-reference assertion.

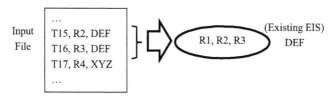

FIGURE 5.9

Reference-to-structure assertion.

Reference-to-Structure Assertion

The second type of convenience confirmation assertion is a reference-to-structure assertion used to add one or more references to an existing EIS. As with a reference-to-reference assertion, a reference-to-structure assertion bypasses the matching rules.

As shown in Figure 5.9, the reference-to-structure assertion transactions require three fields — a transaction identifier, a reference, and an EIS identifier. Grouping is unnecessary for reference-to-structure assertion transactions because each transaction names the specific EIS to which the transaction should be added.

In the example of Figure 5.9, reference-to-structure assertion transactions T15 and T16 add references R2 and R3, respectively, to the EIS labeled DEF which is already in existence and contains reference R1.

EIS VISUALIZATION TOOLS

Visualization can be an effective tool for assessing and managing information (Abu-Halimeh, Pullen, & Tudoreanu, 2013; Gibson & Talburt, 2010). This is especially true for Big Data. Large MDM systems can have millions of entities and source references under management. For systems of this scale, clerical review becomes difficult without tools that allow reviewers to quickly access and understand the contents of EIS indicated for review. Conducting reviews using printouts or on-screen listings can be tedious and error prone. Visualization tools with advanced functionality can considerably ease the review burden and increase reviewer productivity and accuracy (Chen et al., 2013b). Some of the helpful features provided by a good visualization tool allow the reviewer to

- Quickly locate and view EIS called out by clerical review indicators
- Allow multiple reviewers simultaneous access
- Keep track of indicator status in terms of "needing review" or "already reviewed"
- Support undirected, keyword searches over the entire IKB in addition to reviews directed by clerical review indicators
- Automatically generate properly formatted correction and confirmation assertions reflecting reviewer decisions

To illustrate these features, the following section will use, as an example, a browser-based IKB visualization tool called Identity Visualization System (IVS) developed by, and shown here with the permission of, Black Oak Analytics, Inc. All of the information shown in the screen shots were created using synthetic data and do not represent actual persons.

First note that IVS, like most visualization tools, does not directly modify the IKB. As depicted in Figure 5.2, the information from the IKB is extracted to the database in the IVS tool allowing IVS to make queries in real time. During the extraction process, all of the tokens in the EIS are indexed to enable real-time keyword searches of the EIS. In addition, the entropy calculations are made during the extraction by user-defined parameters in the extraction script.

Again as shown in Figure 5.2, the output of IVS is a file of assertion transactions. The decisions reviewers make using IVS are not actually reflected in adjustments to the IKB until these transactions are run against the IKB through an ER assertion process. Although the decoupling of the visualization tool from the IKB by this extraction process gives the visualization tool higher performance, it can also lead to synchronization problems if not properly governed.

The primary issue is that reviewers are working on a copy of the IKB, not the IKB itself. If automated updates are applied to the real IKB before the assertion transactions from the clerical reviews have been applied, some assertion transactions made by reviewers may be rendered invalid because of structural changes made to the IKB by the automated update. Contention between updates is always a potential risk with redundant data. In this case, the copy of the IKB manipulated by the visualization tool is redundant to the actual IKB. Redundancy always introduces the possibility for loss of synchronization between copies of the same data.

ASSERTION MANAGEMENT

The initial login screen for the system is shown in Figure 5.10. By requiring reviewers to login, the system can keep track of which indicated EIS have been reviewed and by which reviewers. The login identifier is also carried forward into all of the assertion transactions generated by the reviewer. When the assertion transactions are applied, the reviewer identifier is inserted into the metadata of the asserted EIS in order to enable the auditability of assertion transactions.

Welcome!

Welcome to Identity Visualization System!

The current IKB is ReviewedTest.idty

Please login first!

| User Name | **Login** |

FIGURE 5.10

Initial login screen.

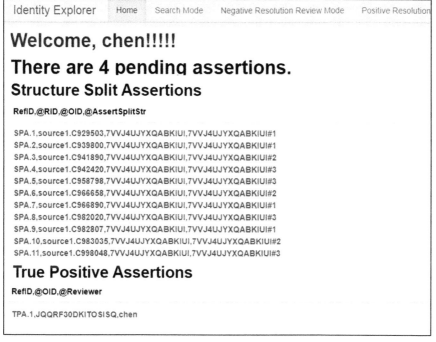

FIGURE 5.11

IVS home page for user chen.

When the reviewer logs into IVS, the system starts on the reviewer's home page. The home page shows the status of work for the reviewer since the last review session. The home page depicted in Figure 5.11 shows that the reviewer "chen" has made four assertions in a previous review session. These assertions are labeled as "pending" because even though the assertion decisions have been made, and the assertion transactions have been generated, the assertion transactions have not yet been applied to the IKB.

An interesting feature of the IVS is the user interface resembling an online shopping model. As reviewers make assertion decisions, the decisions are saved in an "assertion cart" similar to an online shopping cart. When a reviewer makes an assertion decision for an indicator, the asserted indicator is put into the cart. At the same time, the indicated EIS is removed from the reviewer's queue of indicated EIS to review.

At any point in the session the reviewer can view the assertions in the cart, and if he or she so chooses, can "commit" the assertions in the cart. The commit step causes the IVS to generate assertion transactions for the decision in the cart, analogous to "purchasing" the items in a shopping cart. Once the decisions are committed to transactions, the cart is emptied and the assertion transactions become pending assertions as shown in Figure 5.11.

Because the screen shot has been cropped to fit the page, only the assertion transactions generated for two of the four pending assertions can been seen in Figure 5.11. Visible here are 11 structure-split transactions pending for application to the EIS with identifier 7VVJ4UJYXQABKIUI. As discussed in the previous section, each split-assertion transaction has four values — a transaction identifier, a reference identifier, an EIS identifier, and a grouping identifier. For example, the first transaction shown has a transaction identifier of SPA.1, a reference identifier of source1.C929503, the EIS identifier 7VVJ4UJYXQABKIUI, and a grouping identifier of 7VVJ4UJYXQABKIUI#1.

The grouping identifiers have been generated by appending an integer value to the EIS identifier to create a set of unique identifiers for the groups specified by the reviewer. There are three distinct grouping identifiers in the eleven transactions. However, when these 11 transactions are applied to the IKB they will only create two new EIS. The system will automatically select the largest subgroup to retain the base EIS with identifier 7VVJ4UJYXQABKIUI. The two small groups will create two new EIS with new identifiers generated by the system. This process will assure the fewest possible identifiers are changed, and the fewest possible references are given new identifiers.

The top of Figure 5.11 includes tabs showing the three basic operating modes of IVS — Search Mode, Negative Resolution Review Mode, and Positive Resolution Review Mode. The Search Mode allows the reviewer to perform undirected keyword searches of the IKB. Negative Resolution Review Mode shows the reviewer EIS indicated as possible false negatives, and the Positive Resolution Review Mode shows the reviewer EIS indicated as possible false positives.

SEARCH MODE

Figure 5.12 shows the search mode input screen. The reviewer can type any sequence of keywords here to perform an undirected search of the entire IKB. In this case, the search is to be performed on the single token value "michael".

As a result of the search, 100 EIS were found that contained references with the value "michael" in any one of the attribute values. The partial search results are shown in Figure 5.13. The IVS tool will search on multiple keywords both qualified

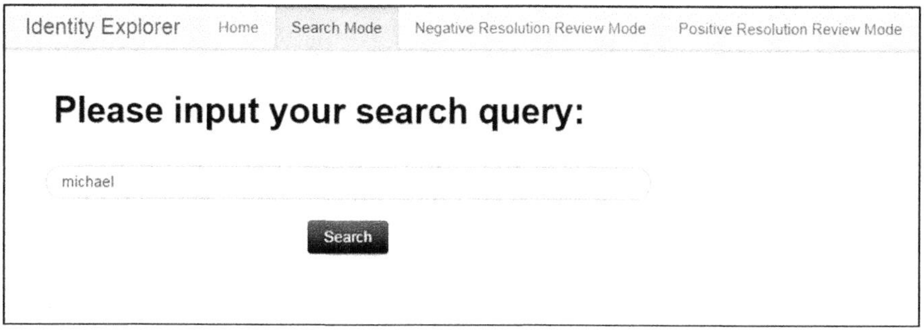

FIGURE 5.12

IVS search mode — undirected search for "michael"

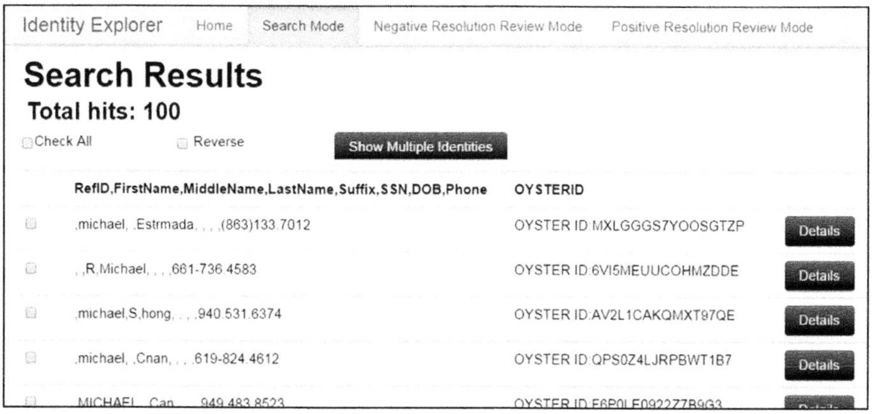

FIGURE 5.13

IVS results for an undirected Search on "michael"

and unqualified. The first reference returned has "michael" in the first name field and the second reference has the value "michael" in the last name field.

In a qualified search the token is prefixed by an attribute name. Figure 5.14 shows a qualified keyword search for references where the token value "michael" is found in the last name field "LastName:michael" and will only search for EIS in the first name field containing the value of "michael".

The results of the directed search are shown in Figure 5.15.

NEGATIVE RESOLUTION REVIEW MODE

Upon entry into the negative resolution review mode, IVS will show the reviewer the EIS groups indicated as possible false negative groups. Because IVS uses the entropy-based clerical review described in the previous section, the groups brought

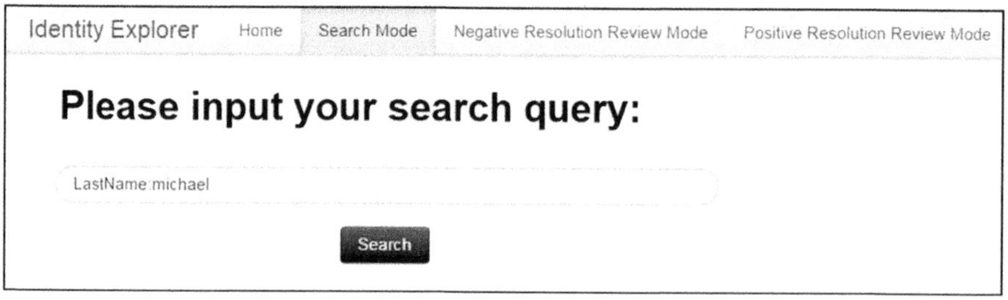

FIGURE 5.14

IVS search mode — directed search for "michael" in Last Name Field.

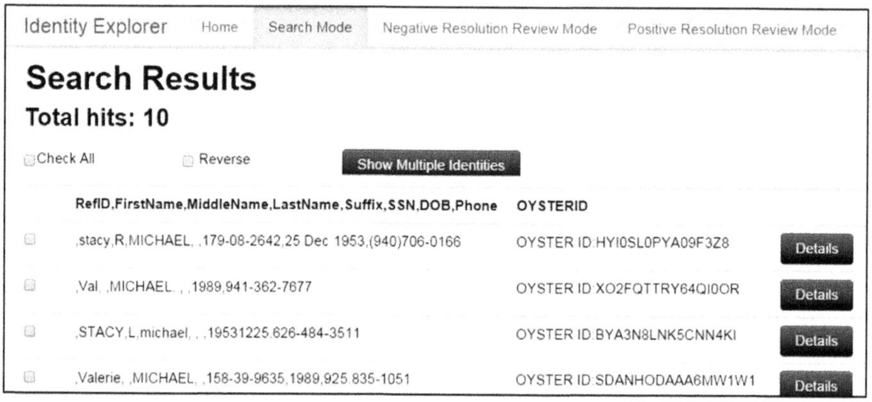

FIGURE 5.15

IVS results for a directed search for "michael" in Last Name Field.

together by the split key are arranged in order from lowest to highest entropy. Figure 5.16 shows the four groups with the lowest entropy when brought together by the split key. In this case the split key is the first 8 digits of the social security number.

To enhance readability for the reviewer, different EIS within a group and different groups have different colored backgrounds. The reviewer can also select different bands of entropy to review. In this example, the band of entropy values between 0.0 and 5.0 entropy is displaying 2,817 EIS groups for review.

At the detail level, the reviewer can see the attribute-level information in each reference. Figure 5.17 shows the detail level of three EIS brought together by a split key. In this example are three EIS brought together by the split key, and each EIS comprises a single reference.

The check boxes at the left of each EIS allow the reviewer to select which EIS should be designated as either true negatives or false negatives that should be merged. After the EIS are selected by their check boxes, the decision is effected by clicking the appropriate button at the bottom of the screen.

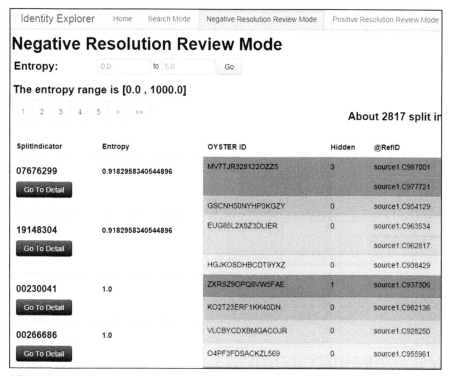

FIGURE 5.16

IVS negative resolution review indicator level.

POSITIVE RESOLUTION REVIEW MODE

The positive resolution review mode function is similar to the negative resolution review mode. Figure 5.18 shows the indicator level list of EIS for positive review mode. In positive review mode the EIS are listed in descending order of entropy scores, since high-entropy EIS are more likely to be false positive.

By clicking the "Go To Detail" button, the reviewer is taken to the detail level screen as shown in Figure 5.19. The EIS shown in Figure 5.19 is the same EIS with identifier value 7VVJ4UJYXQABKIUI shown in Figure 5.18.

Note that in Figure 5.19, the reviewer has already determined the EIS is a false positive and had already selected how the references should be correctly grouped. The groupings are created by selecting an integer value for the drop-down boxes at the left of each reference. After the grouping codes are selected, the reviewer will click the "Assert Structure Split" button at the bottom of the page. The right end of the main menu bar has been moved into view to show the count of assertions currently in the Assertion Cart. By clicking on the Assertion Cart, the reviewer can see all of the assertions that he or she has reviewed since the last commit.

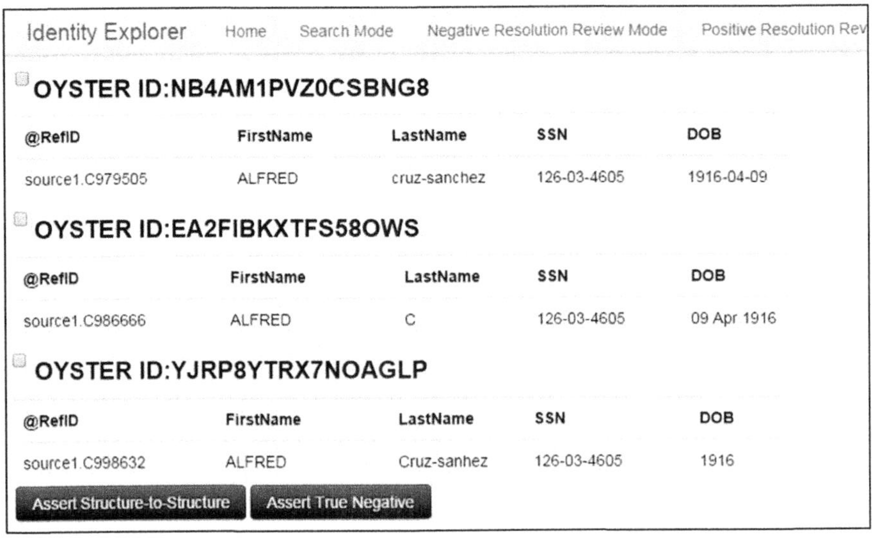

FIGURE 5.17

IVS negative resolution review EIS detail level.

MANAGING ENTITY IDENTIFIERS

The entity identifiers in an MDM system are called "persistent" identifiers rather than "permanent" identifiers for good reason. Because MDM systems are driven by ER processes, and ER processes make mistakes, some entity identifiers are going to change when these mistakes are corrected.

Take, as an example, the false negative error in Figure 5.3. Before the error was discovered, the EIS identified as ABC and DEF were believed to represent different entities. The references R1 and R2 were assumed to reference entity ABC and references R3 and R4 referenced entity DEF. After the correction, only the identifier ABC survived. The result is that reference R3 and R4 changed identifiers.

Similarly, before the false positive error shown in Figure 5.4 was discovered, references R1, R2, R3, R4, and R5 were all believed to reference the entity identified as ABC. After the correction two new entity identifiers are in the system, the identifier DEF for the entity defined by references R3 and R4, and identifier GHI for the entity defined by reference R5. The net result is changed identifiers for reference R3, R4, and R5.

THE PROBLEM OF ASSOCIATION INFORMATION LATENCY

One factor driving the false negative problem, especially with customer entities, is association information often lagging behind existence information. For example, when a customer moves from one address to another, whether postal or electronic

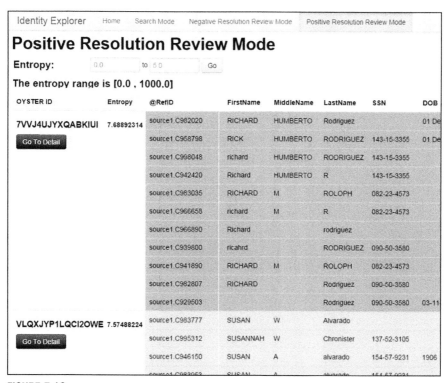

FIGURE 5.18

IVS positive resolution review indicator level.

address, a transaction seen at a new address without reference to an old address often appears to be a new customer. When this happens, the system creates a new EIS and new identifier. It is only later that the association information, such as a postal change-of-address transaction, will appear connecting the customer at his or her new address and old address. In applications where this happens frequently, the result can be a churning effect where new identifiers are created and then quickly retired.

MODELS FOR IDENTIFIER CHANGE MANAGEMENT

Regardless of the cause for identifier changes, these changes must be dealt with. Two basic models include the pull or user-directed model and the push or system-directed model.

The Pull Model

In the pull model all of the source information from client systems is pulled back to the MDM system where it is relinked, i.e. the current identifiers are appended to the

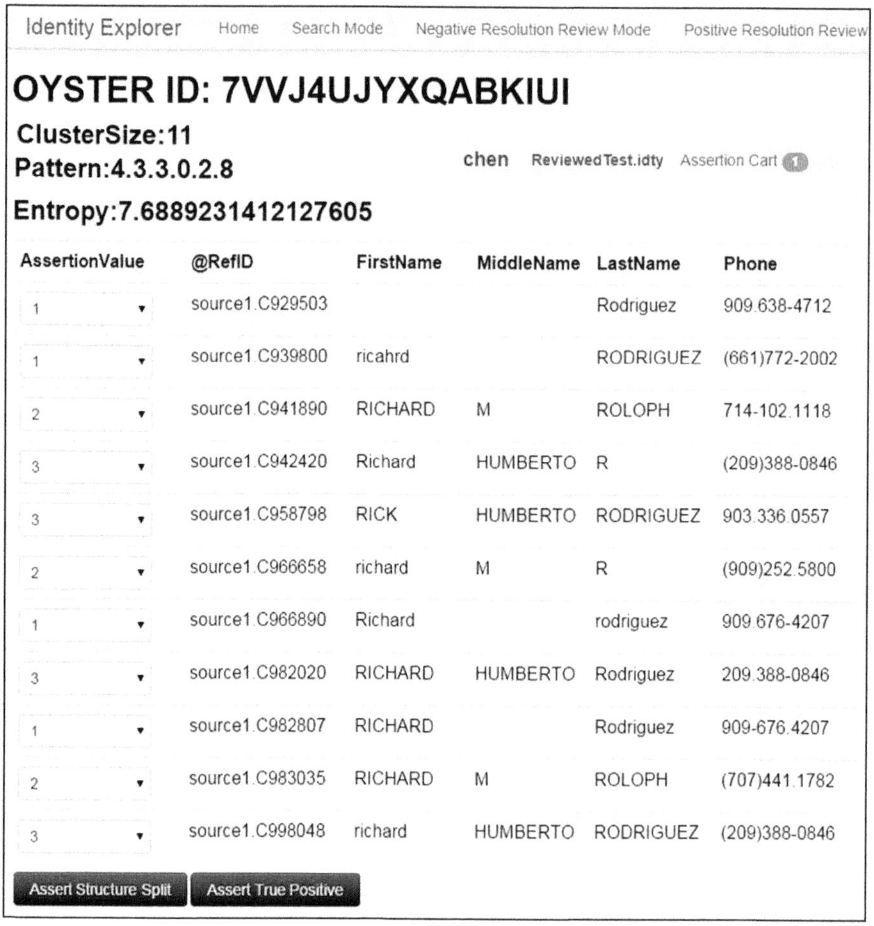

FIGURE 5.19

Positive resolution review mode EIS detail level.

client source records. In this model, it is the client system's responsibility to detect when an identifier has been changed and to take the appropriate actions.

In this division of responsibility, the central MDM system is primarily an identity management system focused on maintaining the identity integrity of its IKB. The central system does not maintain a log of which identifiers have been given to which client systems. The client systems must periodically relink in order to be assured of having the most current identifiers. The pull model is common when there are many client systems using the identifiers, especially when some of the clients are in organizations or information systems separate from the MDM system.

The advantage of the pull model is that from an MDM system viewpoint, it is simpler to manage. By placing the burden on client systems to harmonize identifiers, the MDM system itself is less complex. Of course, the obvious disadvantage of the pull model is the potential loss of synchronization of identifiers across client systems. The extent to which this can happen will depend upon the nature of the application, the volatility of the data, and the frequency of the synchronization process. If updates to the IKB are done on a regular schedule, then relinking can be timed to coincide with the updates in order to minimize the synchronization problem.

The Push Model

In the push model of identifier change management, it is the central system's responsibility to publish changes in identifiers to the client systems. Several different versions of the push model vary in sophistication. In the simpler version, all changes are published to all clients, and it is still the client's responsibility to determine which changes are pertinent to its references and to appropriately adjust the identifiers.

In more sophisticated versions of the push model, the central system keeps track of which identifiers have been given to which clients. In this way the central system can notify (or not notify) each client about changes to identifiers specific to a client. In the most sophisticated approach, the central system and the client systems are integrated to the extent that the central hub actually effects the identifier changes in the client system.

CONCLUDING REMARKS

To obtain the highest level of identity integrity in an MDM system it is necessary to undertake manual, human-in-the-loop correction and confirmation assertions to complement the automated update process. Automated update processes will always produce some level of false positive and false negative errors. Left uncorrected, these errors will accumulate and, over time, will degrade the identity integrity of the system.

At the same time, successful manual updates require support from two other systems- clerical review indicators and EIS search and visualization tools. The review indicators help the MDM data steward focus their attention on the EIS most likely to have these errors. The visualization tool provides them with the capability to rapidly look up these EIS, view them in context, and record their assertion decisions. A robust visualization tool can also assist the data stewards in generating valid assertion transactions, and even help manage and coordinate the overall assertion workflow. This can be especially important when several operators are working concurrently on the same identity knowledge base.

Resolve and Retrieve Phase – Identity Resolution

IDENTITY RESOLUTION

Identity resolution is an EIIM configuration where the input is entity identity information and the output is the identifier of the EIS representing the entity. Identity resolution can be thought of as a recognition process. In other words, does the MDM system recognize the identity information given to it as referencing one of the entities the system has under management? In CDI, the customer version of MDM, identity resolution is often referred to as customer recognition.

Identity resolution is perhaps the most important configuration in EIIM. One of the fundamental principles of information quality is that information only creates value when it is used (McGilvray, 2008; Talburt, 2011). In addition, as McGilvray also points out, the planning, obtaining, storing, sharing, maintenance, and disposal of information are all necessary parts of the information life cycle, but they represent overhead cost. The benefits that offset cost and create information value are only realized when the information is used to accomplish some purpose. In MDM, the purpose is to provide the enterprise with persistent entity identifiers having the highest possible identity integrity.

Two major considerations influencing the implementation of the identity resolution configuration are access mode and universe model.

IDENTITY RESOLUTION ACCESS MODES

Client systems obtain entity identifiers from the IKB through the EIIM identity resolution configuration in two primary ways. The first is batch mode and the second is interactive mode (Kobayashi, Nelson, & Talburt, 2011). Many MDM systems support both modes of identity resolution.

BATCH IDENTITY RESOLUTION

Although batch is often associated with processing large files of records, the fundamental difference between batch and interactive mode is not so much about the quantity as it is about time. When the client system submits entity references to an EIIM identity resolution configuration in batch mode, it is with the expectation that the identifiers for the entities will be returned at a later time. How much later the identifiers are returned can vary considerably from hours to days depending upon the nature of the application. Often the delay between submission and reply is governed by a service level agreement (SLA) setting out requirements for the maximum amount of delay.

The schema for a typical batch identity resolution process is shown in Figure 6.1. The client system submits entity references to the EIIM system for resolution. The references usually undergo standardization and other data quality cleansing and validation operations at the staging step. The entity resolution system attempts to match each input reference to one of the EIS under management in the IKB. If a match is found, then the identifier of the matching EIS is paired with the identifier of the reference in the link index table. If a match is not found, the system will pair the reference with a special identifier discussed in more detail later. After the references have been processed, the system writes the link index table and makes it available to the client system.

It is usually the responsibility of the client system to read the link index table, and to update the original input reference with its resolved entity identifier from the link index table. The first column of the link index table is the list of identifiers for all of the references input into the system. The second column of the table contains the entity identifier corresponding to the reference identifier in the first column. If the input references are in a relational database table, then the link index table can also be written directly to, or loaded into, the same database. At this point the entity identifiers from the link index table can be easily appended to their corresponding references through a simple database join operation.

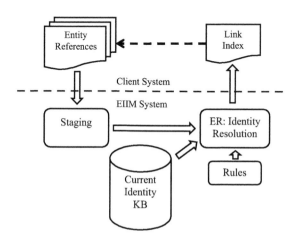

FIGURE 6.1

Schema for batch mode identity resolution.

If the reference file is too large for a traditional relational database, then both the references and link index can be loaded into a NoSQL data store such as the Hadoop Files System (HDFS) or HBase. Big Data stores like HDFS and HBase store data as key-value pairs. Unlike traditional relational databases, the data are often left unnormalized and the keys are not required to be unique. The join operations for these systems are accomplished through Hadoop map/reduce jobs instead of an SQL query.

Some EIIM systems are designed to update the input references directly. Rather than creating a separate link index table, the EIIM system writes the entity identifier directly into a user-designated field of the input reference. In these types of systems, the identity resolution configuration is often referred to as the link append process, because the EIIM system appends the entity identifier value to the input reference.

Managed and Unmanaged Entity Identifiers

The value of the identity resolution process is that it greatly reduces the effort the client system must expend to detect equivalent references. All of the references for the same entity should be paired with (or have appended) the same entity identifier in the link index table. This makes finding equivalent (duplicate) references a simple matter of sorting the link index table by the entity identifier column. Where the link index is in a Big Data store as key-value pairs and the key in the reference identifier, the sort will take the form of a map/reduce step. The mapper inverts the link index, i.e. it makes the entity identifier the key and the reference identifier the value. The reduce step then shuffles (sorts) and brings together all of the references with the same entity identifier.

For example, if the input references represent customer sales transactions and the entities under management are the customers, then after the identity resolution process all of the transactions for the same customer will have the same customer identifier. In this respect, MDM can be viewed as a technique for reuse of ER effort.

An identifier assigned to one of the EIS under management in an MDM system is called a managed entity identifier. To this point the discussion has been based on the assumption there is a matching EIS and, consequently, a managed entity identifier for reference input into the identity resolution process. However, this is not always the case. There may be instances where an input reference does not match any of the EIS under management in the IKB. In this situation, the MDM system will create a default entity identifier. Because the default entity identifier is not saved or maintained in the IKB, the default identifiers are also called unmanaged entity identifiers.

There are two main strategies for unmanaged entity identifiers. The first strategy is to pair the reference identifier with a special identifier value set aside for this purpose. When a value is returned as the identifier it tells the client system no match was found. In this strategy, all no-match references are given this same no-match identifier value. Furthermore, the no-match identifier value is created in a way to guarantee it will not collide with any of the managed entity identifiers. It is the responsibility of the client system to recognize the no-match identifier value and to implement any logic to properly handle it differently than it would a managed identifier.

An alternate no-match strategy is to create a temporary or local entity identifier for references not matching a managed entity. In this case, the unmanaged identifier is created by hashing certain identity attribute values in the reference. For example, in a customer reference, the unmanaged entity identifier might be created by concatenating the first letter of the first name, the first eight letters of the last name, and the street number of the address. Even though these hash keys are unmanaged, they can provide more value to the client system than simply providing the single, no-match indicator of the first strategy.

The reason they are useful is that the unmanaged hash keys are essentially match keys. Two references will only produce the same unmanaged identifier if the identity attribute values used to produce the identifier are similar. Consequently, when the client system brings together references appended with same entity identifiers, there is a higher likelihood the references with the same unmanaged identifiers are equivalent. The likelihood of equivalence may not be as high as it would be for two references given the same managed entity identifier, but nevertheless it provides some guidance to the client system about possible equivalent references. Just as with the special no-match identifier of the first strategy, the unmanaged identifiers created by hashing are formatted in such a way that the client system can easily discriminate between the managed and unmanaged entity identifiers.

The identity resolution configuration of EIIM in Figure 6.1 is similar to the automated identity update configuration shown in Figure 5.1, but with some important differences. The first and most important difference is the IKB is not updated in the identity resolution process. In identity resolution, the input references act only as inquiries into the IKB to retrieve entity identifiers. The content of the IKB is not altered by the identity resolution process.

That is not to say that identity update does not provide identifiers, because it does. The automated update process also provides the client with a link index as one of its outputs, thus it also performs identity resolution. However, the identity resolution provided by the automated update process through the link index is really a byproduct of the process, not its primary purpose. The primary purpose of the update process, both automated and manual, is to enrich the IKB with new entity identity information from high-quality entity reference sources.

Because the IKB is not expected to be altered in the identity resolution configuration, the quality of the input references can be much lower than the threshold required in the identity update configuration. Of course, the garbage-in-garbage-out (GIGO) rule still applies. The quality of a reference input into the identity resolution process will still influence the quality of the output. However, the difference is that in the identity resolution configuration, low quality input references will not lower the identity integrity of the IKB.

INTERACTIVE IDENTITY RESOLUTION

Interactive identity resolution takes place when a client system submits an entity reference to the MDM system with the expectation that the identifier for the corresponding entity will be returned in real time. Because real time is generally understood to mean the client system will hold further processing until the reply is received, the actual amount of time will depend upon the application. Again using the example of customer MDM, if the application is to support a point-of-sale (POS) transaction in a store, the time between entering customer identity information and receiving the managed identifier for the customer may be a matter of a few seconds. As long as the delay does not burden either the customer or the sales person, then it is considered a real-time transaction.

For system-to-system transactions, the bar may be set orders of magnitude higher and subsecond response times may be necessary. Another consideration is the total volume of transactions and the impact on the overall throughput of the system. For example, if a POS transaction needs to be completed in one second for each user, but one thousand user transactions are expected to arrive each second, then each of these requests must be serviced in one-thousandth of a second in order for each user to experience no more than one second of delay. For this reason, an SLA for response-time performance can be even more important for interactive identity resolution than it is for batch identity resolution.

As shown in Figure 6.2, interactive identity resolution is usually mediated through an application programming interface (API). An API is basically a contract between two systems specifying that when a defined set of input values are given, a defined set of output values will be returned. In the case of identity resolution, the inputs are values of entity identity attributes, and the value returned is the entity identifier, either managed or unmanaged.

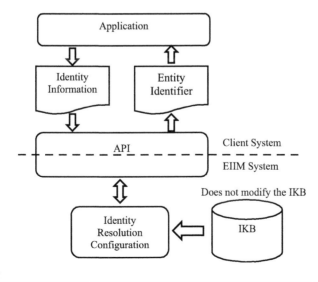

FIGURE 6.2

Schema for interactive identity resolution.

IDENTITY RESOLUTION API

Many options for the implementation of an API for identity resolution follow a number of API standards such as Common Object Request Broker Architecture (CORBA) and the Representational State Transfer (REST) architecture of the World Wide Web (so called RESTful APIs). However, the purpose of the discussion here is not to delve into the details of implementation, but to simply point out some of the high-level design considerations.

The primary trade-off in API design is between control and complexity. Take as an example a simple identity resolution API shown in Figure 6.3 for a student MDM application. Here the client exchanges the student's first name, last name, and date-of-birth for the student's identifier.

The simplicity of the GetIdentifier() design comes with a certain surrender of control by the client. Except for the choice of search values, all other aspects of the exchange are determined by the system hub. For example, the only options for client input are the three identity attributes of first name, last name, and date-of-birth, even though there could be many other searchable attributes such as middle name, address, or gender.

The GetIdentifier() API in Figure 6.3 does not allow the client to specify any matching criteria. In fact, the matching criteria are not exposed. It would be up to the client to understand exactly how matching takes place, and to assess its suitability for a particular application. Understanding the API documentation would also be important to know how likely it is that when GetIdentifier() returns a managed identifier, it is the correct identifier for the reference. For example, if the input reference matches two or more entities, does the API simply select one at random or is other logic invoked? When the GetIdentifier() API returns an unmanaged identifier, how does the client know the reason? Was it because no match was found? Or was it because the reference matched more than one entity?

Giving the client more control is a usually a design choice of making a more complex API to accommodate more client parameters and choices, or to create multiple APIs where each API implements only part of the logic. When a decision is for a family of APIs, then the client may need to make several calls to different APIs to complete a process.

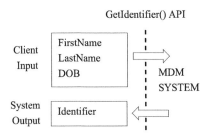

FIGURE 6.3

Simple GetIdentifier() API.

API Families

The notion of an API family is similar to class libraries in object-oriented programming languages such as Java. The API family supports overall objectives such as facilitating identity resolution, but each API in the family is responsible for only one particular task or function. Figures 6.4 and 6.5 show a GetKeywords() API and a GetIdentifierList() API working together to give the client system more control over the identity resolution configuration.

The GetKeywords() shown in Figure 6.4 returns as output a list of string values representing all of the searchable identity attributes for the system named in the input. More specifically, GetKeywords() returns three outputs. The first is an error code signaling the client whether the API transaction was executed successfully, or if not, some indication of why the transaction did not complete. For example, one value of the error code might indicate that the system name given was invalid, or another value that the requested system was unavailable at the time the API was invoked. Providing an error code or completion code to the client is always a good API design choice. The second output of GetKeywords() is the number of keywords returned, and the third output is the actual list of keywords.

For example, suppose the client system is a visualization tool supporting the manual update process as described in Chapter 5. Then the GetKeywords() might be called at system initialization time to populate a dropdown list of search qualifiers or to validate search qualifiers manually entered by the operator.

Unlike the simple GetIdentifier() API of Figure 6.3, the GetIdentifierList() shown in Figure 6.5 allows the client to search on any combination of identity attribute values. For example, suppose the GetKeywords() returns the list "First", "Middle", "Last", "DOB", and "Gender". Then the list given as input to the GetIdentifierList() might look like "First:Geneva", "Gender:F", "DOB:19970507" where the client specifies a search for female students with first name "Geneva" and born on May 7, 1997.

In addition to allowing the client to select its own combination of search terms, the GetIdentifierList() API allows the client more control over the matching process. The assumption for this example is that the GetIdentifierList() API is using a scoring rule such as the one described in Chapter 3 to match search terms to EIS.

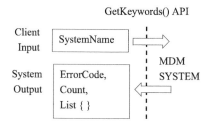

FIGURE 6.4

GetKeywords() API.

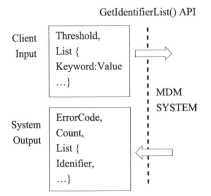

FIGURE 6.5

Simple GetIdentifierList() API.

The first input of the GetIdentifierList(), shown as "Threshold" in Figure 6.5, establishes the minimum score constituting a match.

The output from GetIdentifierList() is similar to the output from GetKeywords(). The client system receives an error code indicating the success or failure of the invocation, the number of EIS matching the search query, and the list of identifiers for the matching EIS.

The APIs given here by no means constitute a complete design. They are only given to illustrate some of the features and considerations going into API design. This family could have many other APIs. For example, another API might be named SetWeights() allowing the client to set the agreement and disagreement weights of a scoring rule that does the matching. Other APIs might be related to security and governance; for example, there could be an API requiring the client to give a user-name and password in exchange for an access token required to invoke other APIs.

CONFIDENCE SCORES

In many respects, the two API examples discussed here represent the extremes. The simple GetIdentifier() makes all of the decisions about the matching and gives the client a single answer. On the other hand, the API family including functions such as GetKeywords() and GetIdentifierList() would give the client access to a detailed level of information and empower more sophisticated decision-making on the client side. An API family providing this level of detail would be needed to support complex applications, such as a visualization tool where domain experts need to review information in detail before making correction and confirmation decisions.

However, if the client is another automated system, then an intermediate strategy is often a better fit, one allowing the client system to participate in making a decision about the output. One technique is to provide the client with a single output identifier, and along with it, a second value called a confidence score or confidence factor. The purpose of the confidence score is to give the client system some quantitative measure of the likelihood the identifier provided by the identity resolution API is the correct identifier for input reference.

Given a reference having some level of match to one or more managed EIS, the calculation of a confidence score needs to take three factors into account — the depth of match, the degree of match, and the match context. The depth of match is measured by how many different identity attribute values participate in the match, whereas the degree of match is how closely the values of each attribute match. Finally, the match context comprises all of the EIS having defined some level of match to the reference in question.

DEPTH AND DEGREE OF MATCH

Decisions about the depth and degree of match not only have a bearing on identity resolution but are also an integral part of the crafting of ER match rules for the capture and update configuration. In considering whether a match rule will predict equivalence, both influences must be considered. Take, as an example, the process of crafting Boolean rules for student MDM. Match depth is about how many identity attributes should participate in a match. Is a match on first name and last name enough? In most cases, probably not. For common names, many different students could share the same first and last name. An extension would be to add agreement on date-of-birth to the rule. Now the question becomes whether there also different students who share the same first name, last name, and date-of-birth. As new attributes are added, it becomes increasingly likely that the references agreeing on all of the values are equivalent and less likely they would not be equivalent.

As a reminder, high-quality MDM can only be attained when the answers to questions like the ones here are answered through data analysis rather than heuristics or intuition, as is so often the case. The effort expended in developing and using the techniques of truth set development, benchmarking, and problem sets discussed in Chapter 3 is an investment that will pay back many times in the long term.

At the same time, the depth of match must be tempered with the degree of match. The pervasiveness of poor data quality usually requires agreement between values that must be defined as something less than identical, i.e. less than an exact match. The recognition that the values of identity attributes will almost always have variations and corruptions has driven the development of a plethora of matching algorithms. Each algorithm is designed to overcome some particular type of variation known to occur in identity attribute values. These approximate or fuzzy matching techniques provide a way to measure the degree of match.

Take, as a simple example, the maximum q-gram similarity, which is a special case of the Jaccard Index character strings. Given two string values, the maximum q-gram similarity is the length of the longest shared substring divided by the length of the longest string. For example, consider the two string values "HALVERS" and "EVERST". The longest substring that they share is "VERS" with a length of

4 characters. Because the longest string "HALVERS" has 8 characters, the maximum q-gram similarity is $4/8 = 0.50$ or 50%. It is also easy to see that the maximum q-gram similarity can only be 100% when the two strings are identical, and the similarity will be 0% for two strings not having any characters in common.

Given a depth of match and a degree of match, a reference-to-reference match may be assigned a score using several methods. Suppose the depth of match is a set of N identity attributes and the degree of match is determined by a similarity function F (like maximum q-gram) taking on values between 0 and 1. If a_j represents the value of the j-th identity attribute of the first reference A, and b_j represents the corresponding j-th attribute of the second reference B, then a commonly used pattern to calculate a match score follows the formulation

$$R2R\_MatchScore(A, B) = \frac{1}{N} \cdot \sum_{j=1}^{N} F(a_j, b_j)$$

The match score is simply the average of the similarity scores between each of the corresponding attribute values of the two references.

For example, suppose $N = 2$, and the two attributes are student first name and last name. Let reference A be ("JON", "HALVERS") and reference B be ("JOE", "EVERST"). Also, let F be the maximum q-gram similarity function. Then

$$R2R\_MatchScore(A, B) = \frac{1}{2} \cdot \left(\frac{2}{3} + \frac{4}{8} \right) = 0.583$$

A more sophisticated version of this formulation allows the user to assign different weights to each attribute. This is helpful when the similarity for certain identity attributes is a better predictor of equivalence than other attributes, as these can be given higher weights.

$$R2R\_MatchScore(A, B) = \frac{1}{N} \cdot \sum_{j=1}^{N} F_j(a_j, b_j) \cdot w_j$$

where

$$\sum_{j=1}^{N} w_j = 1.0 \text{ and } 0.0 \leq F_j(a_j, b_j) \leq 1.0$$

The second formulation also allows attributes to be compared by different similarity functions. For instance, if one of the identity attributes is date-of-birth, then a similarity function designed to measure similarity in the number of days between two date values would be more appropriate than something comparing string similarity like the maximum q-gram similarity function.

All similarity functions are required to return values between 0 and 1 and the weights assigned to each attribute must total 1.0 to ensure the match score value will also be a value between 0 and 1.

However, in identity resolution the match is between a reference and a managed EIS in the IKB. What is needed is a reference-to-structure score. Again, a reference-to-structure match score may be formulated in many ways and will depend upon the architectural design of the EIS. For systems that implement record-based EIS design, as discussed in Chapter 4, a reference-to-structure match score can be easily formulated as follows. Let A represent a reference with N attributes and let S represent a record-based EIS containing M references R_1, R_2, ..., R_M. Then a reference-to-structure match score can be defined by

$$R2S\_MatchScore(A, S) = \max_{1 \leq j \leq M} \left\{ R2R\_MatchScore(A, R_j) \right\}$$

In this formulation, the reference-to-structure match score is simply the largest reference-to-reference match score taken over all of the references comprising the record-based EIS.

MATCH CONTEXT

The third component of an identity resolution confidence score is the match context. While it is important to understand the level of match between a reference and any one particular EIS, it is also important to understand how many other EIS also have some level of match to the same reference. These other EIS and the reference form the match context. However, the way in which a match context interacts with reference-to-structure match scores to create a confidence score will depend upon the universe model of the identity resolution configuration.

Closed and Open Universe Models

An identity resolution configuration is said to use a closed universe model if all of the input references requesting an identifier from the system are references to entities already under management. In other words, only references to managed entities are given as input to the identity resolution configuration. In a closed universe, the question is not whether a reference is to a managed entity; rather it is only which managed entity is being referenced.

On the other hand, an identity resolution configuration is using an open universe model if some of the input references requesting an identifier from the system are references to entities not under management. In an open universe model the system is being asked to recognize whether a reference is to an entity under management with the expectation some references will not be recognized. The identity resolution configuration will return an unmanaged entity identifier in response to an unrecognized reference, but it will not update the system.

Open and closed universe models describe the context of the identity resolution configuration and not the MDM system itself. The same MDM system may run an identity resolution configuration in both open and closed models at different times. Take, as an example, a student MDM system for a school. Suppose all of the students in the school or in a particular class take a standardized examination. When taking the examination students fill in their multiple-choice answers on a scan sheet along with their name and date-of-birth. These answer sheets are then scanned and captured as electronic records. Finally, the answer sheet records are submitted to an identity resolution configuration of the student MDM system to obtain the student's managed identifier.

In this examination scenario, the identity configuration is operating in a closed universe model because the expectation is that every test record references a student under management in the MDM system. However, the closed universe model does not necessarily guarantee every reference will have a managed identifier appended. There could be many reasons why an answer sheet fails to receive a proper identifier, such as a scanning error corrupting the information, a damaged scan sheet, or the student incorrectly entered information. Nevertheless, each record generated from a scan sheet is intended to reference one of the students in the school or class who took the examination.

In a different scenario, the school is sponsoring an event open to the public. However, students of the school sponsoring the event are entitled to a special discount on their registration fee. One of the functions of the event registration system is to pass each attendee's registration information to an identity resolution configuration of the school's MDM system to determine if the attendee is a student. In this open universe scenario, only the registration records for students of the sponsoring school are expected to match and return a managed identifier, while the records for other attendees should not.

CONFIDENCE SCORE MODEL

To understand the confidence score model, first consider the case of closed universe identity resolution. Here the guiding principle is any match is a good match. This is because in a closed universe model the input reference is presumed to match one of the EIS, and therefore, it is presumed to be the EIS with the highest reference-to-structure match regardless of the actual score.

Consider an example where the depth is 3 attributes all with equal weights. Suppose an input reference R has a 0.333 match score with a structure S because it has an exact match on one attribute, but the values of the other two attribute values are missing. Further suppose R has a 0.000 match with all other structures in the IKB, i.e. R and S form the complete context. Even though this is a low match score in absolute terms, because of the closed universe assumption, the confidence score for the match to S is essentially 1.00 or 100%. In other words, the API would give the client the managed identifier of S with a confidence score 1.000 that it is the correct identifier even though the reference-to-structure match score is only 0.333.

Now suppose reference R is more complete with only one attribute value missing. Further suppose the two non-null attributes are an exact match to structure S1 giving it a 0.667 reference-to-structure match score. Also suppose R has a 0.500 match score with structure S2, and a 0.000 match score with all other structures. Even in this case the API should return to the client the managed identifier of

S1 with a confidence of 100%. The reason is that R is known to match one of the structures and because S1 provides the highest match, it must be the one.

The only exception to the highest-score-wins principle is when two structures have the same, or essentially the same, match scores. Now it becomes ambiguous as to which structure is the correct one. For example, if R has a 0.667 match with both structures S1 and S2, then the API would return the identifier for S1 (or S2), but with a confidence score of 0.500 or 50% because there is essentially a 50/50 chance it could be equivalent to either one. Similarly, if R matched S1, S2, and S3 with the same score of 0.667, then the confidence score for the identifier of S1 would be 0.333 or 33%, the equal distribution of the 100% among the three competing EIS.

Although this is greatly simplified, the underlying principle holds. If the structure with the highest match score is a clear winner in the context of other structures, then its identifier should be returned along with the maximum confidence score. If there is a tie for the highest level of match, then the identifier for the one the EIS and confidence score returned is the maximum score divided by the number of matching EIS.

Again due to data quality issues, it is unlikely the confidence score for the highest reference-to-structure match will always be 100%. For example, in a customer MDM, suppose that S1 is a structure representing customer Mary Smith. If Mary were to change her name to Mary Jones, then it would be possible that a reference R with the name Mary Jones may generate a higher reference-to-structure score with some structure R2 representing a different customer, also with the last name of Jones. These and other possible scenarios would indicate that the confidence score would tend to decrease as the highest reference-to-structure score decreases.

The function G plotted in Figure 6.6 shows this relationship. In the closed universe, the confidence remains high even for smaller match scores. However, Figure 6.7 shows that in the open universe model, the behavior of the function G is much different.

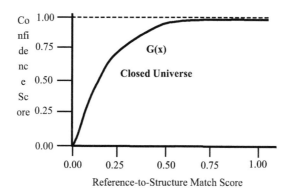

FIGURE 6.6

Confidence score vs. match score — closed universe.

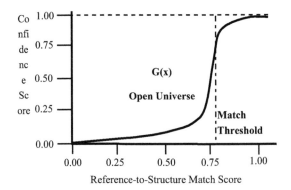

FIGURE 6.7

Confidence score vs. match score — open universe.

In the open universe model the probability that an identifier is correct for a given reference remains small until the value approaches the match threshold. The match threshold is the degree of match equivalent to an ER match rule used in a capture or update configuration.

The only remaining factor is in defining whether the EIS with the highest match score to the reference is a clear winner. Within a given match context, several EIS could have the same or similar match scores as the highest match score. To address this issue, let R be the input reference, let Γ represent the set of EIS having a nonzero match score with R, i.e. R and Γ are the match context. If μ represents the reference-to-structure match score function and E_0 represents the EIS in Γ having the highest match score with R, then define

$$T = |\{E \in \Gamma | \mu(R, E_0) - \mu(R, E) \le \delta\}|$$

T is the count of EIS having match scores within δ of the highest match score. Because this includes E_0, T must be at least 1. Just as with the probability function G, the value of δ should be determined empirically.

Applying these principles, the confidence score for both the closed and open universe models can be formulated as

$$Confidence\ Score(R) = \frac{1}{T} \cdot G(R, E_0)$$

CONCLUDING REMARKS

The resolve and retrieve phase is the most important of all the CSRUD MDM life cycle phases. Resolving an entity reference to its correct entity (EIS) is the primary use case for MDM — the phase producing value for the enterprise.

A major issue for the resolve and retrieve phase is the synchronization of identifiers in the MDM hub with identifiers residing in client systems. As identifiers change in the hub, the changes must somehow be propagated to the clients' systems. The two primary strategies are periodically pulling source records from the clients' systems back to the hub for re-resolution to refresh the identifiers, and pushing changes from the hub to client systems as they occur. The pull model is the simpler of the two strategies, but for some organizations and applications, the pull model may not meet the business and functions requirements for the MDM application.

In addition to synchronization, quantifying the reliability of a resolved identifier is also a problem. The reliability of identification will vary from inquiry to inquiry depending upon the depth, breadth, and context of the match to the EIS in the identity knowledge base. In order to provide guidance to the inquiring client system, some MDM systems compute a confidence score for each inquiry providing the client system with an estimate of the likelihood that a resolved identifier is correct.

Theoretical Foundations

THE FELLEGI-SUNTER THEORY OF RECORD LINKAGE

In 1969, I.P. Fellegi and A.B Sunter, statisticians working at the Dominion Bureau of Statistics in Canada, published a paper titled *A Theory for Record Linkage* (Fellegi & Sunter, 1969) describing a statistical model for entity resolution. Known as the Fellegi-Sunter Model, it has been foundational to ER, and by extension MDM, in several fundamental ways:

- It described record linking, a particular configuration of ER, in a rigorous way using the language of mathematics and statistics.
- Although the structure of the matching rule is no longer used exactly as they described it, it still informs both of the most frequently used styles of matching used today, Boolean rules and scoring rules.
- It emphasized the role and importance of entity resolution analytics. The fundamental theorem is about optimizing match rules with respect to a maximum allowable false positive rate and a maximum allowable false negative rate.
- It defined a method for generating clerical review indicators. The proof of the fundamental theorem relies on the assumption that human reviewers will always be able to correctly decide if a pair of references indicated for review are equivalent or not equivalent.

THE CONTEXT AND CONSTRAINTS OF RECORD LINKAGE

The theory of record linkage is set in a special context of linking across two lists of references. It addresses the problem of finding equivalences between pairs of references where one reference is in the first list and the other reference is in the second list. In the proof of the theorem, they generously assumed the list had no equivalences. In other words, no two references within the same list were equivalent; equivalences could only be found between the two lists. This is much different than the context described in the previous chapters where the input is a single set of references. Although the EIIM configuration of merge-purge is often called record linking, technically record linking and merge-purge are different processes. In the merge-purge configuration of EIIM, a single list of references is partitioned in clusters of presumed equivalent references, whereas record linking takes place only between two separate lists of references.

From an analytical perspective, if X and Y represent the two lists, then the number of pairs to be considered for record linking will be $|X|*|Y|$, the size of the cross product $X \times Y$. In merge-purge, there are $(|X|+|Y|)*(|X|+|Y|-1)/2$ pairs to consider. Moreover, in record linking, the maximum number of equivalences possible will be $\text{Minimum}\{|X|, |Y|\}$ because each reference in List X can only be equivalent to, at most, one reference in List Y. If a reference in List X were equivalent to two references in List Y, then by transitivity of equivalence, the two references in List Y would necessarily be equivalent and contradict the assumption that no two pairs of references in List Y are equivalent. A similar argument holds that each reference in List Y can only be equivalent to, at most, one reference in List X.

However, the confusion is forgivable. Just from a practical viewpoint, starting an ER process with two lists where each list is known to be free of equivalent references is rare. Given two lists of references in the real world there could well be equivalent references within each list as well as between the two lists. As a practical matter, record linking is often implemented by first merging the two lists into a single list, then running a merge-purge or identity capture configuration. If the two lists are truly free of internal equivalences, then each cluster formed in the merge-purge process can comprise only a single reference or two references where each is from a different list. The latter indicates a link between the two lists. On the other hand, if a cluster contains two references from the same list, then the two references are presumably equivalent and this indicates the assumption was not justified. In this way, equivalence references can be found in one process both between the lists and within each list.

THE FELLEGI-SUNTER MATCHING RULE

An understanding of the Fellegi-Sunter matching rule is essential to understanding the overall theorem. Another assumption is the two lists of references have the same number and types of identity attributes. In other words, there is a one-to-one correspondence between the identity attributes in the first list and the identity attributes in the second list. Suppose in the first list, List X, each reference has N identity attributes $x_1, x_2, ..., x_N$, and in the second list, List Y, each reference has the corresponding identity attributes $y_1, y_2, ..., y_N$.

An agreement pattern between two references from Lists X and Y is an N-bit binary number where the k-th bit of the binary number represents the state of agreement between the k-th identity attribute of List X (x_k) and the k-th identity attribute of List Y (y_k). If the k-th bit of the pattern is a 1, then the two attributes agree in value. If the k-th bit of the pattern is a 0, then the two attributes disagree in value.

Take, as a simple example, two Lists X and Y sharing three identity attributes, say first name, middle name, and last name of a customer. Then the agreement patterns will be 3-bit binary numbers. For example, the agreement pattern 101 means the values of the first name attribute agree (1), the values of the middle name attribute disagree (0), and the values of the last name attribute agree (1). In this example of three identity attributes there are $8 = 2^3$ possible agreement patterns corresponding to the 8 binary numbers from 000 to 111. In general, for N corresponding identity attributes there will be 2^N possible agreement patterns.

It should also be noted that agreement does not necessarily mean the two identity attribute values are exactly the same. It could be defined to mean agreement on Soundex code, or having a q-Gram similarity of 80% or larger, or any other type of ER comparator. Moreover, agreement can be defined differently for each attribute.

In this respect, agreement patterns are a special type of Boolean match rule. In the previous example the 101 pattern might be interpreted as the proposition "(First name values agree on Soundex match) AND (NOT(middle name values agree by Exact match)) AND (last name values agree by Exact match)". However, most systems supporting Boolean rules do not implement the NOT operator. Instead, the identity attributes not required to match are not specified in the rule and treated as "don't care" states. In other words, the Boolean rule "First name values agree on Soundex AND last name values agree by exact" would be True as long there was agreement on the first and last name regardless of whether the middle name values agree or not. Thus, this Boolean version of the rule would encompass both the 101 and 111 Fellegi-Sunter agreement patterns.

Given two lists of references, List X and List Y, sharing N identity attributes, define Γ to be the set of 2^N possible agreement patterns. Then a Fellegi-Sunter matching rule is defined by three sets A, R, and V where

1. $A \subseteq \Gamma, R \subseteq \Gamma, V \subseteq \Gamma$
2. $A \cap R = \varnothing, A \cap V = \varnothing, R \cap V = \varnothing$
3. $A \cup R \cup V = \Gamma$

Although A, R, and V are nonoverlapping sets covering Γ, they do not always form a partition of Γ because they are not required to be nonempty subsets of Γ.

Now let $x \in X$, $y \in X$, and let $\gamma \in \Gamma$ represent the agreement pattern between values of the identity attributes of the references x and y. Then the Fellegi-Sunter matching rule $F = \{A, R, V\}$ states

1. If $\gamma \in A$, then always link reference x and y,
2. Else if $\gamma \in R$, then always reject linking (never link) reference x and y,
3. Else if $\gamma \in V$, then a person must verify that x and y are, or are not, equivalent and link accordingly.

All of this is just a mathematical way of saying divide all of the possible agreement patterns into three nonoverlapping groups, A, R, and V. When comparing references from Lists X and Y, if the values of the corresponding identity attributes conform to an agreement pattern in the set A, then the rule is to always link the references together. If the agreement pattern is in the set R, then the rule is to never link the references together. If the agreement pattern is in the set V, then the rule is a person must verify whether the two references should be linked or not.

THE FUNDAMENTAL FELLEGI-SUNTER THEOREM

The crux of the Fellegi-Sunter theory rests on one fundamental theorem. The fundamental theorem adds two more elements to the context besides to the two lists of references. These elements are two constraint values: the maximum allowable false negative rate denoted by λ and the maximum false positive rate denoted by μ.

The fundamental theorem of the Fellegi-Sunter theory says, given the context of two lists X and Y and constraints λ and μ, then it will always be possible to find a Fellegi-Sunter match rule $F = \{A, R, V\}$ that is optimal with respect to the following:

1. The false positive rate from always linking reference pairs with agreement patterns in A will not exceed μ;
2. The false negative rate from never linking reference pairs with agreement patterns in R will not exceed λ; and
3. The number of reference pairs with agreement patterns in V requiring manual verification will be minimized.

Fortunately the proof of the theorem is a constructive proof, i.e. the proof of the theorem shows how to construct the rule $F = \{A, R, V\}$ satisfying these conditions.

The construction starts with the two lists of references X and Y. Let X × Y represent all possible pairs of these references (x, y) where $x \in X$ and $y \in Y$, and $\gamma \in \Gamma$ is one of the agreement patterns. Now let $E \subseteq X \times Y$ represent the pairs of references actually equivalent to each other. The construction of the rule is fairly straightforward and relies primarily on the following formula:

$$R_\gamma = \frac{P(\gamma \in \Gamma | (x, y) \in E)}{P(\gamma \in \Gamma | (x, y) \notin E)}$$

The fraction R_γ is called the Pattern Ratio for pattern γ. The numerator of the ratio is the probability two equivalent references will conform to the agreement pattern γ, and the denominator is the probability that two nonequivalent references will conform to γ. Because these fractions can be very large or very small, the theorem also defines W_γ the Pattern Weight for γ by simply converting the ratio R_γ to its logarithmic value, i.e.

$$W_\gamma = \log_2(R_\gamma).$$

The pattern ratio and pattern weight measure the predictive power of each pattern for equivalence or nonequivalence. If the probability that equivalent references satisfy a given pattern is high and the probability that nonequivalent references satisfy the same pattern is low, the ratio will be very large. It also means the pattern is a good predictor of whether the two references should be linked because it is associated with a high probability of equivalence, thus creating a true positive link. As the numerator approaches 1 and the denominator approaches 0, the value of the ratio becomes unbounded. To avoid the problem of division by zero, the denominator is never allowed to be smaller than a very small, but fixed, value.

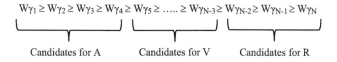

$$W\gamma_1 \geq W\gamma_2 \geq W\gamma_3 \geq W\gamma_4 \geq W\gamma_5 \geq \ldots\ldots \geq W\gamma_{N-3} \geq W\gamma_{N-2} \geq W\gamma_{N-1} \geq W\gamma_N$$

Candidates for A   Candidates for V   Candidates for R

FIGURE 7.1

Candidates for sets A, V, and R based on ordered pattern weights.

On the other hand, if the numerator is small and the denominator is large, the ratio will be small and weight will be a small negative value. In this case the pattern predicts that the references should not be linked because the references are more likely to be true negatives.

From this it is easy to see that the highest weight patterns are the best choices for members of the set A of the rule (always link), and the lowest weight patterns are the best choices for members of the set R of the rule (never link). In the proof of the theorem the patterns are ordered from highest to lowest weight.

The ordering and candidates for the members of the A, V, and R set of the rules are shown in Figure 7.1. The only question is how many of the patterns with high weights should go into A and how many with the lowest weights should go into R. The answers to these questions are determined by the constraints λ and μ.

Note that if a pattern is selected for the set A, then any pair of references conforming to the pattern will be linked. Linking will either result in a true positive or a false positive. Patterns in A never create false negative links. They can only make true or false positives. Also, unless the denominator of the pattern ratio equals 0, the pattern will make some false positive links, i.e. it will link two nonequivalent references. The false positive rate for a pattern in A is the ratio of the number of nonequivalent pairs of references it links together to the total number of nonequivalent pairs.

The algorithm for selecting patterns for membership in A proceeds as follows, starting with A empty and the cumulative false positive rate equal to zero. Start with the pattern having the highest weight. If the pattern's false positive rate is greater than μ, then the algorithm stops and A remains empty. Otherwise add the pattern to A, add its false positive rate to the cumulative false positive rate, and select the pattern with the next highest weight. If the cumulative false positive rate plus the false positive rate of the next pattern is greater than μ, then the algorithm stops. Otherwise add this pattern to A, add its false positive rate to the cumulative false positive rate, and select the pattern with the next highest weight. This process continues until a pattern is selected causing the cumulative false positive rate of the patterns in A to exceed μ, the maximum allowable false positive rate.

After the members of A are selected, the next step is to select the agreement patterns for R. If a pattern is selected for the set R, then any pair of references conforming to the pattern will not be linked. Therefore, patterns in R can only create true negatives or false negatives. When two equivalent references conform to a pattern in R, then the pattern will create a false negative. The false negative rate of a pattern in R is the ratio of the number of equivalent pairs satisfying the pattern to the total number of equivalent pairs.

The algorithm for selecting patterns for membership in R follows a similar algorithm to the one for A, starting with R empty and the cumulative false negative rate equal to zero. Start with the pattern having the lowest weight. If its false negative rate is greater than λ, then the algorithm stops and R remains empty. Otherwise add the pattern to R, add its false negative rate to the cumulative false negative rate, and select the pattern with the next lowest weight. If the cumulative false negative rate plus the false negative rate of the next pattern is greater than λ, then the algorithm stops. Otherwise put this pattern in R, add its false negative rate to the cumulative false negative rate, and select the pattern with the next lowest weight. This process continues until a pattern is selected that causes the cumulative false negative rate of the patterns in R to exceed λ or until there are no other patterns remaining to select (not already selected for A).

The members of set V are determined by default. If after selecting the members of A and R patterns still remain, then these patterns comprise V. The construction of the Fellegi-Sunter rule $F = \{A, R, V\}$ is now complete.

Since its original publication, a number of authors have described many extensions and improvements of the Fellegi-Sunter Model. Most notably William Winkler at the U.S. Bureau of the Census has published on the application of expectation-maximization methods (Winkler, 1988) ways to adjust for lack of conditional independence among attributes (Winkler, 1989a), and the automation of weight calculations (Winkler, 1989b).

ATTRIBUTE LEVEL WEIGHTS AND THE SCORING RULE

Although the theorem and the construction of the Fellegi-Sunter rule are elegant, the theory presents some practical challenges in its implementation. One of the biggest problems is with the number of possible patterns that must be analyzed. It might not be uncommon in an application to have 10 identity attributes. To develop a Fellegi-Sunter rule for such an application would require the analysis of $1,024 = 2^{10}$ agreement patterns.

However, if prepared to make the assumption that the identity attributes are conditionally independent, then the problem can be greatly simplified. The conditional independence assumption is that the probability of agreement or disagreement between two values of one identity attribute does not affect the probability of agreement or disagreement between two values of any other identity attribute. Of course in most applications, this is not entirely true. For example, if two addresses were to agree on a state, then the agreements on city will be limited to the names of cities in that state. However, in general, the benefits of assuming conditional independence outweigh these concerns.

The benefit of assuming conditional independence of the identity attributes is that the calculation of the pattern weight can be estimated by calculating the weight of each identity attribute. In their book, Herzog, Scheuren, and Winkler (2007) give

an excellent exposition of the method for calculating pattern weights from the estimated probabilities of agreement and disagreement on individual identity attributes.
Given the attributes are conditionally independent, the pattern weight calculation is

n = number of attributes

m_i = probability that equivalent references agree on attribute i

u_i = probability that non-equivalent references agree on attribute i

$$w_i = \begin{cases} \log_2\left(\dfrac{m_i}{u_i}\right) & \text{if agreement in attribute i} \\[2ex] \log_2\left(\dfrac{(1\text{-}m_i)}{(1\text{-}u_i)}\right) & \text{otherwise} \end{cases}$$

$$\log_2(W_\lambda) = \sum_{i=1}^{n} w_i$$

By using this calculation, the estimate for each pattern weight can be calculated
by summing the ratios associated with individual attributes. Using the previous
example of the agreement pattern 101, then

$$\log_2(W_{101}) = \log_2\left(\frac{m_1}{u_1}\right) + \log_2\left(\frac{(1\text{-}m_2)}{(1\text{-}u_2)}\right) + \log_2\left(\frac{m_3}{u_3}\right)$$

where m_1 is the probability that equivalent records agree on first name, and u_1 is the
probability that nonequivalent records agree on first name. The values of m_2 and u_2
are for similar probabilities on values of middle name, and m_3 and u_3 for values of
last name.

In this scheme each attribute has two weights, an agreement weight and a
disagreement weight. These weights are summed to estimate the weight of the
complete pattern. When implemented in software, this "on-the-fly" generation of
the pattern weight is called a scoring rule as discussed in Chapter 3. The example
given in Figure 3.4 shows the automatic generation of the weight for the agreement
pattern 10110.

When scoring rules are implemented in ER systems, the patterns comprising the
A subset of patterns in the Fellegi-Sunter linking rule (always link) are determined
by a value called the match threshold. Just as shown in Figure 3.4, if two references
conform to an agreement pattern generating a weight above the match threshold,
the references are linked. This corresponds to a value between $W\gamma_4$ and $W\gamma_5$ in
Figure 7.1 defining the boundary of the A patterns. In addition, many scoring rule
systems implement a second threshold called the review threshold that is smaller
than the match threshold. Pairs of references generating a pattern weight smaller
than the match threshold but greater than the review threshold are logged for clerical
review. The review threshold corresponds to a value between $W\gamma_{N-3}$ and $W\gamma_{N-2}$ in
Figure 7.1, separating the V patterns from the R patterns.

FREQUENCY-BASED WEIGHTS AND THE SCORING RULE

One further refinement of estimating pattern weight from attribute weights is called frequency-based weights. Frequency-based weighting is simply a reinterpretation of the probability m_i and u_i from agreement on attributes to agreement on specific attribute values. Thus, if v is a value of the i-th identity attribute then

$m_i(v) =$ probability equivalent references agree on the value v in attribute i
$u_i(v) =$ probability nonequivalent references agree on the value v in attribute i

In this scheme, each identity attribute has many weights, potentially one for every value the attribute can take on. However, as the name implies, the value weights are usually only generated for the most frequently encountered values. The assumption is that more frequently encountered values are more likely to be associated with many different entities and consequently should have a lower weight than less frequently used values, which are more likely associated with fewer entities.

A case in point for party entities are name attributes. For example, consider first name. Given a population, it may be determined that many different customers have the first name "JOHN" versus many fewer different customers having the first name "FREDRICK". If the first name is the first identity attribute, this means the probability nonequivalent references will agree on "JOHN" is greater than the probability nonequivalent references will agree on "FREDRICK", i.e. u_1("JOHN") > u_1("FREDRICK"). The net effect will be the weight for agreement on "JOHN" in the first name attribute will be smaller than the weight for agreement on "FREDRICK".

The nuanced adjustment in weight based on frequency can make the scoring rule an accurate tool in certain MDM domains. The trade-off is the increased analytical effort to initially determine the weights and the ongoing effort to keep the weights in adjustment. Another issue with both frequency-based and attribute-based weights in general is they do not perform well on sets of references with identity attributes having a significant number of missing values. The setting of the weights depends on the probabilities of agreement and disagreement, but when one or both values are missing, agreement and disagreement cannot be determined.

THE STANFORD ENTITY RESOLUTION FRAMEWORK

Another significant contribution to the theory of entity resolution is the Stanford Entity Resolution Framework (SERF) developed by researchers at the Stanford InfoLab led by Hector Garcia-Molina (Benjelloun et al., 2009). The main contributions of the SERF are:

1. It changed the context of ER from the Fellegi-Sunter model of linking pairs of references between two different lists to the problem of finding clusters of equivalent references within a single dataset similar to the merge-purge configuration of EIIM.

2. In addition to a pair-wise matching operation, it described a new operation merging (creates clusters of) references to form new objects (the EIS of EIIM) that can also be acted upon by the match and merge operations.
3. Using abstract mathematical descriptions of the match and merge operations, it formally defined what it means for a set of objects (clusters) produced by the match and merge operations acting on a set of references to comprise the entity resolution of those references.
4. It established the properties the match and merge operations must satisfy in order to assure the unique entity resolution of a set of references will exist.
5. In the case where the match and merge operations have the properties necessary to produce a unique entity resolution of a set of references, it defined an algorithm for applying the match and merge operations to the set of references always ending with the clusters that comprise their entity resolution.

ABSTRACTION OF MATCH AND MERGE OPERATIONS

The foundation of SERF is an abstraction of the match and merge operations as functions operating on an abstract set of entity references. Whereas the Fellegi-Sunter model focuses on the actual mechanics of matching in terms of agreement and disagreement of identity attribute values, the SERF takes a more abstract approach. If M represents the match operation and D represents its domain, then the match function M is defined as

$$M : D \times D \rightarrow \{True, \; False\}$$

M is simply a function assigning each pair of elements in its domain a True or False value. Similarly for the same domain D, the merge operation μ is defined as

$$If \; x, y \in D \; and \; M(x, y) = True, \; Then \; \mu(x, \; y) \in D$$

The merge function simply maps pairs of matching elements in D to another element in D. Because both x and y are elements in D, it is possible in some instances either $\mu(y, x) = x$ or $\mu(x, y) = x$. When this happens, then x is said to "dominate" y.

So what is the domain D? If R is a set of entity references, then the domain D is the closure of R with respect to M and μ. In other words, D is the set of all objects possibly formed by starting with R, then repeatedly finding matching references and merging the matching references.

As a warning, even though these operations are called match and merge, and R is said to be a set of entity references, this is strictly a set theoretic definition, and at this point in the model, these names do not imply any particular real-world behavior or structure. For example, there is nothing in the definition of M that requires $M(x, x) = True$. In other words, the elements of D are not required to match themselves, a fairly basic expectation of real data matching. There is also no assumption that $M(x, y) = M(y, x)$ or that $\mu(x, x) = x$.

To illustrate this point, consider the case where $R = \{1\}$, the set containing only the integer value of one. Furthermore, define the operations M and μ as follows

$$\text{If } x, y \text{ are integers, } M(x, y) = \begin{cases} True & \text{if } x \text{ is odd} \\ False & \text{if } x \text{ is even} \end{cases}$$

$$\text{If } M(x, y) = True, \text{ then } \mu(x, y) = x + y$$

Having defined R, M, and μ, the next question is what is D? Given that R only has one element 1, the only place to start is with the question: Is $M(1, 1)$ True or False? Because 1 is odd, the answer is True. Therefore, the merge function can operate on the pair $(1, 1)$ resulting in a new object $\mu(1, 1) = 1 + 1 = 2$.

At this point D has expanded from $\{1\}$ to $\{1, 2\}$. Now there are 4 pairs in D to test for matching with M. If any of those pairs match, then the merge function can be applied and will possibly generate new objects in D. As it turns out, $M(1, 2) =$ True, thus $\mu(1, 2) = 3$ thereby expanding $D = \{1, 2, 3\}$. By following this pattern it is easy to see D can be extended to include all positive integers $Z^+ = \{1, 2, 3, ...\}$ an infinite set.

THE ENTITY RESOLUTION OF A SET OF REFERENCES

Given a set of entity reference R, a match operation M, and a merge operation μ, then a set ER(R) is said to be the entity resolution of R, provided ER(R) satisfies the following conditions:

1. ER(R) $\subseteq D$. This condition requires ER(R) to be a subset of D.
2. If $x \in D$, then
   a. Either $x \in$ ER(R), or
   b. There exists a $y \in$ ER(R) such that $\mu(x, y) = y$ or $\mu(y, x) = y$.
   This condition states every element of D must either be in the entity resolution of R or be dominated by an element in the entity resolution or R.
3. If $x, y \in$ ER(R), then
   a. Either $M(x, y) = False$, or
   b. $\mu(x, y) \neq x$, $\mu(x, y) \neq y$, $\mu(y, x) \neq x$ and $\mu(y, x) \neq y$.

This condition states for any two elements in the entity resolution of R, they either don't match, or if they do match, then one does not dominate the other.

Given the previous example where $R = \{1\}$ and $D = Z+$, what is ER(R)? The first thing to note is by the definition of the merge function, no two elements of D can ever dominate each other. Because x and y are positive integers, and $\mu(x, y) = x + y$, it follows that $x + y > x$ and $x + y > y$. Therefore by Condition 1 of the definition, the only candidate for ER(R) is D. However, for D to be ER(R), D must also satisfy Condition 2. For Condition 2, there are two cases for $x, y \in D$ to consider. One is when x is even. If x is even, then $M(x, y) = False$ and Condition 2 is satisfied. On the other hand if x is odd, then $M(x, y) = True$. However, $\mu(x, y) = x + y$ can't be equal to x or y by the same argument as in Condition 1. Thus ER(R), the entity resolution of R exists and is unique, but it is infinite. It is not difficult to construct other examples where ER(R) does not exist or where there is more than one ER(R).

CONSISTENT ER

The SERF also answers the question of when the match and merge operations will produce a unique and finite ER(R), called consistent ER. Consistent ER will occur if and only if the match and merge operations have the following properties, called the ICAR properties:

- For every $x \in D$, $M(x, x)$ =True, and $\mu(x, x) = x$ (Idempotent)
- For every $x, y \in D$, $M(x, y) = M(y, x)$, and $\mu(x, y) = \mu(y, x)$ (Commutative)
- For every $x, y, z \in D$, $\mu(x, \mu(y, z)) = \mu (\mu (x, y), z)$ (Associative)
- If $M(x, y) = M(y, z) = $ True, then $M(x, \mu (y, z)) = M(\mu (x, y), z) = $ True (Representativity)

THE R-SWOOSH ALGORITHM

The SERF also includes a number of algorithms for actually producing the set of elements in D comprising the ER(R). The most important of these is the R-Swoosh algorithm. Given match and merge operations satisfying the conditions of the consistent ER, the R-Swoosh algorithm was shown to require the least number of operations to produce ER(R) in the worst case scenario. The details of the R-Swoosh ER algorithm are discussed in the next chapter.

The next chapter also compares the R-Swoosh algorithm with the One-Pass algorithm. The One-Pass algorithm is simpler (requires fewer operations) than the R-Swoosh algorithm, but it is only guaranteed to produce ER(R) when additional conditions are applied to the match and merge functions. However, these extra conditions are often imposed for typical EIIM and MDM systems; thus R-Swoosh is not often used in commercial applications.

ENTITY IDENTITY INFORMATION MANAGEMENT

Entity Identity Information Management (EIIM) is the main theme of this book, and has been discussed extensively in previous chapters. As stated in Chapter 1, EIIM is the collection and management of identity information with the goal of sustaining entity identity integrity over time (Zhou & Talburt, 2011b). While the primary focus of the EIIM model is on addressing the life cycle of entity identity information, EIIM draws from, and is consistent with, both the Fellegi-Sunter and the SERF models of ER.

EIIM AND FELLEGI-SUNTER

The manual update configuration of EIIM discussed in Chapter 5 and the importance of assessing ER outcomes discussed in Chapter 3 are both drawn directly from the work of Fellegi and Sunter. As noted earlier, the proof of their fundamental theorem of record linkage depends on the assumption that some number of matches will require manual review. Furthermore, it prescribes a method for identifying the pairs of references needing to be reviewed, namely the pairs having agreement patterns comprising the verify subset V of the Fellegi-Sunter matching rule. Although the method of the theorem minimizes the number of pairs satisfying these "soft" rules, they do require verification by a domain expert. Unfortunately, this important aspect of ER is absent in many MDM systems that rely entirely on automated ER matching decisions.

The reliance on automated ER coupled with a lack of ER analytics is a recipe for low-quality MDM if not outright failure. Even at small levels, false positive and false negative errors will accumulate over time and progressively degrade the level of entity identity integrity in an MDM system.

In addition to clerical review of matching, the Fellegi-Sunter Model is framed around accuracy in the form of limits on false positive and false negative rates. However, these constraints are meaningless if these values are not known. Measurement of entity identity integrity attainment is yet another important aspect of ER absent in many MDM systems. Few MDM stewards can offer reliable, quantitative estimates of the false positive and false negative rates of their systems. Even though almost every chief data officer (CDO) or chief information officer (CIO) would state that their goal is to make their MDM systems as accurate as possible, few actually undertake systematic measures of accuracy. Without meaningful measurements it is difficult to tell if changes aimed at improving accuracy are really effective.

EIIM AND THE SERF

The EIIM Model elaborates on several features of the SERF. For example, it explores in more detail the characteristics of the merge operation. In the EIIM Model, the results of merging references are characterized as entity identity structures (EIS). The EIIM further describes the interaction between the match and merge operations in terms of EIS projection. The next chapter discusses EIS projection in more detail and also investigates the consequences of design choices for both EIS and EIS projection. These include the most commonly used designs of survivor record, exemplar record, attribute-based, and record-based EIS. In particular, the chapter shows that a simplified version of the R-Swoosh algorithm called One-Pass is sufficient to reach ER(R) when the record-based projection of EIS is used.

The EIIM automated update configuration is equivalent to the SERF notion of incremental resolution (Benjalloun et al., 2009). Whereas the SERF focuses primarily on the efficiency of resolution, the focus of EIIM is on sustaining entity identity integrity through the incremental resolution (update) cycles including the use of manual update (assertion).

CONCLUDING REMARKS

The primary theoretical foundations for ER are the Fellegi-Sunter Theory of Record Linkage and the Stanford Entity Resolution Framework. Their basic principles still underpin ER today. Deterministic matching, probabilistic matching, ER metrics, ER algorithms, clerical review indicators, and clerical review and correction all have their origin in these models. However, in order for ER to effectively support MDM, some additional functionality is required. EIIM describes additional functionality in terms of creating and maintaining EIS. The EIS are essential for preserving entity identity information and maintaining persistent entity identifiers from ER process to ER process.

The Nuts and Bolts of Entity Resolution

THE ER CHECKLIST

Even in its most basic form, entity resolution (ER) has many moving parts that must be fit together correctly in order to obtain accurate and consistent results. The functions and features that are assembled to support the different phases of the CSRUD Life Cycle are called EIIM *configurations*. The focus of this chapter is on the configurations supporting the capture and the automated update phases. From a design perspective, these configurations are essentially the same, and must address the following questions:

1. What rules will match pairs of references?
2. How will references be systematically matched? The configuration should systematically compare pairs of references so that the largest number (if not all) of the matches can be found, and at the same time, make as few comparisons as possible.
3. What rules will match clusters? Once two or more references have been linked together to form a cluster, there have to be rules for matching a single reference to a cluster of references, and rules for matching two clusters.
4. What is the procedure for reorganizing matching clusters? If an input reference and a cluster match, or there are two matching clusters, then there must be a procedure for reorganizing them into a single cluster.

DETERMINISTIC OR PROBABILISTIC?

One of the first questions faced in the design of a new ER/MDM system or the selection of the third-party system is whether the base rule for matching a pair of references should be a Boolean rule (misnamed deterministic) or a scoring rule (misnamed probabilistic). The basic design for both types of rules was discussed in Chapter 3 and both have advantages and disadvantages. The choice between Boolean versus scoring rules, or some combination, will depend upon the nature of the data, the application, and level of maturity of the organization (Wang, Pullen, Talburt, & Wu, 2014a).

Consider the example of a Boolean rule set from Chapter 3 for student enrollment records, shown here.

Rule 1:
(First: Soundex) AND (Last: Exact) AND (School_ID: Exact)
Rule 2:
(First: Exact) AND (Last: Exact) AND (Street_Nbr: Exact)

Rule 1 and Rule 2 represent the OR clauses of the overall Boolean rule and can be thought of as subrules. The obvious advantage of a Boolean rule is that it is easy to understand and create. In addition, its subrules (OR clauses) operate independently of each other. If a new matching condition needs to be addressed, it can easily be added as a new subrule without impacting the effects or actions of the other subrules.

Another advantage is that different subrules can use different comparators for the same attribute. In the example given here, the student first name is compared using the SOUNDEX comparator in Rule 1, but the student first name is compared using the EXACT comparator in Rule 2. In contrast, in the basic design of the scoring rule, each attribute has only one comparator. Another advantage of a Boolean rule is that it is easier to address the issue of misfielded items or cross-attribute comparison. For example, a subrule can be added that compares the first name to the last name and vice versa to address cases where the first and last names have been reversed. Similar comparisons can be made on attributes like telephone numbers.

Another advantage of the Boolean rule is that it is easier to align it with the match key index than a scoring rule. Blocking and match key indexing are discussed in more detail in the next chapter. In general, a Boolean rule is easier to design and refine than a scoring rule.

The biggest advantage of the scoring rule is that it provides a fine-grained matching capability that for certain types of data can be much more accurate than Boolean rules. This is because a scoring rule can adjust its matching decision based on the actual values of the attributes. For example, consider the case where a Boolean rule specifies an exact match on student first name, such as required in Rule 2 of the example. The first name comparison will give a True result if the two first names are "John" or if they are "Xavier" as long as they are both the same. However, scoring rules operate by assigning weight to the agreement and defer in the final decision on matching until all of the weights have been added together. This means that if analysis shows that the first name "John" is shared by many different students but the first name "Xavier" is only shared by a few students, then agreement on "Xavier" can be given a higher weight than agreement on "John" because agreement on "Xavier" has a higher probability of predicting that the enrollment records are equivalent. The following XML segment shows how this might look in a script defining a scoring rule for an MDM system.

```
<ScoringRule Ident="Example" MatchScore="800" ReviewScore="750">
   <Term Item="StudentFirst" Similarity="Exact"
         DataPrep="Scan(LR, Letter, 0, ToUpper, SameOrder)"
         AgreeWgt="300" WgtTable="Ex1SFirst" DisagreeWgt="-20" />
   <Term Item="StudentLast" Similarity="Exact" ...
```

In this script a scoring rule named "Example" is defined. The total score needed to declare a match is 800, and all comparisons that score between 800 and 750 should be reviewed, i.e. all such scores will produce a review indicator. The script also shows that the first term of the scoring rule compares the attribute "Student-First," which has the student's first name. The comparator for the first name is required to be an EXACT match. However, before the first name values are compared, the first name string goes through a data preparation using an algorithm called SCAN that extracts only letter characters and changes the letters to all upper case.

In addition to an agreement weight of 300 and a disagreement weight of -20, the definition also points to a Weight Table named "Ex1SFirst". This means that in the operation of this rule, if two first names agree (after data preparation), the Weight Table is searched. If the name value is found, then the agreement weight given in the table is added to the overall score; otherwise the default agreement weight of 300 is added. If the first names do not agree, then the disagreement weight of -20 is added to the score.

CALCULATING THE WEIGHTS

The algorithm used to calculate the agreement weights and disagreement weights is the Fellegi-Sunter probabilistic model for estimated weights under the assumption of conditional independence of the identity attributes (Herzog, Scheuren, & Winkler, 2007). To illustrate how this algorithm works, let a_i represent the i-th attribute of a set of identity attributes, and let R be a set of references. Then define

$E =$ number of equivalent pairs of references in R
$\sim E =$ number of nonequivalent pairs of references in R
$E_i =$ number of equivalent pairs of references in R that agree on the value a_i
$\sim Ei =$ number of nonequivalent pairs of references in R that agree on a_i

Using these counts m_i, the probability that equivalent pairs will agree on a_i is calculated by

$$m_i = E_i / E$$

Similarly, u_i, the probability that non-equivalent pairs will agree on a_i is calculate by

$$u_i = \sim E_i / \sim E$$

The agreement weight for a_i is calculated by

$$Agree_i = log_2\left(\frac{m_i}{u_i}\right)$$

And the disagreement weight for a_i is calculated by

$$Disagree_i = log_2\left(\frac{(1 - m_i)}{(1 - u_i)}\right)$$

If v represents a particular value of a_i, then it is only necessary to restrict the counts to references in R. As in the example of student enrollment records let $v = $ "John", then E_i would now represent the number of all equivalent pairs of records in R that agree on "John" and $\sim E_i$ would represent the number of all nonequivalent pairs of records in R that agree on "John." Otherwise, the calculations are calculated in the same way.

There are two principal disadvantages to the scoring rule. The first is that it is hard to calculate the weights and to determine the optimal match threshold score. The calculation of the weights is an iterative process (Wang, Pullen, Talburt, & Wu, 2014b), and the determination of the match threshold can require considerable trial-and-error and assessment of results. The use of the scoring rule definitely requires good ER knowledge and skills along with good tools to objectively measure ER results.

A second potential problem with scoring rules is that they are more sensitive to the missing values than Boolean rules. When using a scoring rule, if one or both of the values of the attribute being compared are missing (null), then it is not clear what weight value should be used. Many implementations simply use a default weight of zero for missing value comparisons. Despite the advantage of granularity in matching, a scoring rule may not perform as well as a Boolean rule on data where there is a large percentage of missing identity values.

CLUSTER-TO-CLUSTER CLASSIFICATION

The answers to Questions 2 (how to systematically match references), 3 (how to match clusters), and 4 (how to reorganize clusters) in the opening section are interrelated. Interestingly, most of the design decisions hinge on the answers to Question 3: what rules will match a reference to a cluster of reference? And what are the rules for comparing clusters of references?

The problem is that the base matching rule is designed to only classify pairs of references, rather than a set of references. As discussed earlier, the two most common approaches to pair matching are Boolean rules or scoring rules. In the case of a Boolean rule, the classification categories are simply matching pair (true) or nonmatching pair (false). In the case of the scoring rule, the classification can be matching pair (score is above the match threshold), possible matching pair that needs review (score is below the match threshold, but above the review threshold), or nonmatching pair (score is below the review threshold).

Before considering the general problem of comparing two clusters, first consider the problem of comparing a single input reference to a cluster of references that are already linked together and are presumed to represent a single entity. The assumption is that this comparison should utilize the base rule that performs pair matching. In order to do this, two important questions need to be answered:

1. How to select a set of attribute values from the cluster to match against the attributes of the new input reference so that the base rule can be invoked?

2. Of the possible attribute value selections, how many of these selections must match in order for the overall reference-to-cluster comparison to be considered a match?

The first factor describes what is called a cluster (or a structure) projection. Figure 8.1 shows an example of an input reference R3 and a cluster of previously linked references R1 and R2. In this example, the pair-wise matching rule states that two references are classified as a match if they agree on first name and last name, or if they agree on employer identifier ("ID").

The two most common types of projections are record-based projection and attribute-based projection (Zhou & Talburt, 2011c). In record-based projection, the incoming reference simply participates in pair-wise matching with each reference in Cluster C1. In other words, the answer to the question about how to select attribute values to use in the base rule is that the attribute values selected must come from the same reference in the cluster.

In the example of Figure 8.1, there are two previously processed references R1 and R2 that form Cluster C1 because they satisfied the base match rule by agreeing on the ID value. In the scenario shown, an input reference R3 comes into the system to be compared to Cluster C1. In a record-based projection model, there are two possible selections. The attribute values of R3 can be compared to the attribute values of R1 and R2. However, it is easy to see that neither of these would be classified as a matching pair. When R3 is compared to R1, the first names agree, but the last names and ID values disagree. When R3 is compared to R2, the last

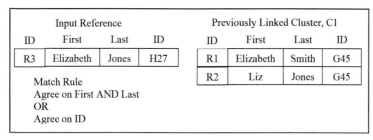

Input Reference					Previously Linked Cluster, C1			
ID	First	Last	ID		ID	First	Last	ID
R3	Elizabeth	Jones	H27		R1	Elizabeth	Smith	G45
					R2	Liz	Jones	G45

Match Rule
Agree on First AND Last
OR
Agree on ID

FIGURE 8.1

Reference-to-cluster match scenario.

names agree, but the first names and ID values disagree. In record-based projection, the projections of the cluster correspond to the individual references in the cluster. In other words, a cluster comprising 10 references would produce 10 projections.

In this example, part of the answer to how many matches must succeed seems obvious. If the input reference does not match any of the references in the cluster, then the overall reference-to-cluster comparison should be classified as a no-match. On the other hand, if the input reference matches one or more of the references in the cluster, how many is enough to say that the reference should be part of the cluster? In general, the answer is that one is enough, i.e. if the input reference matches at least one of the projections from the cluster then the overall reference-to-cluster comparison is considered a match. The reason for this is the "principle of transitive closure" that will be discussed later. However, requiring only a single match is not universally true in all systems. In some cases, the requirement may be set higher — for example, that the input reference must match every projection from the cluster.

In an attribute-based projection, the attribute values used to compare to the input reference are not required to come from the same reference in the cluster. If an attribute-based projection is used in the example of Figure 8.1, the input reference R3 could be compared to four possible projections of the First, Last, and ID values in Cluster C1. These are shown in Table 8.1.

Note that projections P1 and P4 correspond to references R1 and R2, respectively. However, projections P2 and P3 do not correspond to actual references but are combinations of attributes taken from R1 and R2. In this case, the input reference R3 would match projection P3 according to the first condition of the base match rule, i.e. First and Last values agree.

The fact that R3 matches one of the attribute-projections of the cluster again brings up the question of how many projections should match in order to say that the reference matches the entire cluster. And again the answer is that in most systems matching one cluster projection is sufficient for the overall reference-to-cluster comparison to be considered a match.

The same logic for record-based and attribute-based projection can be extended to the more general case of cluster-to-cluster classification. Reference-to-cluster classification is just a special case of cluster-to-cluster classification, where one cluster comprises a single reference. In the general case, each projection from the

Table 8.1 Attribute-based Projections of C1

	First	Last	ID
P1	Elizabeth	Smith	G45
P2	Liz	Smith	G45
P3	Elizabeth	Jones	G45
P4	Liz	Jones	G45

first cluster is compared to each possible projection of the second cluster until, or if, enough pair-wise projections are classified as a match in order for the cluster-to-cluster classification to be considered a match.

The number of attribute-based projections can grow dramatically. Just as a simple example, suppose that references have three identity attributes A1, A2, and A3. Also, suppose that cluster C1 contains three references and cluster C2 contains four references. A record-based cluster-to-cluster comparison would require at most 12 (3 times 4) reference-to-reference comparisons. On the other hand, in the worst-case scenario where all of the attribute values are unique within the cluster, then the number of distinct attribute-based projections from cluster C1 would be 27 (3^3) and from cluster C2 there would be 64 (4^3). Together these would yield 1,728 possible projection-to-projection comparisons. However, the actual number will typically be much smaller since the expectation is that references in the same cluster will share many of the same attribute values, and will not all be unique. In the example of Figure 8.1, Table 8.1 shows that even though a cluster of two references with three attributes could produce eight (2^3) attribute-based projections, there are actually only four projections of C1 because the attribute ID has only one value "G45".

THE UNIQUE REFERENCE ASSUMPTION AND TRANSITIVE CLOSURE

The next question is this: once the conditions are defined for classifying a cluster-to-cluster comparison as a match, what should happen to the clusters? Most often, the two clusters are merged into a single cluster, and all references in the merged cluster are given the same link value. Such an approach is in alignment with the Unique Reference Assumption that states "every reference is created to refer to one and only one real-world entity."

Given this assumption, suppose that the system has determined that reference R1 is equivalent to R2, i.e. R1 and R2 refer to the same real-world entity E1. Suppose now a third reference R3 is determined equivalent to R2, i.e. R2 and R3 refer to the same real-world entity E2. Because R2 references both E1 and E2, it follows by the Unique Reference Assumption that E1 and E2 are the same entity, therefore R1, R2, and R3 are all equivalent because they all reference the same entity.

If a relationship has the property that "A relates to B" and "B relates to C" implies that "A relates to C," then it is called a *transitive* relationship. The unique reference assumption provides the argument that reference equivalence is a transitive relationship among references. In other words, R1 is equivalent to R2, and R2 is equivalent to R3, implies that R1 is equivalent to R3. From an ER perspective that means that all three references R1, R2, and R3 should be linked together. Transitivity of reference equivalence also explains why in reference-to-cluster classification, even if an input reference matches only one reference (or attribute-projection) in a cluster, it is equivalent to all of them. The reference can be classified as a match for the entire cluster and can be merged into the cluster.

It often happens that an input reference can match two or more clusters. Even in this case, the same rule of transitive closure of reference equivalence is usually followed, and all of the clusters that match the input reference are merged together along with the input reference itself into a single cluster. A reference that matches and causes the merger of two or more references is sometimes called a *glue record*.

It is important to note that even though reference equivalence is transitive, matching itself is not transitive. If reference R1 matches reference R2, and R2 matches reference R3, it does not follow that R1 will match R3. For example, consider a simple match rule that says two strings match if they differ by at most one character. Then for this match rule it would be true that "ABC" matches "ADC", and that "ADC" matches "ADE", but it is not true that "ABC" matches "ADE".

SELECTING AN APPROPRIATE ALGORITHM

Once the cluster-to-cluster classification method has been decided, the next question is which ER algorithm should be used to systematically compare each input reference to previously processed references. The most desirable algorithm should have three characteristics:

1. It should find all possible matches. It should select and compare references in a way that whenever two reference match they will be compared, i.e. for a given base rule for pair matching and a cluster-to-cluster classification method, if a reference-to-reference match, or a reference-to-cluster match, or a cluster-to-cluster match is possible given the references in the input source, then the algorithm will systematically select the references and clusters in such a way that these comparisons will be made.
2. It should be efficient. At the same time it does not lose matches, it should try minimizing the number of attempted comparisons among references and clusters to find those matches, i.e. it should avoid spending time on comparisons that will not result in a match. For example, one way to find all possible matches is to use the "brute force" method that exhaustively compares every cluster to every other cluster. However, brute force is not efficient.
3. It should be sequence neutral, i.e. the clusters created at the final step should be the same regardless of the order that the input references are processed by the algorithm. This property is really a corollary of the first characteristic provided the algorithm obeys transitive closure.

The degree to which possible matches are found (Characteristic 1) is called the *recall* of the algorithm. If R is a set of N references, and P is the set of all distinct, unordered pairs of references from R, then the number of pairs in P is given by

$$|P| = \frac{N \cdot (N - 1)}{2}$$

For a given match rule, let M represent the pairs of references in P that would actually match by the rule. In general the size of M will be much smaller than P. Given an algorithm A for selecting pairs in P for matching, let pairs found by A that actually match be represented by F. Then the match recall of A is given by

$$Recall(A) = \frac{|F|}{|M|}$$

It is easy to guarantee that Recall(A) is 100% by having the algorithm compare every pair of references in P. However, according to the first formula the number of pairs in P grows with the square of N, the number of references in R. Even for fast processing systems using an ER algorithm that makes every possible comparison between references, time performance will be unacceptable. In addition, ER does not easily lend itself to parallel and distributed processing.

For practical purposes the ER algorithm A must select only some subset of P as candidates for matching. Let C represent the set of pairs in P that are selected by the algorithm A. Then the efficiency of the algorithm (Characteristic 2) called its match *precision* is given by

$$Precision(A) = \frac{|C \cap M|}{|C|}$$

The match precision of A measures the ratio of matching pairs found by A to the total number of pairs compared by A.

As noted earlier, the recall of an algorithm (Characteristic 1) and its ability to be sequence neutral (Characteristic 3) are related to each other. If the algorithm is sensitive to the order in which the references are processed, it may miss some matches that it might have found if the references were processed in a different order. In addition, there is a dependency upon the choice of cluster projection used for cluster-to-cluster matching. An algorithm that has all three characteristics when record-based projection is used may fail in some characteristics if attribute-based projection is used.

To help illustrate these concepts, a series of examples will be shown. For each example, the input and base rule for matching pairs of references will be the same. Table 8.2 shows the input references used in the examples.

Table 8.2 List of Input References

RefID	First	Last	SID
R1	John	Smith	H7
R2	Marie	Jones	K9
R3	John	Smyth	F1
R4	Mary	Dell	H2
R5	Jon	Smith	F1
R6	Marie	Jones	H2

Similar to the previous example concerning cluster projections, each reference has four attributes: a record identifier (RefID), a first name value (First), a last name value (Last), and a school identifier (SID).

In addition, all of the examples will use the same base rule for pair matching:

Base (Boolean) Rule for matching pairs of references

(First values agree) AND (Last values agree)

OR

(SID values agree)

THE ONE-PASS ALGORITHM

The One-Pass Algorithm is a simple algorithm that is more efficient than brute force yet still able to find all possible matches for certain cluster-to-cluster classification schemes. Its name comes from the fact that each input reference is only processed one time, i.e. one pass through the input references.

The algorithm starts with a list of input references and an empty output list of clusters. Each input reference is processed in order by comparing it to all of the clusters in the output list. If it matches one or more clusters in the output list, then all of the clusters that it matches are merged together, including the input reference itself, to form a new cluster. In the case where the input reference does not match any one of the clusters in the output list, it forms a new single-reference cluster appended to the end of the cluster list. This continues until all of the input references have been processed.

EXAMPLE 8.1 ONE-PASS ALGORITHM USING RECORD-BASED PROJECTION

Configuration Choices for Example 8.1:
1. Base rule for matching reference pairs: Boolean rule (First Agree) AND (Last Agree) OR (SID Agree)
2. Cluster projection: Record-Based
3. Cluster-to-Cluster Match Rule: Single Match
4. Transitive Closure: Yes
5. ER Algorithm: One-Pass

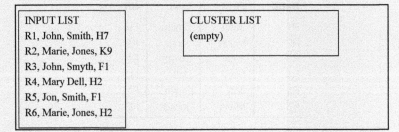

FIGURE 8.2

Starting conditions for Example 8.1.

The starting conditions for the example input are shown in Figure 8.2. When the first input reference R1 is processed, there are no clusters to compare it with, and therefore it is simply made into the single-reference cluster C1 as the first item in the Cluster List, as shown in Figure 8.3.

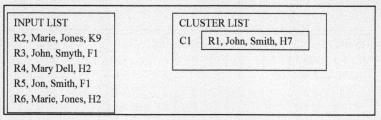

FIGURE 8.3

After processing the first input reference R1.

In the next step, Reference R2 is processed. In this case, there is only one reference-to-cluster comparison of R2-to-C1. The cluster projection for this example is record-based projection. This means that C1 only projects one set of values to be compared to R2, namely the values that comprise R1. Because the R1 values do not march the R2 values according to the base rule, R2 creates a new cluster C2 as shown in Figure 8.4.

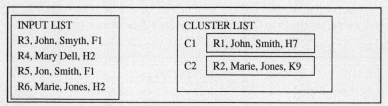

FIGURE 8.4

After processing the second input reference R2.

In the third step, Reference R3 is processed. Now there are two reference-to-cluster comparisons of R3-to-C1 and R3-to-C2. Again, C1 only projects the R1 values and these do not match R3 by the base rule. C2 only projects the R2 values and these do not match R3 either. Therefore, R3 creates a new cluster C3, as shown in Figure 8.5.

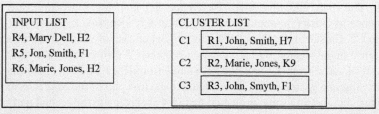

FIGURE 8.5

After processing the third input reference R3.

In the fourth step, Reference R4 is processed and there are three reference-to-cluster comparisons of R4-to-C1, R4-to-C2, and R4-to-C3. Each cluster only projects one set of values from the single reference in the cluster. The values of R4 do not match any of these projections, and therefore, it creates a new cluster C4 as shown in Figure 8.6.

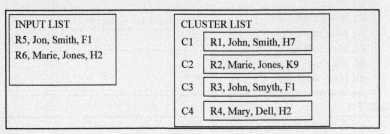

FIGURE 8.6

After processing the fourth input reference R4.

In the fifth step, Reference R5 is processed and there are now four reference-to-cluster comparisons of R5-to-C1, R5-to-C2, R5-to-C3, and R5-to-C4. Again, each cluster only projects one set of values from the single reference in each cluster. However, in this step the SID value in R5 matches the SID value projected from C3 according to the second part of the base rule. Consequently, R5 is merged with Cluster C3 to form a new Cluster C5 as shown in Figure 8.7.

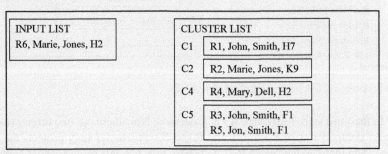

FIGURE 8.7

After processing the fifth input reference R5.

In the sixth and final step, Reference R6 is processed. There are four reference-to-cluster comparisons of R6-to-C1, R6-to-C2, R6-to-C4, and R6-to-C5. Clusters C1, C2, and C4 only project one set of values from the single reference in the cluster. By record-based project, C5 projects two sets of values, one set of value from R3 and one set values from R5. At this step, R6 matches name values projected from C2 according to the first part of the base rule, and R6 also matches the SID value projected from C4 according to the second part of the base rule. In this case, R6 acts as a glue record causing R6, C2, and C4 to merge into a single cluster C6 as shown in Figure 8.8.

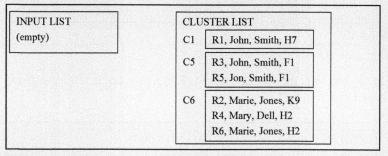

FIGURE 8.8

After processing the sixth input reference R6.

The final result is that the six input references are linked together into three clusters, cluster C1 comprising reference R1, cluster C5 comprising references R3 and R5, and cluster C6 comprising references R2, R4, and R6. However, this result is dependent upon all of the configuration choices stated at the beginning. Change any of these parameters and the clustering results for the same input dataset may be different, as will be shown in later examples.

EXAMPLE 8.2 ONE-PASS ALGORITHM USING RECORD-BASED PROJECTION (INPUT REORDERED)

The configuration choices for Example 8.2 are the same as for Example 8.1, the only difference being that the input has been reordered so that reference R1 now appears at the end of the input list instead of at the beginning as shown in Figure 8.9.

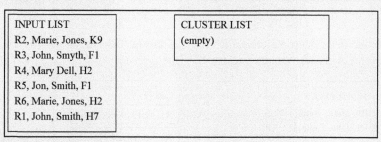

FIGURE 8.9

Starting conditions for Example 8.2.

The first input reference R2 forms the single-reference cluster C1 as shown in Figure 8.10.

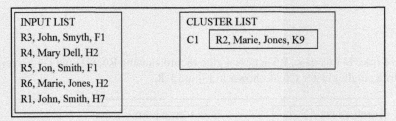

FIGURE 8.10

After processing the first input reference R2.

In the next step, the second reference R3 forms a single-reference cluster C2 as shown in Figure 8.11.

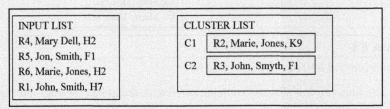

FIGURE 8.11

After processing the second input reference R3.

In the third step, Reference R4 is processed and forms the single-reference cluster C3 as shown in Figure 8.12.

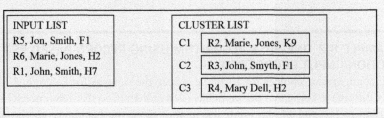

FIGURE 8.12

After processing the third input reference R4.

In the fourth step, Reference R5 matches cluster C2 and merges to form cluster C4 as shown in Figure 8.13.

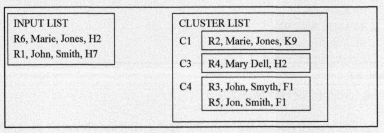

FIGURE 8.13

After processing the fourth input reference R5.

In the fifth step, Reference R6 matches both C1 and C3 to form the new cluster C5 as shown in Figure 8.14.

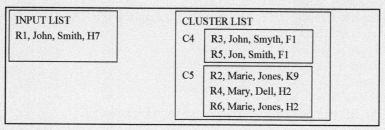

FIGURE 8.14

After processing the fifth input reference R5.

In the sixth and final step, Reference R1 is processed and does not match any of the projections from clusters C4 and C5, and forms the new single-reference cluster C6 as shown in Figure 8.15.

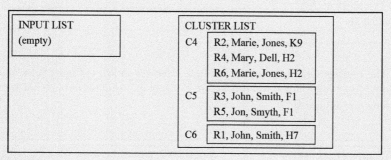

FIGURE 8.15

After processing the sixth input reference R1.

The final result is that the six input references are linked together into three clusters, cluster C4 comprising references R2, R4, and R6, cluster C5 comprising references R3 and R5, and cluster C6 comprising reference R1. The important point here is that even though the cluster labels are different, the clustering is the same as in Example 8.1 as shown in Figure 8.8, i.e. the order of processing did not affect the ER results, the same references were clustered together. Although this does not constitute a proof, it is true that One-Pass is sequence neutral when record-based projection is used for cluster-to-cluster matching. The next two examples show that One-Pass is not always sequence neutral when attribute-based projection is used.

EXAMPLE 8.3 ONE-PASS ALGORITHM USING ATTRIBUTE-BASED PROJECTION

Configuration choices for Example 8.3:

1. Base rule for matching reference pairs: Boolean rule (First Agree) AND (Last Agree) OR (SID Agree)
2. Cluster projection: Attribute-based
3. Cluster-to-Cluster Match Rule: Single Match
4. Transitive Closure: Yes
5. ER Algorithm: One-Pass

The first part proceeds much the same as in Example 8.1.

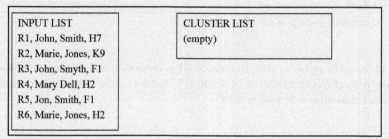

FIGURE 8.16

Starting conditions for Example 8.3

The starting conditions for the example input are shown in Figure 8.16. When the first input reference R1 is processed, it forms the single-reference cluster C1 as shown in Figure 8.17.

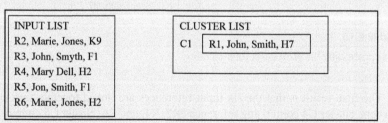

FIGURE 8.17

After processing the first input reference R1.

In the next step, reference R2 creates a new cluster C2 as shown in Figure 8.18.

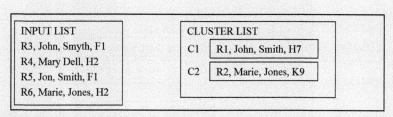

FIGURE 8.18

After processing the second input reference R2.

In the third step, reference R3 creates a new cluster C3 as shown in Figure 8.19.

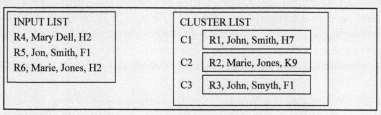

FIGURE 8.19

After processing the third input reference R3.

In the fourth step, Reference R4 creates a new cluster C4 as shown in Figure 8.20.

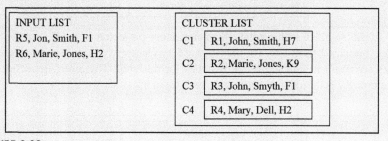

FIGURE 8.20

After processing the fourth input reference R4.

In the fifth step, Reference R5 matches C3 and a new Cluster C5 is formed by the merger as shown in Figure 8.21.

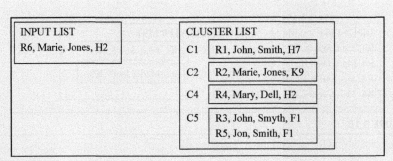

FIGURE 8.21

After processing the fifth input reference R5.

In the sixth and final step, Reference R6 is processed. Just as before, there are four reference-to-cluster comparisons of R6-to-C1, R6-to-C2, R6-to-C4, and R6-to-C5. Even though this example uses attribute-based projection, Clusters C1, C2, and C4 only project one set of values from the single reference in the cluster. However, in the R6-to-C5 comparison, C5 produces three projections that are shown in Table 8.3.

Table 8.3 Attribute-based Projections of C5

	First	Last	ID
P1	John	Smyth	F1
P2	Jon	Smyth	F1
P3	John	Smith	F1
P4	Jon	Smith	F1

At this step, R6 still matches the name values projected from C2, and the SID value projected from C4. The fact that C5 produces two additional projections does not result in any additional matches for this step. Therefore, the result for Example 8.3 is the same as for Examples 8.1 and 8.2 as shown here in Figure 8.22.

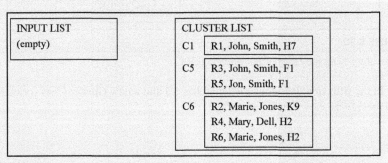

FIGURE 8.22

After processing the sixth input reference R6.

EXAMPLE 8.4 ONE-PASS ALGORITHM USING ATTRIBUTE-BASED PROJECTION (INPUT REORDERED)

The configuration choices for Example 8.4 are the same as for Example 8.3; the only difference is the input has been reordered so reference R1 now appears at the end of the input list instead of at the beginning as shown in Figure 8.23. The purpose of this example is to show the One-Pass algorithm is not sequence neutral when used in conjunction with attribute-based projection.

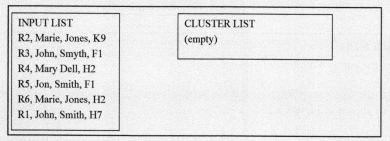

FIGURE 8.23

Starting conditions for Example 8.4.

The first input reference R2 forms the single-reference cluster C1 as shown in Figure 8.24.

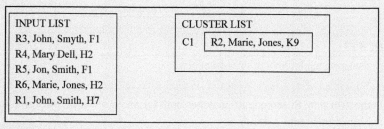

FIGURE 8.24

After processing the first input reference R2.

In the next step, the second reference R3 forms a single-reference cluster C2 as shown in Figure 8.25.

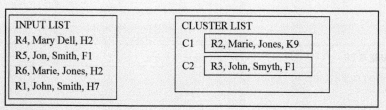

FIGURE 8.25

After processing the second input reference R3.

In the third step, Reference R4 is processed and forms the single-reference cluster C3 as shown in Figure 8.26.

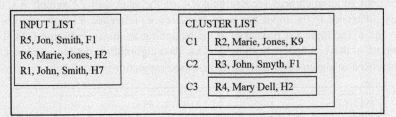

FIGURE 8.26

After processing the third input reference R4.

In the fourth step, Reference R5 matches cluster C2 and merges to form cluster C4 as shown in Figure 8.27.

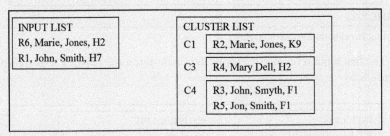

FIGURE 8.27

After processing the fourth input reference R5.

In the fifth step, Reference R6 matches both C1 and C3 to form the new cluster C5 as shown in Figure 8.28.

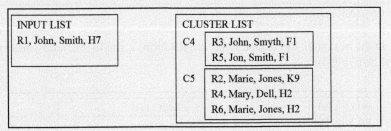

FIGURE 8.28

After processing the fifth input reference R5.

In the sixth and final step, something different happens. Cluster C4 now produces four projections, the same projections that were produced from Cluster C5 in the previous example and shown in Table 8.3. In particular, R1 matches projection P3. Therefore, R1 is merged into C4 to produce a new cluster C6 as shown in Figure 8.29.

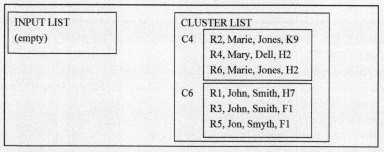

FIGURE 8.29

After processing the sixth input reference R1.

The final result is that two clusters of three references are fundamentally different than the results in Examples 8.1, 8.2 and 8.3. In particular, this example shows that the One-Pass algorithm is not always sequence neutral when attribute-based projection is used. When the configuration choice is attribute-based projection, then an ER algorithm stronger than the One-Pass algorithm is required.

The R-Swoosh Algorithm

The R-Swoosh ER algorithm was developed at the Stanford InfoLab oun, Garcia-Molina, Su, & Widom, 2005). The R-Swoosh algorithm is part of a larger body of ER research called the Stanford Entity Resolution Framework (SERF). As described in Chapter 7, the SERF model describes entity resolution in terms of abstract match and merge functions, and shows the conditions that must hold for these functions so the ER process will always arrive at a finite, unique, and sequence-neutral outcome. An important component of SERF is the Swoosh family of ER algorithms, of which R-Swoosh is the most basic.

The R-Swoosh algorithm is similar to the One-Pass in that it starts with a list of input references and an empty output list of clusters. The primary difference is that clusters from the output list are sometimes pushed back into the input list for reprocessing. Here is how that happens. When an item on the input list is selected for processing, it is compared in order to each cluster in the output list. If a comparison results in a match, the input item is removed from the input list and merged with the matching cluster. The new merged cluster is removed from the output list and appended to the end of the input list. The algorithm continues by processing the next item in the input list until the input list is empty. In the case where an input item does not match any of the clusters in the output list, it forms a new single-reference cluster that is appended to the end of the cluster list the same as in the One-Pass algorithm. The algorithm continues until all of the input items have been processed.

EXAMPLE 8.5 R-SWOOSH ALGORITHM USING ATTRIBUTE-BASED PROJECTION

Configuration choices for Example 8.5:
1. Base rule for matching reference pairs: Boolean rule (First Agree) AND (Last Agree) OR (SID Agree)
2. Cluster projection: Attribute-Based
3. Cluster-to-Cluster Match Rule: Single Match
4. Transitive Closure: Yes
5. ER Algorithm: R-Swoosh

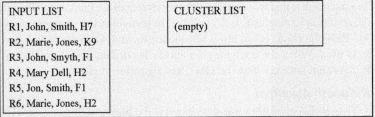

FIGURE 8.30

Starting conditions for Example 8.5.

Because there are no matches among the first four references, these all create single-reference clusters as shown in Figure 8.31.

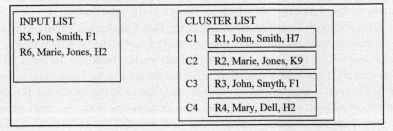

FIGURE 8.31

After processing input references R1, R2, R3, and R4.

Up to this point, R-Swoosh behaves the same as One-Pass. However, in the fifth step there is a difference. In the R5-to-C1 and R5-to-C2 comparisons there is no match, but R5-to-C3 is a match on SID. In the R-Swoosh algorithm R5 is merged into C3 to form a new cluster C5. R5 and C3 are removed from the input list and output list, respectively, and the new cluster C5 is appended to the end of the input list for reprocessing as shown in Figure 8.32.

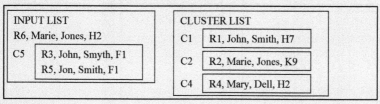

FIGURE 8.32

After processing the fifth input reference R5.

Unlike the previous examples, the sixth step is no longer the final step because there are now two items still in the input list. When reference R6 is processed, the first match it finds is to C2. This stops the comparisons, and R6 is merged with Cluster C2. The new merged cluster C6 is appended to the input list as shown in Figure 8.33.

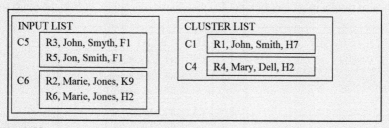

FIGURE 8.33

After processing the sixth input reference R6.

In the seventh step, cluster C5 is compared to C1. By attribute projection, cluster C5 will produce four projections, the same as those shown in Table 8.3, and in fact, project P3 of Table 8.3 is a match to the single projection of C1. Consequently, clusters C5 and C1 are merged into a new cluster C7 that is appended to the input list as shown in Figure 8.34.

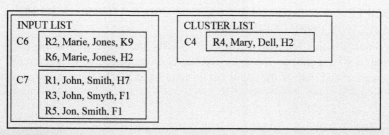

FIGURE 8.34

After processing the seventh input item C5.

In the eighth step, cluster C6 is compared to C4. Because these two clusters match, they are merged into a new cluster C8 that is an appended input list as shown in Figure 8.35. Although the cluster list is empty, the algorithm does not stop until the input list is empty.

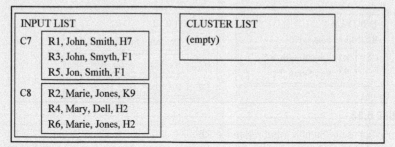

FIGURE 8.35

After processing the eighth input item C6.

In the ninth step, cluster C7 is simply moved to the empty cluster list. In the tenth and last step, cluster C8 is compared to cluster C7. Because these two clusters do not match, cluster C8 is also moved to the end of the cluster list as shown in Figure 8.36. This also results in an empty input list and so the algorithm ends at the tenth step.

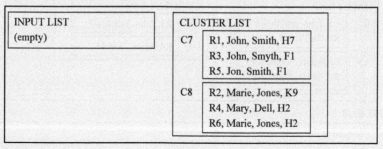

FIGURE 8.36

After processing the ninth and tenth input items C7 and C8.

EXAMPLE 8.6 R-SWOOSH ALGORITHM USING ATTRIBUTE-BASED PROJECTION (INPUT REORDERED)

The configuration for this example is exactly the same as for the previous Example 8.5 except that the input list has been reordered so that reference R1 is placed at the end of the input list instead of at the beginning, as shown in Figure 8.37.

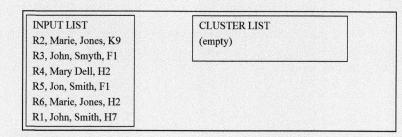

FIGURE 8.37

Starting conditions for Example 8.6.

Because there are no matches among the first three references, these all create single-reference clusters as shown in Figure 8.38.

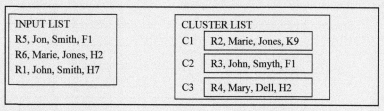

FIGURE 8.38

After processing input items R2, R3, and R4.

In the fourth step, reference R5 matches cluster C2. Following the R-Swoosh algorithm, R5 and C2 are merged to create new cluster C4 that is appended to the input list as shown in Figure 8.39.

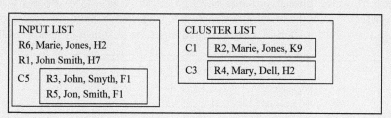

FIGURE 8.39

After processing input item R5.

In the next step, reference R6 is found to match cluster C1. R6 and C1 are merged to form a new cluster C6 that is appended to the input list, as shown in Figure 8.40.

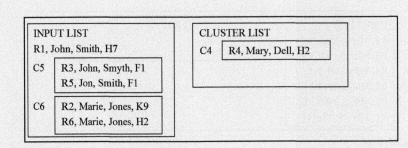

FIGURE 8.40

After processing input item R6.

In the sixth step, reference R1 is compared to cluster C4 and found not to be a match. Reference R1 forms a new cluster C7 that is appended to the cluster list as shown in Figure 8.41.

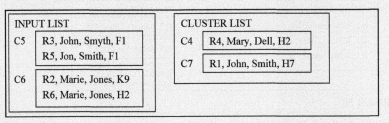

FIGURE 8.41

After processing input item R1.

In the seventh step, cluster C5 is first compared to C4 and found not to be a match. However, through attribute-based projection, cluster C5 is a name match to cluster C7 as in the previous Example 8.5. Clusters C5 and C7 are merged to form a new cluster C8 that is an appended input list as shown in Figure 8.42.

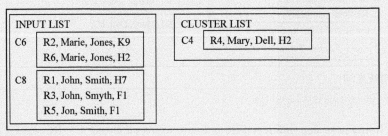

FIGURE 8.42

After processing input item C5.

In the eighth step, cluster C6 matches and merges with C4 to form cluster C9 that is appended to the input list as shown in Figure 8.43.

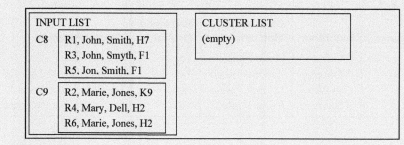

FIGURE 8.43

After processing input item C6.

At this point, the algorithm is essentially complete. In the ninth step, cluster C8 is moved to the cluster list, and in the tenth step, cluster C9 is compared to cluster C8, but does not match. Therefore, cluster C9 is appended to the cluster list and the algorithm ends with an empty input list as shown in Figure 8.44.

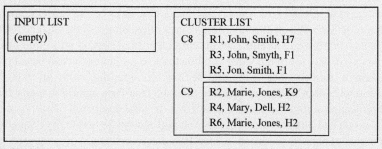

FIGURE 8.44

End of algorithm after processing input items C8 and C9.

Although these examples do not establish a proof, at least Examples 8.5 and 8.6 show that the R-Swoosh algorithm produces the same results for attribute-based projection when presented with the differently ordered lists that caused the One-Pass to give different results when using attribute-based projection as demonstrated in Examples 8.3 and 8.4.

CONCLUDING REMARKS

The previous examples have shown that some combinations of ER design choices will lead to undesirable results. Examples 8.1 and 8.2 show the combination of the One-Pass algorithm with record-based cluster matching produces the same clustering results for two different orderings of the input list. It is not difficult to show

Table 8.4 Summary of ER Design Scenarios for Same Input and Base Rule

Scenario	Algorithm	Cluster Matching	Sequence Neutral	Cluster Results
1	One-Pass	Record-based	Yes	N Clusters
2	R-Swoosh	Attribute-based	Yes	M Clusters where M ≤ N
3	One-Pass	Attribute-based	No	Varies by Order of Input
4	R-Swoosh	Record-based	Yes	N Clusters, but Inefficient

this combination is actually sequence neutral, i.e. will give the same clustering results for any ordering of the input list.

However, Examples 8.3 and 8.4 demonstrate that the combination of the One-Pass algorithm with attribute-based projection cluster matching is not sequence neutral. They show that different orderings can produce different clustering results. Examples 8.5 and 8.6 show that the combination of the R-Swoosh algorithm with attribute-based cluster matching gives the same clustering results for both orderings. Benjelloun et al. (2009) have shown that this will always be the case, i.e. the combination of R-Swoosh and attribute-based cluster matching will be sequence neutral.

It is also worthwhile to note that because an attribute-based projection can produce more pair-wise attribute value combinations to test than a record-based projection, then it follows that using the R-Swoosh algorithm with attribute-based projection will often find more matches than the One-Pass algorithm using record-based projection. From this it also follows that the total number of clusters produced by R-Swoosh and attribute-based projection will always be less than or equal to the total number of clusters produced by One-Pass and record-based projection as shown in Examples 8.1 and 8.5. Acting on the same input list, One-Pass using record-based projection produced three clusters in Example 8.1 while R-Swoosh using attributed-based projection produced two clusters in Example 8.5. The reason is that with transitive closure, more matches yields a higher likelihood of producing a glue record that will merge two clusters. In other words, more matching means fewer clusters.

A summary of these design combinations is shown in Table 8.4. Note that even though Scenario 4 is a valid sequence neutral combination, it would be better to use Scenario 1 instead. Using R-Swoosh with record-based matching is inefficient because the extra comparisons are not necessary to achieve the correct result. One-Pass will give the same clustering result with fewer comparisons.

Blocking

BLOCKING

As necessary as the considerations discussed in Chapter 8 are to the design of a logically sound ER system, they are not sufficient to implement a usable ER system. As a practical matter, neither the One-Pass algorithm nor the R-Swoosh algorithm should be implemented exactly as described. The number of comparisons will be overwhelming. For both of these algorithms the number of comparisons grows as the square of the number of references processed. Twice as many references require four times as many comparisons, and three times as many references require nine times more, and so on. Implementing any of the design scenarios as described in a computer language such as C or Java will produce a system that will never be able to process more than a few thousand references in a reasonable amount of time, even with a fast computer.

To actually implement a practical ER system, one more ingredient is required for the ER recipe and that is *blocking*. For a given set of input references to an ER process, this simply means performing the ER process on specific subsets of the input instead of on the entire set of references. These subsets are called blocks, hence the name *blocking*. For example, if the input has 1,000 references, if an ER process is performed on the entire 1,000 references, processing will require on the order of $1,000^2$ or 1,000,000 comparisons to complete. However, if the references are partitioned into 10 disjoint blocks of 100 references, then the effort to perform the ER algorithm on each block will require on the order of 100^2 or 10,000 comparisons. Thus, the overall effort for all 10 blocks will be on the order of 10×100^2 or 100,000 comparisons, an order of magnitude less than performing the algorithm on the entire 1,000 references.

Of course, there is an obvious problem. Suppose that references R1 and R2 in the input match by the ER base rule. If the blocking process assigns R1 to block B1, and assigns R2 to a different block B2, then R1 and R2 will not be compared and the ER process will not find this match. The ER process will only make comparisons among the references within block B1 and within B2, but not between B1 and B2. Consequently, unless the blocking is done in such a way that the records that match are in the same block, the ER process will not be accurate.

This presents another ER conundrum. Putting the references into the proper block requires knowing ahead of time whether they will match or not. But finding equivalent references by matching is the whole purpose of the ER process. So if it were already known which references match, then there would be no need for the ER process in the first place.

In reality, the best that can be done is to assign references to the same block based on the likelihood that they will match. Because it is only a probability, some matching references may still end up in separate blocks, causing those matches to be lost and the overall accuracy of the process to be reduced. Like so many things in ER, blocking is a trade-off. In the case of blocking, the trade-off is between accuracy and performance.

TWO CAUSES OF ACCURACY LOSS

As discussed earlier, ER is about finding equivalent references, not just matching. The first loss in ER accuracy is introduced simply because matching is the primary tool for resolving equivalence. The fact that two references have similar values for identity attributes only increases the likelihood they are equivalent; it does not guarantee it. As discussed in Chapter 3, the loss of ER accuracy due to matching is measured in terms of false positive (FP) and false negative (FN) errors. From the perspective of matching, the accuracy of the ER process can be measured as

$$Linking\ (Matching)\ Accuracy = \frac{|TP| + |TN|}{|TP| + |TN| + |FP| + |FN|}$$

The introduction of blocking can further decrease the accuracy of ER. Blocking will never create new matches, so it cannot cause an increase in false positive links. However, it can increase the number of false negatives. Assume the majority of matches found by an ER process result in true positive links rather than false positive links and then the effect of blocking is to increase the number of false negatives. This happens when references that would have matched and created true positive links are placed into separate blocks where they remain unlinked. Although as a general rule blocking reduces accuracy by increasing false negatives, it is not absolute. There is always a small probability blocking could prevent a false positive match and increase the number of true negatives, thereby increasing accuracy.

Blocking is said to be in alignment with the ER process when it is true that every match that could have been found without blocking will still be found with blocking in place, i.e. the blocking does not prevent any matches. However, the fact that blocking is in 100% alignment with the ER process does not mean that the ER process is 100% accurate. The accuracy of the ER process is dependent on the false positive and false negative rates of the matching in the ER process itself. The point is accurate ER results depend upon both accurate matching and accurately aligned blocking.

Measuring the reduction of comparisons from blocking is easier than measuring the loss of accuracy from blocking. An empirical method to test the potential loss of accuracy from blocking is to first select some subset of the references small enough that the ER process can run without blocking. By analyzing the cluster results of running these references with blocking and without blocking it is possible to estimate the loss of matching that blocking has introduced. If no matches are lost by the blocking, then the cluster results should be identical.

It should also be noted that if some matches are lost by blocking, then the ER results with blocking will always have more clusters than the results without blocking. This is because all ER processes (except for certain types of assertion configurations) that link references together by matching rules and transitive closure will never split clusters apart, they will only bring clusters together. Therefore, with more matches found, the number of clusters decreases as the sizes of the clusters increase. In the extreme, if all references were to match, then the output would only be one cluster comprising all input references. At the other extreme, if no references were to match, then every reference will form its own cluster, i.e. N references will form N clusters, each containing a single reference.

BLOCKING AS PREMATCHING

The central issue of blocking is how to organize the references into subsets that contain the references most likely to match. The fact that matching is the primary tool for determining equivalence drives the blocking decisions. In essence, blocking is prematching. Blocking typically focuses on the similarity between references by one or two of their identity attributes to form the block, and then leaves the ER algorithm and the base matching rule to do the fine-grained resolution into clusters.

For example, if the base rule matches two customer references based on having similar names and addresses, then the strategy might be to organize the references into blocks according to the same postal code (e.g. zip code in the U.S.). The idea is that if two complete addresses match, they will have the same postal code. This example can be used to highlight some of the factors that influence the accuracy of blocking.

The first and most obvious factor is that the blocking value needs to be highly correlated to the matching logic. Using the postal code for blocking implies all references are expected to agree on address. If there are other agreement patterns that do not require agreement on address, then blocking by postal code may not be effective in bringing together the references that match by those patterns.

The second factor is the importance of data preparation. If the references being processed in this example had customer addresses that were entered by the customer, then some of the postal codes may be incorrect. Customers may not know their correct postal code or they might be mistyped. An important step would be to standardize the references using the appropriate postal authority so that each address has the correct postal code.

A third factor is the problem of missing values. If a blocking value is missing in a reference, then it is impossible to know to which block the reference should be assigned. In the example of the postal code, it may be possible to overcome the problem of missing values. If the street address and city-state elements of the address are complete, then it might be possible to determine the value of the postal code by using tables supplied by the relevant postal authority. However, in other cases it might be more difficult. For example, if blocking were by year-of-birth, then there may not be a way to impute a missing value based on other information in the reference.

Missing values are a problem for both blocking and matching. Just as a missing value can prevent a reference from being assigned to a block, it can also prevent references from being matched. If a match rule required agreement on the customer's account number and the account number value in a reference is missing, then that reference cannot be matched to another reference based on account number agreement.

Because of the problem of missing values, matching is often based on more than one pattern of agreement. For example, student enrollment records might be matched based on the agreement of the student's first name, student's last name, and date-of-birth. If data analysis shows that some of the dates-of-birth are missing, the rule may be augmented to also allow a match based on the agreement of the student's first name, student's last name, and the house number of the student's address. Allowing a match by either pattern could help compensate for instances where a reference is missing either a date-of-birth or the house number. However, this would not help if both are missing. Yet a third might be required that supports a match on other identity attributes when both date-of-birth and house number are missing.

Another important consideration for blocking is uniformity in block size. The uniform distribution of references to blocks is not an accuracy issue, but a performance issue. The purpose of blocking is to improve performance, but it is important to understand that the principle of blocking does not work based on the average size of the blocks; rather it depends on the absolute size of each block. Recalling the previous example, it does not help to partition 1,000 references into 10 blocks with an "average" size of 100 references if one of the blocks has 900 references. The loss in performance in processing the approximately 900^2 or 810,000 comparison in the large block will negate any gains from faster processing of the 9 smaller blocks. So, in addition to the problem of organizing blocks by likelihood of matching, there is the additional consideration of uniform block size. The latter is sometimes called the "large entity" problem where the nature of the references and the base match rule interact to form very large clusters.

BLOCKING BY MATCH KEY

Many approaches to blocking have been developed. Christen (2012), Isele, Jentzsch and Bizer (2011), and Baxter, Christen, and Churches (2003) describe a number of these, including inverted indexing, sorted neighborhoods, Q-gram indexing, suffix-array indexing, canopy clustering, and mapping-based indexing. However, inverted indexing, sometimes called match key indexing or standard blocking (Christen, 2006), is one of the most common approaches to blocking in ER systems. In addition, match key blocking plays an important role in addressing ER and MDM for Big Data that will be discussed in the next chapter.

The example of blocking records by postal code described earlier is also a simple example of blocking by match key. The value used to partition references into blocks, such as the postal code, is called the match key. Sometimes the match key is simply the value of a single attribute of the reference such as the postal code. In other cases, the value may be modified in some way. The transformations that modify values to form the match key are called hashing algorithms, and the resulting values are sometimes called hash keys instead of match keys. The routines that create match keys are called *match key generators*.

Phonetic encoding algorithms such as Soundex (Holmes & McCabe, 2002), NYSIIS (Borgman & Siegfried, 1992), and Double-Metaphone (Philips, 2000) are commonly used hashing algorithms used to overcome phonetic variation in names. For example, the Soundex has an algorithm that transforms both "SMITH" and "SMYTHE" into the string value (hash value) of "S530." There are many other hash algorithms including those that are simply string manipulation functions such as uppercasing letters, extracting specific character types such as digits, or extracting specific substrings. At the other extreme, some hashing functions perform mathematical operations on the underlying bits of the character string, transforming the string into an integer value. All of these hash functions can be used to create match keys.

In some cases, the match key is created from the values from several attributes. For example, if the base match rule requires agreement on the customer's name as well as the address, then the size of each block can be reduced by constructing a compound match key by concatenating the customer's last name with the postal code. As long as this is the only matching pattern, then using this compound key would improve performance without decreasing accuracy. The reason is the longer match key now requires two conditions to be met and would create smaller blocks. At the same time agreement on name also implies agreement on last name and agreement on address implies agreement on postal code, and therefore, the match key is aligned with the agreement pattern of the rule. Any pair of references that would match by the name and address pattern would be placed in the same block by the last name and postal code match key.

MATCH KEY AND MATCH RULE ALIGNMENT

As noted earlier, blocking is in 100% alignment with the base matching rule if any two references that match by the rule are always in the same block. For match key blocking, 100% alignment can be expressed this way. If it is true that whenever two references match by the rule, they also generate the same match key, then the match-key and rule are in alignment. For match key blocking, misalignment occurs when two references match each other, but do not generate the same match key.

A secondary goal of match key generation is to minimize the number of references that generate the same match key, but that do not match by the rules. So a natural question to ask is: why not make the match key generators the same as the match rules? In some simple scenarios this might be possible, but in most cases they must be different. The reason can be explained by the following example.

For simplicity, suppose that there is a single match rule for student enrollment records with a pattern that requires the last names to be the same (exact match), but allows the first name values to be nicknames for each other, e.g. for English names allowing "JAMES" and "JIM" to be a match. In this case using a match key made by combining the first and last name will not work properly. For example, the two records "JAMES DOE" and "JIM DOE" will match by the rule, but their match keys "JAMESDOE" and "JIMDOE" are not the same. Therefore, they would not be assigned to the same match key block and would never be compared and brought together in the same cluster.

Another match key strategy for this same rule might be to use the LeftSubstring(1) hash generator for the first name. Now the enrollment records "JAMES DOE" and "JIM DOE" match by the rule and also generate the same match key "JDOE". However, this would still not bring the match key generator into 100% alignment with the rule. Take for example the enrollment records "ROBERT CAMP" and "BOB CAMP". Because for English names, Bob is a common nickname for Robert, these two references would match by the rule, but their match keys "RCAMP" and "BCAMP" are not the same. Thus, the rule and the index generator are still not in 100% alignment.

THE PROBLEM OF SIMILARITY FUNCTIONS

The problem with the previous example is caused when the comparator used in a rule is based on a similarity function rather than a hashing algorithm. A similarity function requires two input values in order to give a match result. In the example just given, the similarity function is the Nickname function. It takes the two first name values and looks them up in a table to see if one is a nickname for the other. On the other hand, a hashing algorithm operates on a single value to transform it, such as the SOUNDEX has an algorithm that transforms "Smith" into the value "S530." When a hash function such as SOUNDEX is used as a comparator, it simply checks if two attribute values give the same hash value.

However, the nickname comparator can only operate when it knows both values. It is not a hash function because it is not possible to design an algorithm in such a way that if two names are processed independently by the algorithm, the names will produce the same output (hash) value if and only if they are nicknames of each other. In other words, a hash algorithm does not need information from other attribute values to produce its output.

It turns out many similarity functions are commonly used in ER matching rules. One example is the Levenshtein edit distance function discussed in Chapter 3. Given the string "KLAUS," there are a hundreds, if not thousands, of other strings that are within 1 edit distance just by changing a single character, e.g. first character substitution "ALAUS", "BLAUS", "CLAUS", etc. second character substitutions "KAAUS", "KBAUS", "KCAUS", etc. and so on. Again, there is not a hashing algorithm that can act on every one of these variant strings independently and produce the same output value.

The worst case for match key blocking is when all of the comparators used in an agreement pattern of a rule are similarity functions that do not have corresponding hash algorithms. For example, consider a rule that matches student enrollment records by the pattern where first name is a nickname match and the last name is within one Levenshtein edit distance. In this case, a match key generator based on hashing algorithms cannot be constructed that will guarantee when two references match, their match keys will be the same. The blocking for a rule like this would best be done using a different technique other than match key blocking such as q-gram blocking as described by Christen (2012).

However, if the ER system is constrained to use match keys for blocking, other strategies can be adopted. One is to break the rule into multiple patterns in which each pattern has at least one comparator that corresponds to a hash generator. For example, instead of one agreement pattern of nickname match on the first name and edit distance of one on the last name, use two patterns. The first agreement pattern uses nickname on the first name, but requires an exact match on the last name. Then the second pattern could require exact match on the first name, but allow one edit distance difference on the last name. This would not be a perfect solution; at least it would allow for blocking by match key that would find those matches where the variation was only in the first name or the last name, but not in both.

DYNAMIC BLOCKING VERSUS PRERESOLUTION BLOCKING

The example just given also shows why it is sometimes beneficial to create more than one match key per reference, when the match rule allows for more than one agreement pattern. However, the use of more than one match key leads to an implementation issue. The issue is the point in the process at which references are assigned to blocks. There are two approaches. One approach is to organize the input into blocks prior to starting the ER process (preresolution blocking), and the other approach is to create the blocks as the ER algorithm is executing (dynamic blocking or indexing).

First consider the case where there is only a single match key such as the postal code. In this case, preresolution blocking could be easily done by sorting all references by postal code before the ER process starts. Each block of references with the same postal code could then be read into the system and processed by the match rules and ER algorithm one block at a time. Because each block is independent of every other block, the blocks could be processed in parallel. By doing so, there will not only be a gain in performance by applying the ER algorithm to the smaller blocks of data, there will be an additional gain in performance by processing the blocks concurrently in different processor threads or on different processors.

The other approach is dynamic blocking by using an inverted index. In dynamic blocking, the input references do not have to be sorted or preordered. Instead, as each reference is read into the system, its match key is generated, and the reference is indexed in memory by its match key. In other words, the system keeps track of each reference through an inverted index built using the match key. When a new input reference is read into the system, its match key is generated and then through the inverted index, the match key is used to look up all of the previous processed references that also generated the same match key.

The set of references brought back by the inverted index is sometimes called the candidate list because the references returned by the index are the most likely to match the incoming reference. The candidate list produced by the inverted index comprises the block for that match key, at least as it exists at that point in the process. The blocks grow in size as each new input record is read and indexed by the system.

Now consider the case where there is more than one match key generator. For simplicity, suppose each student enrollment record generates two match keys, one based on first name and another based on last name. In this case, preresolution blocking can't be done by sorting because there are two ways to sort, one by first name and the other by last name. On the other hand, the dynamic blocking by inverted index is largely unaffected. For example, if a reference for "John Doe" is read, then the system uses the inverted index to look up all previously processed references with the first name "John" and all previously processed references with the last name "Doe." The union of these two sets of references then forms the candidate list of references that should be compared to the incoming reference "John Doe."

PRERESOLUTION BLOCKING WITH MULTIPLE MATCH KEYS

When performance considerations require more than one match key, the problem of preresolution blocking becomes much more difficult. In dynamic match key blocking using an inverted index, the candidates for an input reference are assembled on demand as each input reference is processed. Because the inverted index is in memory, it is a simple matter to recall the relevant candidates for a given input.

That is not possible to do in preresolution blocking where all combinations have to be anticipated. For example, consider the same reference with the name "John Doe" in the case where both the first name and second name values act as match keys. In preresolution blocking the system needs to anticipate that the reference "John Doe" may match with other references with the first name "John" and the last name "Doe" just as in dynamic blocking. Therefore, all references with the first name "John" and the last name "Doe" must be brought into the same block.

However, if one of the references in the block with the first name "John" has the last name "Smith", then preresolution blocking must anticipate this reference could match with other references that have the last name of "Smith". Therefore, all references with the last name of "Smith" should also be brought into the block. If a reference with the last name "Smith" is brought into the block that has a first name of "James", then by the same reasoning it is necessary to bring into the block all of the references with the first name of "James" as they may match. This chaining or transitive closure of the match keys can go on and on and potentially create very large blocks of references, exactly the opposite of what is desired.

The essential difference is that dynamic match key blocking by inverted index has the luxury of only dealing with one degree of connection (references with the same first name or same last name as the input reference) as each input reference is processed. On the other hand, preresolution match key blocking must anticipate all degrees of connection in advance by forming the transitive closure of all first and last name connections.

From this example it might appear dynamic blocking is the preferred method because it can easily accommodate multiple match keys. This is true as long as the volume of data to be processed allows the entire inverted index to reside in main memory. As data volumes grow into the big data range, this may no longer be possible or at least practical, from a systems implementation standpoint. Approaches to preresolution match key blocking for big data when multiple match keys are required will be discussed in the next chapter.

BLOCKING PRECISION AND RECALL

Just as match rules can be evaluated in terms of precision and recall, the same measure can be applied to blocking, especially match key blocking. Match keys can be thought of as an information retrieval (IR) strategy. Consider the case of dynamic match key blocking. As a new input reference enters the system, the goal is to retrieve all previously processed references likely to match the input reference. In the match key approach, the match key generated from the input reference is like a query that returns a list of candidates. Basically, two measures can be applied to the retrieved candidate list.

The first question is what proportion of the candidates in the list actually matches the input reference? The answer to this question is the precision measure of the match key query. In other words, if every candidate returned by the inverted index matches the input record, the query has 100% precision.

The second question to ask is whether there are references that match the input reference, but were not in the candidate list. The answer to this question is the recall measure of the match query. Recall is the proportion of all references that actually match the input reference that are actually returned in the candidate list. In other words, if every reference that will match the input reference is returned in the candidate list, then the query has 100% recall.

Yet another way to express match-key-to-rule alignment is to say that the match key index has 100% recall. In other words, if there is any reference that will match the input reference, then it will be in the candidate list produced by the match key query to the inverted index. The precision measure is not important for alignment (accuracy), but it is important for performance. The nonmatching references returned by the index represent overhead in the process as they force the system to make additional, nonproductive comparisons in order to find the actual matching references.

The scenarios in Figure 9.1 illustrate various relationships between precision and recall as Venn diagrams. If R is a set of references, then the background of the

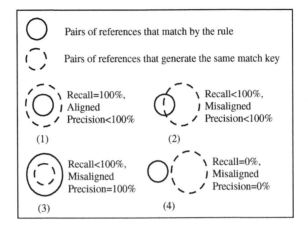

FIGURE 9.1

Schematics for match key recall and precision.

diagram represents all possible unordered pairs of references from R. The area enclosed by the solid circle represents the set of all pairs of references from R that satisfy the matching rule. The area enclosed by the dashed circle represents the set of all pairs of references from R that generate the same match key.

Alignment occurs when the recall measure is 100%, meaning the solid circle is completely enclosed in the dashed circle as shown in Scenario (1). The area between the two circles (inside the dashed and outside the solid) represents pairs that generate the same match key, but do not match by the rule. For this reason, the precision shown in Scenario (1) is less than 100%. In Scenario (2), the match key index recalls some, but not all, of the matching references along with many pairs that do not match. Both precision and recall in Scenario (2) are less than 100%.

In Scenario (3), every pair of references recalled by the match key index are matching references, and therefore, the precision of this scenario is 100%. The area between the circles (inside the solid and outside the dashed) represents matching pairs that are not recalled by the match key index, and therefore, the recall of Scenario (3) is less than 100%.

Scenario (4) shows complete misalignment between the rule and the match key index. None of the pairs that share the same match key match by the rule, and conversely, none of the pairs that match are returned by the index. In Scenario (4) both precision and recall are 0%.

The scenario shown in Figure 9.2 illustrates the strategy of using multiple match key generators. Each match key individually has less than 100% recall, but taken together (their union), they do achieve 100% recall. The areas outside of the solid oval but enclosed by one or more dashed circles represents the loss of precision, i.e. pairs that generate the same match key and are recalled by an index but do not match by the rule.

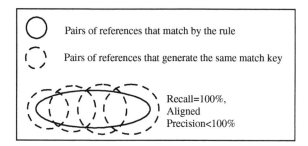

FIGURE 9.2

Schematic for multiple match keys.

MATCH KEY BLOCKING FOR BOOLEAN RULES

The following XML segment shows how dynamic match key blocking might be defined for a Boolean rule in an ER system performing ER on school enrollment records (Zhou, Talburt, & Nelson, 2013).

```
<IdentityRules>
   <Rule Ident="SLN">
     <Term Item="SSN" DataPrep="Scan(LR, DIGIT, 0, ToUpper, SameOrder)"
        Similarity="EXACT"/>
     <Term Item="FirstName" Similarity="SOUNDEX"/>
   </Rule>
   <Rule Ident="FLD">
     <Term Item="FirstName" DataPrep ="Scan(LR, LETTER, 0, ToUpper,
SameOrder)"
        Similarity=NICKNAME/>
     <Term Item="LastName" DataPrep ="Scan(LR, LETTER, 0, ToUpper,
SameOrder)"
        Similarity=Exact/>
     <Term Item="YOB" DataPrep="Scan(LR, DIGIT, 0, KeepCase, SameOrder)
        Similarity=Exact/>
   </Rule>
</IdentityRules>
<Indices>
   <Index Ident="1">
     <Segment Item="SSN" Hash="Scan(LR, DIGIT, 0, KeepCase, SameOrder)"/>
     <Segment Item="FirstName" Hash="SOUNDEX"/>
   </Index>
   <Index Ident="2">
     <Segment  Item="LastName"  Hash="Scan(LR,  LETTER,  0,  ToUpper,
SameOrder)"/>
     <Segment Item="YOB" Hash="Scan(LR, DIGIT, 0, ToUpper, SameOrder)"/>
   </Index>
</Indices>
```

The first section of the XML segment enclosed by the <IdentityRules> element defines the Boolean rule comprising two agreement patterns. The first agreement pattern is an exact match on social security number (SSN) and a SOUNDEX match on the first name. The second agreement pattern is a nickname match on first name and an exact match on both last name and year-of-birth (YOB).

The second section of the segment enclosed by the <Indices> element defines two match-key generators. Both generate compound keys. The first key comprises a simple hash of the SSN by the SCAN algorithm. The SCAN algorithm parameters specify a left-to-right (LR) scan to extract digits (DIGIT) up to the full length of the string (0), keeping the original case (KeepCase), and keeping the digits in the same order as in the original string (SameOrder). The second component of the first match key is the SOUNDEX hash of the first name.

The first match key index is in 100% alignment with the first agreement pattern, and in this case, it also achieves 100% precision. This is because every candidate brought back by the first index will match to the incoming reference because agreement on the match key is exactly the same as agreement on the rule pattern.

The second match key definition is necessary because the second agreement pattern uses the nickname similarity function for the first name attribute. To assure alignment, the second match key brings back candidates that agree on last name and year-of-birth. Both of the agreements are necessary but insufficient to satisfy the second rule pattern. In other words, candidates brought back by the second match key may not always match by the second pattern (because first names are different), but if any references do match by the second pattern, they will be brought back as candidates by this index.

Note that it is not always necessary to create a separate match key generator for every agreement pattern. Whether a new match key generator is needed will depend on the nature of the rules. Take as an example a Boolean rule for student enrollment that has two patterns. The first pattern requires exact agreement on first name, last name, and the difference in age value is 0, −1, or 1 (i.e. ages are within one year of each other). The second pattern requires exact agreement on first name, last name, and street number of the student's address. A single match key comprised of the student's first name and last name together would be in alignment with both patterns.

MATCH KEY BLOCKING FOR SCORING RULES

The examples shown so far have been based on Boolean rules. Match key generation and rule alignment are essentially the same for scoring rules. The difference is the agreement patterns of Boolean rules are explicit in the definition of the rule, whereas understanding the agreement patterns for a scoring rule requires some analysis.

An agreement pattern in a Boolean rule is an AND clause, i.e. a sequence of comparator terms joined by the AND operator and separated from other patterns by the OR operator. In a Boolean rule, it is easy to find and examine each agreement pattern, then determine whether it requires defining a new match key generator, or if it is already in alignment with a previously defined match key.

For a scoring rule, it is not as simple. Scoring rules have patterns, but they are not obvious from inspecting the rule. For simplicity, suppose that a scoring rule compares four identity attributes A1, A2, A3, and A4, and the comparators for these attributes correspond to a hash algorithm. Further assume the scoring rule does not use value-based (frequency-based) weights, i.e. there is only one agreement and one disagreement weight for each of the four attributes.

This means when comparing any two references there are a total of 16 (2^4) possible patterns of agreement and disagreement, i.e. they could agree or disagree on A1, agree or disagree on A2, and the same for A3 and A4. Each of these patterns can be represented by a four-bit binary number where a 0 bit means disagreement and a 1 bit means agreement. For example, 1010 would represent agreement on A1, disagreement on A2, agreement on A3, and disagreement on A4.

Now assume each attribute has the following agreement and disagreement weights, A1(10, 0), A2(3, −4), A3(7, −1), A4(5, 2) where the first number of the ordered pair is the agreement weight and the second number is the disagreement weight. For example, the disagreement weight for A2 is −4. Given these weights, a total score can now be calculated for each of the 16 possible agreement patterns. For example, the pattern "1010" would have a score of $10 - 4 + 7 + 2 = 15$.

Table 9.1 shows each of the 16 patterns ranked in descending order by their total score. Now suppose the match threshold set for this rule is 8, i.e. any pattern that gives a score of 8 or more will be considered a match. From this table it is clear

Table 9.1 Pattern Scores in Descending Order

Pattern	Score
1111	25
1110	22
1011	18
1101	17
1010	15
0111	15
1100	14
0110	12
1001	10
0011	8
1000	7
0101	7
0010	5
0100	4
0001	0
0000	−3

the agreement patterns for the scoring rule are the first 10 patterns in Table 9.1 that have a score greater than or equal to 8.

The pattern with the smallest score that satisfies the threshold value of 8 is the pattern "0011". With the assumption that all of the comparators correspond to a hash algorithm, it is possible to define a match key for each 10 patterns. For example, the match key for the pattern "0011" would be the hash value of A3 concatenated with the hash value of A4 (A3 + A4). This match key would clearly be in alignment with the pattern "0011" that it was generated from.

However, it is not necessary to define 10 different match keys in order to achieve alignment with all 10 match patterns. For example, the match key A3 + A4 derived from the pattern "0011" is also in alignment with the patterns "1111", "1011", and "0111" because these patterns also require agreement on A3 and A4. Next consider the pattern "1001" just above "0011". A match key for this pattern would be A1 + A4. This match key would also be in alignment with the pattern "1101". Thus, two match keys A3 + A4 and A1 + A4 align with 6 of the 10 patterns above the threshold. Furthermore, the match key A2 + A3 is in alignment with the pattern "0110" and "1110", the match key A1 + A2 aligns with pattern "1100", and finally match key A1 + A3 aligns with pattern "1010". Thus, 5 match keys are sufficient to properly align with all 10 of the agreement-disagreement patterns of the scoring rule.

Although this example is simplistic, this approach to finding match keys for a scoring rule is basically sound. The actual analysis becomes more complicated when frequency- or value-based weights are used. Also, the assumption that each comparator corresponds to a hash algorithm may not hold in every situation.

CONCLUDING REMARKS

Even though blocking contributes to some loss of ER accuracy, it is absolutely essential. Even with the use of parallel and distributed computing, the power of $O(n^2)$ will eventually overwhelm any system that does not employ blocking. Although there are several strategies for blocking, the most commonly used is match key blocking. The loss of accuracy with match key blocking can be minimized by properly aligning the match keys with the matching rules. Match-key-to-rule alignment is easier to achieve in systems using Boolean rules, especially rules that rely primarily on hash function comparators rather than similarity functions. Match-key-to-rule alignment is more difficult in systems that use scoring (probabilistic) rules.

CSRUD for Big Data

LARGE-SCALE ER FOR MDM

As noted earlier, in the world of ER small data can quickly become big data because ER is fundamentally an $O(n^2)$ problem. Match key blocking, as discussed in Chapter 8, is one of the primary strategies for addressing the problem of large-scale ER (Bianco, Galante, & Heuser, 2011; Kirsten et al., 2010; Yancey, 2007). This is because properly aligned match key blocking will partition the set of input references into disjoint subsets that can be resolved independently of one another. This makes match key blocking ideal for distributed processing applications such as Hadoop Map/Reduce that do not support or require processor-to-processor communication. However, this approach will only work as long each block is small enough to fit into the memory of any single processor.

The Hadoop Map/Reduce is a processing layer that sits on top of the Hadoop File System (HDFS). In the Hadoop architecture, a mapper function outputs key-value pairs. The system then brings together all of the key-value pairs into blocks that share the same key. These blocks are then processed by reducer functions. This paradigm fits nicely with match key blocking in which the key of the key-value pair is the match key, and the value of the key-value pair is the reference.

LARGE-SCALE ER WITH SINGLE MATCH KEY BLOCKING

Suppose for a base ER rule there is a single, properly aligned index generator. Alignment of the index generator with the match rule implies all pairs of references that match by one of the rules also generate the same index value. Therefore, from an entity resolution standpoint, this means all of the matches that can be found by the match rule are going to be found between references within the same block. By the assumption of alignment, references from different match key blocks should not match. Consequently in the case of a single index generator, the complete resolution of a dataset can be accomplished in a relatively simple, two-step process as shown in Figure 10.1.

The first step is the generation of the match key values. At this first step, the partitioning and distribution D1 of the input references to different processors is arbitrary and can simply be based on uniformly sized groupings of references. This is

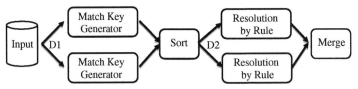

FIGURE 10.1

Distributed workflow based on single index generator.

because the match key value produced by a match key generator only depends upon the values of the identity attributes in each reference, and there are no dependencies on other references. In the Hadoop Map/Reduce framework, algorithms such as match key generation that operate independently on individual records are usually run in a map step. The output of a map step is always a key-value pair. In this case the key of the key-value pair is the generated match key, and the value of the key-value pair is the reference that generated the match key.

After each block of input references has been processed by the match key generator running at each of the nodes, each reference will produce a single match key. These match key-reference pairs are then merged and sorted into match key value order. In the Hadoop Map/Reduce framework, sorting by key value is performed by a shuffle step that follows the map step and precedes the reduce step. Unless otherwise specified, the shuffle sorts the mapper output in key value order by default.

After the references are sorted into match key order, Hadoop automatically creates key-blocks. Each key-block comprises all of the key-value pairs that share the same key value. In this case, it will be blocks of references where all of the references in the same block share the same match key value.

In the reduce step, the key-blocks are distributed to different processors where the final resolution of blocks into clusters takes place. Again, this fits well with the Hadoop map/reduce framework that guarantees all of the records in a key-block are processed together on the same processor. One processor could be given multiple blocks, but the reducer function of Hadoop assures blocks are not split across processors.

Once a block of key-value pairs is sent to a processor, it can be processed by an ER algorithm and base match rule to link the references into clusters. Consequently, in a Hadoop framework the ER process itself works best in a reduce step. Taking again the example of blocking by postal code, the key of the key-value pair would be the postal code and the value of the key-value pair would be the actual reference. In this way, all references with the same postal code would be sent to the same processor. The reduce step guarantees blocks with the same postal code will be sent to the same processor provided the postal code block does not exceed the capacity of a single processor. Typically key blocks will be smaller than the single process capacity, allowing the system to send several key blocks to the same processor. The reducer provides an iterator function that allows the code resident on the processor to access each key-value pair in the key-block sequentially. In the final reduce step each postal code block becomes the input to an ER algorithm that will further refine the block into clusters according to the matching rules of the ER process.

Decoding Key-Value Pairs

From the viewpoint of a map/reduce process, all records only have two fields, a key field and a value field separated by a special character, by default a tab character. Although the keys and values can be typed, they are usually handled as text (character strings). Therefore, it is the responsibility of the application developer to interpret the value portion of the key-value pairs as a reference comprising several attribute-value pairs, i.e. subvalues of a value string. The subvalues representing the attribute values of the reference can be encoded into the overall string representing the single-value of the key-value pair in many different ways. For example, the encoding can be comma-separated values (CSV) or even traditional fixed-field width record format. Talburt and Nelson (2009) have developed a Compressed Document Set Architecture (CoDoSA) that uses short metadata tags in the string to separate and identify the subvalues encoded into an overall string. CoDoSA encoding resembles a lightweight XML document. CoDoSA is the standard for encoding references in the EIS of the OYSTER Open Source Entity Resolution system (Talburt & Zhou, 2012, 2013). An example of an OYSTER EIS using CoDoSA reference encoding is shown in Figure 1.3 of Chapter 1.

In the case of a single index as shown in Figure 10.1, both distributions D1 and D2 actually create true partitions of the datasets A and B, respectively — i.e. the distributed segments are nonoverlapping. D1 can partition the input by simply counting off equal size blocks of references. D2 partitions the match key-value pairs because each reference has only one match key value; thus the match key blocks cannot overlap.

THE TRANSITIVE CLOSURE PROBLEM

However, there is a problem associated with the process described in Figure 10.1. The problem is that, in most large-scale entity resolution applications, a single match key is not sufficient to bring together all of the references that should be compared. Data quality problems such as typographical errors in attribute values, missing values, and inconsistent representation of the values will require the use of more than one match key in order to obtain good resolution results with a reasonable amount of comparison reduction. This problem is particularly acute when the base match rule is a scoring rule. As described in Chapter 9 in the section titled "Match Key Blocking for Scoring Rules," a simple scoring rule comparing only a few identity attributes may need support from dozens of match key generators.

When each input reference can potentially create more than one match key, the processing method outlined in Figure 10.1 will not always lead to the correct resolution of the references in the input. The reason is the requirement for transitive closure of an ER process. Transitive closure states if a reference R1 is linked to a reference R2, and reference R2 is linked to a reference R3, then reference R1 should be linked to reference R3.

To see how having multiple match key generators disrupts the process described in Figure 10.1, suppose there are three distinct references R1, R2, and R3, and two match key generators Gen1 and Gen2. Table 10.1 shows the results of applying the two match key generators to the three references.

Because each reference generates two keys, the final result is a set of six match key-value pairs. These pairs in sorted order by match value are shown in Table 10.2.

The four distinct key values partition the key-value pairs into four blocks. The first block has two key-value pairs that share the match key value of K1. The second block formed by the match key K2 has only a single key-value pair. The third block has two key-value pairs formed by the match key K3, and finally the last block is a single key-value pair formed by the match key K4.

The first observation is that, even though the keys partition the key-value pairs, they do not partition the underlying set of references. The references in the K1 block overlap with the references in the K2 and K3 blocks at references R1 and R2, respectively. Any reference that generates two or more distinct match keys will be duplicated in each of the blocks for those match keys.

Now suppose in a distributed processor scheme the K1 and K2 blocks are sent to processor P1, and the K3 and K4 blocks are sent to another processor P2. Further suppose when the ER process running on P1 processes the K1 block, it finds that R1 and R2 are matching references and links them together. Similarly suppose when the ER process running on P2 processes the K3 block, it finds that R2 and R3 are matching references and links them together.

Table 10.1 Match Key Values

Reference	Gen1	Gen2
R1	K1	K2
R2	K1	K3
R3	K4	K3

Table 10.2 Pairs Sorted by Match Key

Key	Value
K1	R1
K1	R2
K2	R1
K3	R2
K3	R3
K4	R3

The combined output of this process comprises four clusters: {R1, R2}, {R1}, {R2, R3}, and {R4}. However, this result is not consistent with the principles of ER. The final output of an ER process should be a true partition of the original input, i.e. each reference should be in one, and only one, cluster, and the clusters should not overlap with each other. Clearly when references can generate multiple match keys, the simple process shown in Figure 10.1 no longer works.

The approach to solving the multiple-index problem depends upon whether the ER processes are using record-based resolution or attribute-based resolution as described in Chapter 8. The solution for multiple match keys when the ER system is using record-based projection is simpler than one using attributed-based projection, so it will be discussed first.

DISTRIBUTED, MULTIPLE-INDEX, RECORD-BASED RESOLUTION

The workflow for multiple match key resolution as shown in Figure 10.2 begins in the same way as the process outlined in Figure 10.1 for a single index workflow. The problem is that simply sorting and distributing by match key blocks is no longer adequate. As discussed in the previous example, simply sorting to create distribution D2 may cause the final result to contain clusters of overlapping references.

One solution to the problem shown here is to replace the sort process with a transitive closure process where the closure is with respect to shared match key values. This can most easily be understood by looking at the references and relationships in the form of a graph.

TRANSITIVE CLOSURE AS A GRAPH PROBLEM

In graph theory an undirected graph is simply a set N of nodes and a set of E of edges, where E is a subset of $P(N)$, the set of all subsets of N that contain two elements. As a simple example consider, $N = \{a, b, c, d, e\}$ and $E = \{\{a, b\}, \{b, c\}, \{d, e\}\}$. N and E form an undirected graph of five nodes and three edges depicted in Figure 10.3.

A connected component of a graph is a maximal subset of nodes in the graph having the property for any two nodes in the subset, there exists a path of edges that connects them together. In Figure 10.3, it is easy to see the graph has two

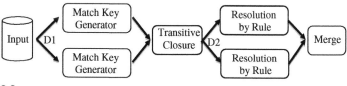

FIGURE 10.2

Distributed workflow for multiple match keys.

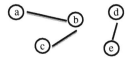

FIGURE 10.3

Undirected graph of *N* and *E*.

connected components {a, b, c} and {d, e}. Even though node "a" and node "c" do not share an edge, there is a path from "a" to "b" and from "b" to "c" that connects them. It will also be true the connected components of a graph form a partition of the nodes, i.e. every node in the graph is in one, and only one, component.

A connected component represents the transitive closure of the nodes in the component with respect to connections between nodes. The standard algorithm for finding the components of a graph uses this principle (Sedgewick & Wayne, 2011). It starts by selecting any node in the graph, and then finds all of the nodes connected to it. Next, all of the nodes connected to these nodes are found, then the nodes connected to these, and so on until no new connections can be made. The set of nodes found in this way comprises the first component of the graphs. The next step is to select any node not in the first component and form its component in the same way as the first. This process stops when there are no more nodes outside of the components that have already been found.

REFERENCES AND MATCH KEYS AS A GRAPH

References and their match keys can also be given a graphical interpretation. Consider the following example of 11 references {A, B, C, D, E, F, G, H, I, J, K} and 3 index generators. For simplicity, the match key values in Table 10.3 are given

Table 10.3 Match Keys

Reference	Generator 1	Generator 2	Generator 3
A	11	21	
B	12	16	1
C	18	2	13
D	22	3	8
E	12	16	4
F	11	3	8
G	19	20	4
H	18	2	9
I	6	2	13
J	15	5	10
K	19	7	4

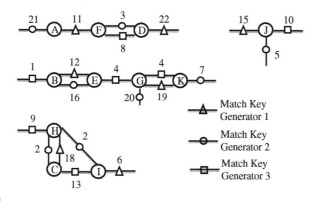

FIGURE 10.4

Graph interpretation of Table 10.3.

as integer values. By the design of the match key generators, the values produced by one generator will be different from the set of values produced by a different generator. However, in general there will be duplication among the values produced by the same generator.

The references and match keys in Table 10.3 can be interpreted as a graph in which the references are the nodes of the graph and match keys shared by two references form an edge in the graphs. Figure 10.4 shows the graph interpretation of Table 10.3.

One notable difference between the match key graph in Figure 10.4 and the graph in Figure 10.3 is the match key graph is noisy. The noise is created by the fact that some references may generate unique keys not shared with any other reference, e.g. keys 21 and 22. A unique match key does not form an edge in the graph. Another source of noise is that some references share more than one match key, e.g. nodes F and D.

Although this noise makes the graph in Figure 10.4 look somewhat different from the graph in Figure 10.3, they still have the same essential features. Two references are connected if and only if they share at least one match key between them. It is also much easier to see the connected components of the references in the graph representation in Figure 10.4 than by inspecting Table 10.3. It is apparent the graph in Figure 10.4 has four connected components {A, D, F}, {J}, {B, E, G, K}, and {C, H, I}.

AN ITERATIVE, NONRECURSIVE ALGORITHM FOR TRANSITIVE CLOSURE

The standard algorithm for finding the connected components of a graph is a breadth-first search algorithm that uses recursion (Sedgewick & Wayne, 2011). Although elegant, it has a limiting feature when working with Big Data. The standard recursive algorithm for transitive closure needs to have access to all the node and edge information in one memory space to work efficiently. In other words, the algorithm assumes it can directly access any part of the graph at any given point in the algorithm. For very large datasets this may not be practical or even possible.

Distributed processing using the Hadoop framework works best when it is operating on large key-value sets by successively performing record-level operations (mapper functions) followed by operations on key-values blocks (reducer functions). To better fit the processing paradigm, the authors have developed an iterative algorithm for finding the connected components of a match key graph like the one shown in Figure 10.4. The purpose of the algorithm is to perform the transitive closure of a graph through the iterative, sequential processing of a large set of key-value pairs without the need to create large, in-memory data structures.

The context and notation for the pseudo-code of this algorithm is that R represents a set of references, and G represents a set of N match key generators. If r is a reference in R, then $r1$, $r2$, $r3$, ..., rN represent the key values generated by each of the index generators acting on r (some values may be null). The algorithm has three parts: an initial bootstrap phase, an iteration phase, and a final deduplication phase. Here is a general description of each phase and the key-value pairs they use.

- **Bootstrap**: In the bootstrap phase, the key of the key-value pair is a match key and the value of key-value pair is the reference. Each reference can generate up to N key-value pairs, one key-value pair for each non-null match key generated by the reference. In the bootstrap, the key value pairs are sorted by match key to find the connected pairs of references. The output of the bootstrap phase is a list where each item in the list is a set of reference identifiers of the references connected to each other by a shared match key value.
- Starting with the bootstrap phase, and in each following step, the items in the output list are sets of record identifiers. These sets of record identifiers are the proto-components of the graph, i.e. components in formation. At the bootstrap these proto-components are usually singleton sets or pairs of identifiers. The algorithm takes a bottom-up approach by first finding connected pairs of references in the bootstrap phase, then finding overlapping pairs in the first iteration phase to form triples, then quadruples in the next iteration, and so on. At the end of the bootstrap phase the match key values and the actual contents of the reference are discarded. Only reference identifiers are carried forward into the iteration phase. After the match keys have been generated, the attribute-value pairs of the reference are not needed for the actual transitive closure process and can be discarded for storage efficiency. At the end of the transitive closure process, the actual reference value can be recovered for use in the ER process by performing a simple join of the reference identifiers with the original input.

- **Iteration**: Each iteration phase starts with a list of proto-components. In the case of the first iteration, it is the list of proto-components from the bootstrap. In other iterations it is the list of proto-components output from the previous iteration. Each iteration begins by taking each proto-component produced in the previous step and expanding it into a set of key-value pairs where the key is a single reference identifier taken from the proto-component and the value is the entire proto-component. This means that if a proto-component contains N reference identifiers, then it forms N key-value pairs, one for each reference identifier in the proto-component. For example, if the proto-component comprises three reference identifiers {R1, R2, R3}, then it forms three key value pairs of (R1, {R1, R2, R3}), (R2, {R1, R2, R3}), and (R3, {R1, R2, R3}). After the expansion, the key-value pairs are sorted by key value. After the key-value pairs are sorted, all of the proto-components with the same key block are merged (set union) to produce a new proto-component. The new list of proto-components becomes the input for the next iteration. The iteration continues until no new proto-components are created at the merge step, i.e. the proto-components cease to grow in size as a result of the merging of all of the proto-components in the same key-value block.
- **Deduplication**: Due to the nature of the algorithm and the noise inherent in the match key graph, the same component may appear in different positions in the list. The final phase is to deduplicate the final list of components into a set of unique connected components. This is done by creating key-value pairs where the key value is the first reference identifier in the final component, and the value of the key-value pair is the entire component. After these key-value pairs are sorted by key value, only the first component in each key-value block is kept. This is because during the iteration phase, the reference identifiers are maintained in the proto-component sets in sorted order. Therefore, if two components agree on the first reference identifier, then they are the same component.

BOOTSTRAP PHASE: INITIAL CLOSURE BY MATCH KEY VALUES

Let kList be a list of items where each item has two attributes. The first attribute is a non-null, match key value for a reference. The second attribute is the identifier (RefID) of the reference; kList should have one record for each possible combination of a reference r in R and a non-null match key value produced by one of the index generators in G acting on r. If kItem represents an item in kList, then kItem.key represents the value of the first attribute (match key value), and kItem.rid represents the value of the second attribute (RefID).

Let sList represent another list where each list item has two attributes; for sList the first attribute is an integer value and the second attribute is a set of RefIDs. If sItem represents an item of sList then sItem.int is the integer value and sItem.refSet is the list of RefIDs.

```
Bootstrap Start
Sort kList primary by key and secondary by RefID.
\\ Write proto-components to sList by processing kList sequentially
1 → compNbr
kList.getNextItem() → kItem
kItem.rid → prevRid
kItem.idx → prevIdx
Declare compSet a Set of RefID
∅ → compSet
∅ → sList
While(More items in kList)
        If((kItem.rid == prevRid) OR (kItem.idx) == prevIdx))
        Then
                compSet.insert(kItem.rid)
        Else
                compNbr → sItem.int
                compSet → sItem.refSet
                sList.append(sItem)
                compNbr + 1 → compNbr
                kItem.rid → compSet
        kList.rid → prevRid
        kList.idx → prevIdx
        K.readNextRecord()→ kRec
End of While Loop
compNbr → sItem.int
compSet → sItem.refSet
sList.append(sItem)
```

ITERATION PHASE: SUCCESSIVE CLOSURE BY REFERENCE IDENTIFIER

Let sList be the same list of items produced in the bootstrap phase, and let tList represent a list of items where the first attribute is a single RefID, and the second attribute is a Set of RefIDs.

```
\\ This is an iterative process, stops when changeCnt is zero
1 → changeCnt
∅ → tList
While(changeCnt>0)
        // Expand sList into tList
        While(More items in sList)
                sList.readNextItem()→ sItem
                (sList.refSet).sizeOf()→ setSize
```

```
              For J from 1 to setSize
                      sList.refSet.getSetElement(J) → refID
                      refID → tItem.refID
                      sList.refSet → tItem.refSet
              End J Loop
      End While Loop
      // Sort tList
      Sort tList by first column refID
      // empty sList to hold the new proto-components
      0 → sList
      1 → compNbr
      0 → changeCnt
      Declare compSet to be a set of RefIDs
      // Process tList in order by key to create new set of proto-components
      tList.getNextItem() → tItem
      tItem.refSet → compSet
      tItem.rid → prevRid
      While(More items in tList)
              If((tItem.refSet ∩ compSet not 0) or (tItem.rid == prevRid))
                      Then
                              compSet.setUnion(tRec.refSet)
                              If(compSet.SizeOf() > (tRec.refSet).
                                                     SizeOf())
                                      changeCnt+1 → changeCnt
                      Else
                              compNbr → sItem.int
                              compSet → sItem.refSet
                              sList.append(sItem)
                      tItem.rid → prevRid
                      tItem.refSet → compSet
                      compNbr+1 → compNbr
                      tList.getNextItem() → tItem
      End of While Loop
      compNbr → sItem.int
      compSet → sItem.refSet
      sList.append(sItem)
End of While Loop
```

DEDUPLICATION PHASE: FINAL OUTPUT OF COMPONENTS

Start with Table S at the end of the iteration phase.

```
0 → tList
While(More items in sList)
      sList.getNextItem() → sItem
      (sList.refSet).getSetElement(1) → tItem.refID
```

```
                    sItem.refSet → tItem.refSet
                    tItem.append(tItem)
End While Loop
Sort tList by key (refID)
Ø → sList
1 → compNbr
tList.getNextItem() → tItem
tItem.rid → prevRid
While(More items in tList)
        If(tItem.rid<>prevRid)
                    compNbr → sItem
                    tItem.refSet → sItem.refSet
                    sList.append(sItem)
                    compNbr + 1 → compNbr
        tItem.rid → prevRid
        tList.getNextItem()→ tItem
End While Loop
compNbr → sItem
tItem.refSet → sItem.refSet
sList.append(sItem)
```

The bootstrap phase and first iteration in applying this algorithm to the match key graph of Figure 10.2 is shown in Table 10.4. The first two columns of Table 10.4 with the heading of kList show the information from Table 10.3 flattened into a single column and sorted in order by match key values. The next two columns with the heading sList show the first set of proto-components formed by collapsing the key blocks in the second column under kList. The two columns with the heading tList(raw) show the expansion step of the first iteration in which each proto-component in the input is expanded into key-value pairs.

The two columns with the heading tList(sorted) show the same key-value pairs under the heading tList(raw), but in sorted order by the key value (reference identifier). The final step of the first iteration is to merge the values (lists) in the same key-value block. This creates a list of 10 proto-components under the heading of sList(merged), which will become the input into the second iteration.

It is also important to note that in the final merge step, every key-value block changed except for the key-value block with the key value of J shown highlighted in Table 10.4.

Table 10.5 shows the remaining iterations and final deduplication phase for this example. For brevity the expansion steps (tList(raw)) have been omitted as has the last merge step. The final tList(sorted) columns signal the final iteration because there are no changes in when proto-components in the same key-value block are merged. The final result comprises the four components of the match key graph shown in the Figure 10.4.

For simplicity, the pseudo-code and example shown here use the simplest form of the algorithm. In following the steps it is easy to see the many opportunities to

Table 10.4 Bootstrap and First Iteration for Figure 10.3

kList#	kList	sList#	sList	tList(raw)	tList(sorted) key	tList(sorted)	sList(merged)#	sList(merged)
1	B	1	B	B	A	A	1	A,F
2	C	2	C,H,I	C	A	A,F	2	B,E
2	H	3	D,F	H	B	B	3	C,H,I
2	I	4	E,G,K	I	B	B,E	4	D,F
3	D	5	J	D	B	B,E	5	B,E,G,K
3	F	6	I	F	C	C,H	6	A,D,F
4	E	7	K	E	C	C,H,I	7	E,G,K
4	G	8	D,F	G	C	C,I	8	C,H,I
4	K	9	H	K	D	D	9	J
5	J	10	J	J	D	D,F	10	E,G,K
6	I	11	A,F	I	D	D,F		
7	K	12	B,E	K	E	B,E		
8	D	13	C,I	D	E	B,E		
8	F	14	J	F	E	E,G,K		
9	H	15	B,E	H	F	A,F		
10	J	16	C,H	J	F	D,F		
11	A	17	G,K	A	F	D,F		
11	F	18	A	F	G	E,G,K		
12	B	19	D	B	G	G,K		
12	E			E	H	C,H		
13	C			C	H	C,H,I		
13	I			I	H	H		
15	J			J	I	C,H,I		
16	B			B	I	C,I		
16	E			E	I	I		
18	C			C	J	J		
18	H			H	J	J		
19	G			G	J	J		
19	K			K	K	E,G,K		
20	G			G	K	G,K		
21	A			A	K	K		
22	D			D				

Table 10.5 Iterations 2 through 3 and the Deduplication Phase

sList(merged)		tList(sorted)		sList(merged)		tList(sorted)		Merge&Dedup
1	A,F	A	A,F	1	A,D,F	A	A,D,F	A,D,F
2	B,E	A	A,D,F	2	B,E,G,K	A	A,D,F	B,E,G,K
3	C,H,I	B	B,E	3	C,H,I	B	B,E,G,K	C,H,I
4	D,F	B	B,E,G,K	4	A,D,F	B	B,E,G,K	J
5	B,E,G,K	C	C,H,I	5	B,E,G,K	B	B,E,G,K	
6	A,D,F	C	C,H,I	6	A,D,F	C	C,H,I	
7	E,G,K	D	D,F	7	B,E,G,K	C	C,H,I	
8	C,H,I	D	A,D,F	8	C,H,I	D	A,D,F	
9	J	E	B,E,G,K	9	J	D	A,D,F	
10	E,G,K	E	E,G,K	10	B,E,G,K	D	A,D,F	
		E	E,G,K			E	B,E,G,K	
		F	A,F			E	B,E,G,K	
		F	D,F			E	B,E,G,K	
		F	A,D,F			F	A,D,F	
		G	B,E,G,K			F	A,D,F	
		G	E,G,K			F	A,D,F	
		G	E,G,K			G	B,E,G,K	
		H	C,H,I			G	B,E,G,K	
		H	C,H,I			G	B,E,G,K	
		I	C,H,I			G	B,E,G,K	
		I	C,H,I			H	C,H,I	
		J	J			H	C,H,I	
		K	B,E,G,K			I	C,H,I	
		K	E,G,K			I	C,H,I	
		K	E,G,K			J	J	
						K	B,E,G,K	
						K	B,E,G,K	
						K	B,E,G,K	
						K	B,E,G,K	

reduce the effort. For example, whenever a proto-component has not changed during the merger, it does not need to be expanded into the next step. Its cross-product key-value pairs no longer have any contribution to make to the transitive closure of other components. Another improvement is to deduplicate the input sList before expanding the sList into the tList key-value pairs.

One final observation is that the algorithm is symmetric with respect to reference identifiers and match keys. It is a simple matter to reverse the map output from the key generation so the key-value pairs input to the bootstrap have the reference identifier as the key and the match key as the value. In this case, instead of discarding the match key, the reference identifier is discarded and the iteration proceeds by performing the transitive closure on the match keys instead of the reference identifiers. If there are relatively few match key generators, then closure on the match keys can be more efficient than closure on the reference identifiers because the cross-products are smaller. The only difference is that at the end, it will take two joins to recover the original reference value, one to join the match key to the reference identifier and another to join the reference identifier to the reference value.

Although not shown in the example given in Figure 10.4, another practical problem that must be addressed is the possibility that some references will not generate a match key by any of the generators. Although this is clearly an indication of a poor quality record, it could happen for certain sets of references and match key generator configurations. One approach is to write these references out as exceptions and not carry them through the transitive closure process.

By the fact that a reference does not generate a match key value, it is already known it will not match with any other references. Therefore, references that do not generate a match key will form their own, single-reference clusters in the final output. If these references are carried forward to participate in the transitive closure process rather than output as exceptions, then they should each be assigned an auto-generated match key value. However, if they are all given the same default match, instead of forming many, single-reference clusters, they will form one large component that can degrade the overall performance of the system. In order to prevent this, the autogenerated match key should be unique across all references. In a distributed processing environment such as Hadoop, assigning a value unique across all processors in the system can be a challenge. Autogenerated keys for this purpose should use some local processor variable such as node name together with a sequence number to prevent different processors from assigning the same key value.

EXAMPLE OF HADOOP IMPLEMENTATION

The following code for the bootstrap phase of the transitive closure is implemented as a Reducer class in Hadoop. The Bootstrap reducer essentially reads the kList and creates the tList(raw) shown in Table 10.4. Note the sList in Table 10.4 is only shown for clarity. The building of the sList is not a required step in the algorithm.

The input coming into the Bootstrap reducer is a series of key-value blocks similar to the kList. Each block comprises one key and series of values. The values are presented to the reducer as an iterable list. The Bootstrap class overrides the "reduce()" method of the parent Reducer class. The first argument of the "reduce()" method is the key of the block labeled as "inputKey". The second argument is the iterable list of values labeled "values". The first two arguments are inputs. The third argument is the output Context labeled "context".

```
/** @author Cheng @date 08/25/2014 */
public class Bootstrap extends Reducer<Text, Text, Text, Text> {
        @Override
        public void reduce(Text inputKey, Iterable<Text> values,
                        Context context) throws
                        IOException, InterruptedException {
                TreeSet<String> group = new TreeSet<String>();
                for (Text value : values) {
                        group.add(value.toString());
                }
                if(group.size()>1){
                        for (String aa : group) {
                                context.write(new Text(aa.trim()),
                                        new Text(printArray(group)));
                        }
                }
        }
        private static String printArray(TreeSet<String> group) {
                String result = "";
                int i = 0;
                for (String aa : group) {
                        if (i == 0) {
                                result += aa.trim();
                        } else {
                                result += "\u0007" + aa.trim();
                        }
                        i++;
                }
                return result;
        }
}
```

The Bootstrap input is coming from a mapper that generated a set of match keys for each reference. The mapper writes its key-value pairs to its Context with the generated match key as the key of the key-value pair, and the reference identifier as the value of the key-value pair. A shuffle step prior to the reducer brings together the pairs having the same match key and block passed to the Bootstrap reducer. So for the Bootstrap reducer, the key of each key-block is a match key, and the values are the reference identifiers that produced the match key similar to the kList in Table 10.4. For example, in Table 10.4, match key value "1" was only produced by Reference B, and match key "2" was produced by References C, H, and I.

In the Bootstrap class, the first operation is to iterate over the values in the block and add each one to a Java TreeSet structure labeled "group". A TreeSet structure is used because it will insert new items in sorted order. It is important for the operation of the algorithm that the list of reference identifiers output from each iteration step is in sorted order.

All of the values in the block are cast and manipulated as Java String objects. In the next step, the values are made into a single string that uses a Bell character as a delimiter to separate the different reference identifiers. The construction of the delimited string is carried out by the "printArray()" method. The "printArray()" method iterates over reference identifiers in the TreeSet and concatenates these values in sorted order into a string labeled "result". All values except for the first value are preceded by an ASCI "\u0007" (Bell) character. The Bell character serves as a delimiter to make it easier for the string to be parsed into individual reference identifiers at a later point in the algorithm.

After the string is constructed, the reducer writes a single key-value pair to Context where the key value is the first reference identifier in the TreeSet ("aa") and the value is the concatenated string of all reference identifiers in the block (the "result" returned from "printArray()"). However in this code, no key-value pair is written for blocks containing only one value. Again this is departure from the example shown in Table 10.4 implemented for performance efficiency. When a match key block only contains one reference identifier, either that reference is connected to other references in another block, or the reference is not connected to any other reference. For the "1" block only containing B, it is the former. Reference B is connect to reference E in the "12" and "16" blocks of kList. Hence, reference B will be retained in the bootstrap because it is present in other match key blocks with more than one value.

However, some references may be lost entirely during bootstrap because they do not connect with any other reference. For example, the reference J only occurs in the kList in the single-value blocks "5", "10", and "15". Therefore, the reference J is lost during bootstrap. However, this is not a problem because the final step of the transitive closure process is to perform an outer join between the reference identifiers remaining at the end of the transitive closure process with the original input of reference identifier-reference pairs. Because it is an outer join, all of the original references will be recovered at the end of the process. It will also signal that any reference recovered by the outer join will form a single-reference component of the graph.

ER USING THE NULL RULE

It is important not get lost in the details of the transitive closure process and lose sight of the overall objective, which is ER. As shown in Figure 10.2 the transitive closure is only an intermediate step to partition the set references to be resolved into manageable sized blocks. In this case the blocks are the connected components of the match key graph of references. Each component becomes the input to an ER process which applies an ER algorithm and matching rule to find the clusters and create the final set of EIS.

However, there are situations where it is possible to end the ER process with transitive closures. This is possible when the match rule is a Boolean rule set, and where each one of the comparators used in the rules are hash functions. In this case, match key generators can be constructed in such a way that they are equivalent to the match rules. In other words, two references share the same match key if, and only if, the references match by the rule that corresponds to the match key. In this case the components found from the transitive closure of the match keys represent the final clusters of the ER process, and the ER process is said to use the "Null Rule."

Here is a simple example. Suppose an ER process for matching student records uses a two-part Boolean rule. The first part is two enrollment records are a match if they agree on first, middle, and last name values. The second part is they are considered a match if they agree on the last name, have the same date-of-birth, and the first names agree on Soundex value. Since simple agreement (exact match) and Soundex agreement are both hash function comparators, then the enrollment records can be resolved using the null rule.

To use the null rule for this example requires building two match key generators, one for the first rule that creates a match key by concatenating the characters of the first, middle, and last names (presumably with some cleansing such as upper casing and removing punctuation). The second match key generator would create a match key by concatenating the four-character Soundex value of the first name with the character of the last name and digits of the date-of-birth (again with some cleansing and standardization). So, clearly if two enrollment records share one of these keys, the records are going to match according to the rule that corresponds to the key. Therefore, a component formed by the transitive closure of the enrollment records by these two match keys contains all of the records that are equivalent by the Boolean match rule.

The null rule cannot be used if any of the comparators of the proposed matching rule are similarity functions rather than hash functions — for example, comparators such as Levenshtein edit distance or Q-gram. In these cases, the match keys can only approximate the match conditions up to hash function levels. The final components from the transitive closure of the approximate match keys must be further refined by applying the full match rule.

Using the previous example, suppose the second part of the rule were changed to require the first name values to be within one Levenshtein edit distance of each other instead of having the same Soundex value. Now the second match key generator would have to be revised. Because Levenshtein is a similarity function rather than a hash function, the new index generator would have to omit the first name and only concatenate the last name and date-of-birth. However, this change would now allow enrollment records with completely different first names to come into the same component as long as they agree on last name and date-of-birth. Therefore, the references in these components would have to be compared using the complete match rule in order to make the final determination of clusters.

THE CAPTURE PHASE AND IKB

The only thing that differentiates merge-purge ER from the capture phase of CSRUD is the transformation of clusters into EIS and storing them in an IKB. The flows in Figures 10.1 and 10.2 are essentially the same for both except for capture, the merged output from the ER flow into a storage system. In the distributed processing storage environment, both the Hadoop File System (HDFS) and HBase follow the key-value pair paradigm. Because they do not follow the relational data base model and do not directly support structure query language (SQL) they are often referred to as "Not only SQL" or NoSQL databases. Following the Hadoop model for distributed process used up to this point, the design for a distributed IKB will follow an HDFS file system implementation.

In order to retain the full functionality present in a nondistributed file system, a distributed IKB requires a number of tables, except that in HDFS tables correspond to folders. Again each folder contains one set of key-value pairs and possibly other folders. Because it is a distributed file system, HDFS only presents the user with a logical view of a file as a folder. Underneath the folder HDFS may be managing the physical file as segments distributed over several different underlying storage units. Figure 1.3 in Chapter 1 shows a segment of a nondistributed IKB created in a capture configuration of the OYSTER ER system. OYSTER stores its IKB as an XML document with a hierarchical structure. The IKB comprises the IKB-level metadata (<Metadata>) and the EIS (<Identities>). Each EIS (<Identity>) comprises a set of references (<References>) that in turn comprise a reference value (<Value>) in CoDoSA format and reference metadata (<Traces>).

In the HDFS distributed data store, both data and metadata reside in folders created by map/reduce processes. Each folder corresponds to a logic dataset comprising key-value pairs. The physical segments of the dataset may actually reside in different locations managed by HDFS.

There are three essential key-value folders in the HDFS version of the IKB. The text in parentheses after the name of the folder describes the key-value pair definitions for the folder.

- References — (Source identifier + Reference identifier, reference value) the store of all references under management. Note the key value is a concatenation of the source identifier for the reference with the unique reference identifier within the source. This is required to give each reference in the IKB a unique identifier across all sources. The reference value is a CoDoSA encoded string where each attribute value is preceded with an escape character (ASCI Bell) followed by an attribute tag. The meaning of the attribute tag is defined in the CoDoSA Tags table of the IKB.

- Entities — (Entity identifier, Entity-level metadata) The key is the entity identifier and the value is a string that is a concatenation of various entity-level metadata items such as the identifier of the run (process) in which the entity was created and the identifiers of any runs in which the entity was modified. This is where any assertion metadata would be stored as well as including true positive assertion tags and negative structure-to-structure assertion tags generated by correction or confirmation assertions as discussed in Chapter 5.
- Reference-to-Entity — (Source identifier + Reference identifier, Entity identifier + Reference-level metadata) Key-value pairs in the Entities folder have the same key as the References folder, but have a different value structure. The value string is a concatenation of the entity identifier and various reference-level metadata. The primary purpose of the Entities folder is to indicate for each reference the entity to which it belongs. This folder defines the EIS of the IKB. All of the references with the same entity identifier comprise an EIS. The remaining portion of the value string following the entity identifier contains various metadata pertaining to the relationship between the reference and the entity to which it belongs. For example, the reference-level metadata could include the identifier of the run (process) in which the reference was merged into the EIS. It might also include the identifier of the rule that caused the reference to merge into the EIS.

There are several additional folders that can be added to the IKB. These folders are primarily to hold IKB-level metadata and are generally small enough that they can hold physical tables (text files) rather than virtual key-value pairs. These include

- Run Identifiers — A sequence number or other unique identifier for each run of the system for traceability and auditing. Run identifiers are primarily used to associate other metadata with a particular run of the system.
- CoDoSA Tags — A two-column table where each row has a CoDoSA attribute tag followed by its description. These tags are used to encode the string representing the reference value in the References folder.
- Sources — A four-column table where each row has a unique source identifier, path to the source, name of source, and description of the source.
- Other tables to store copies of the Run Scripts (control scripts) for each run, Reports generated from each run, log files generated for each run, and any other run-level metadata.

THE IDENTITY UPDATE PROBLEM

Another important EIIM configuration is the automated update configuration in the update phase of the CSRUD Life Cycle. When new references are introduced, the system uses the matching rule to decide if each new reference is referring to an entity already represented in the IKB by an existing EIS, or if it is referring to some new entity not yet represented in the system. In the former case, the system should integrate the new reference into the EIS of the matching identity. In the latter case, the

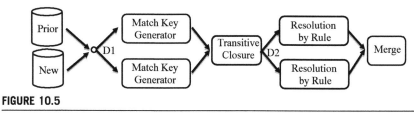

FIGURE 10.5

The basic workflow for the update configuration.

system must create a new EIS and add it to the IKB to represent the new identity. This means there will be two inputs to the update process including the existing (prior) EIS created in a previous process and the new references.

Figure 10.5 shows the general approach to the update configuration for a distributed processing environment that is basically the identity capture workflow of Figure 10.4 with an added input of prior EIS to be updated.

One problem in adapting the identity capture workflow of Figure 10.4 to identity update is that the identity capture workflow was based on the assumption that all of the inputs are single references, each with a unique reference identifier, but in Figure 10.5 the Prior input comprises EIS rather than references.

If the Prior EIS have a record-based structure, then it is possible to recover (reconstruct) the references used to create each of the prior EIS. If not, then it may still be possible to recover these references as long as the aggregate set of references used to create the Prior EIS has been saved or archived in some way. In either case it means the workflow in Figure 10.5 is essentially a recapture of the prior references combined with the new references.

However, there are still two problems with the recapture approach. The first issue concerns the evolution of matching rules. Over time, the matching rules may be modified to improve the entity identity integrity of EIS or to accommodate changes in the reference data. Therefore, the matching rules used to create or update the prior EIS may be different from the matching rules currently in effect. A simple recapture process will apply the current identity rules to the prior references as well as the new references. In other words, the identities represented by the prior EIS from D are essentially discarded, and the identities represented by the EIS in E are based entirely on the current rules. This issue may or may not be a problem, but it is an artifact of the recapture approach that should be noted.

The second problem in using a recapture approach is a much more fundamental issue related to the issue of persistent identifiers for the identities represented in the system.

PERSISTENT ENTITY IDENTIFIERS

An important goal of EIIM is to create and maintain persistent entity identifiers for each identity under management, i.e. each EIS retains the same identifier from process to process. This is not the case for basic ER systems that do not create and maintain EIS. In these systems the link identifier assigned to a cluster of references at the end of the process is transient because it is not part of a persistent identity structure. The entity identifiers assigned by these systems are only intended to represent the linking (identity) decisions for a particular process acting on a particular input. Typically these system select one survivor record from each link cluster to go forward into further processing steps. After the survivor record has been selected, the link identifier is no longer needed.

If the only objective were to build the identities represented by combining the references from Prior EIS with the new references, then a recapture approach to the workflow shown in Figure 10.5 would be sufficient. The problem is even though the EIS in the merged output bring together all of the references that represent the same identity, a Prior EIS and a corresponding EIS in the output that represent the same entity may be assigned different identifiers. In other words, from an EIIM perspective, simply performing a capture process on the combined references would have the undesirable side effect that the identifiers for the same entity identity could change after each update process.

Fortunately, there is a fairly simple solution to the problem, and that is to treat the EIS identifier as a match key in the transitive closure process. To see how this works, consider a simple example in which there is only one Prior EIS, one new reference, and a single match key generator G1 as shown in Figure 10.6.

In the scenario of Figure 10.6 there is a single Prior EIS with Identifier E1 that comprises two references R1 and R2, two new reference R3 and R4, and a single match key generator G1 that produces three distinct match key values 1, 2, and 3. For purposes of the example, assume the generator G1 is aligned with the base match rule, and R2 and R3 match by the base rule. Remember the alignment between the match rule and the generator means if two references match they must generate the same match key; however, if they generate the same match key, they do not necessarily match by the rule.

Also, notice in the scenario of Figure 10.6 that R1 and R2 do not generate the same match key even though they are in the same EIS. Assuming generator

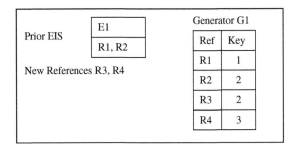

FIGURE 10.6

Simple update scenario.

alignment, this means R1 and R2 do not match by the base rule because they generate different match keys. However, it is important to remember EIS are designed to store equivalent references and not all equivalent references match. For example, suppose these are customer references and the base rule is they must match on name and address. The references R1 and R2 may be for the same customer who has changed address, i.e. the address in R1 does not match the address in R2. If the generator G1 is aligned with the name+address match rule, then it is unlikely the hash value produced by the address in R1 will be the same as the hash value produced by the address in R2; consequently the match keys for R1 and R2 will be different.

Nevertheless, these references are equivalent and therefore belong in the same EIS. This EIS may have been formed in a previous automated ER process that used a different base rule, e.g. match on name and telephone number, or these references may have been asserted together in a manual update process.

Given these assumptions, then a simple capture process on the combined reference would result in three output EIS shown in Figure 10.7 as F1, F2, and F3.

The problem is the result shown in Figure 10.7 is incorrect. Given R1 and R2 are equivalent, and R2 matches R3, then by transitive closure of equivalence, R1, R2, and R3 should all be in the same EIS. In order to solve the problem, the knowledge of prior equivalence must be carried forward into the preresolution transitive closure process. This can be accomplished by treating the Prior EIS identifiers as supplemental match keys, as shown in Figure 10.8.

If the transitive closure of the references is determined based on both the match key and the EIS identifier, then the graph will only have two components {R1, R2, R3} and {R4}. This is because R1 and R2 are connected by the shared identifier E1, and R2 and R3 are connected by the shared match key 2. Thus, R1, R2, and R3 form a single connected component.

In order to complete transformation of the capture process into a proper update process, two more changes must be made. The first is that not only should the Prior EIS identifiers be used to form the transitive closure of the references, but also these identifiers need to be carried forward into the ER process. In other words, when the

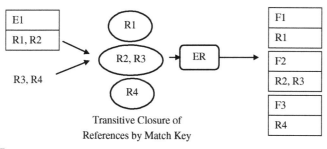

Transitive Closure of
References by Match Key

FIGURE 10.7

Results of capture based on transitive closure of match keys.

Prior EIS	E1		Generator G1		
	R1, R2		Ref	Key	EIS
			R1	1	E1
New References R3, R4			R2	2	E1
			R3	2	-
			R4	3	-

FIGURE 10.8

Simple update scenario with supplemental EIS keys.

ER process sees a reference, it also needs to know if it came from a Prior EIS, and if it does, it needs the Prior EIS identifier value.

Secondly, the matching logic of the ER process needs to be augmented. Regardless of the base match rule, any time two references are determined to have come from the same Prior EIS, they should be considered a match. In other words, the base match rule is supplemented with an assertion rule. Furthermore, the EIS created by the ER process should reuse the Prior EIS identifiers in those cases where the output EIS contains a reference from a Prior EIS.

Figure 10.9 shows the correct result obtained by making these three changes, i.e. adding the Prior EIS identifier as a supplemental match key for transitive closure, carrying the Prior EIS identifier forward into the ER process, and augmenting the ER base rule with the assertion rule for references originating from the same Prior EIS. Note the first output EIS has been labeled with the Prior EIS identifier E1 because it represents the same identity updated with a new reference R3. On the other hand, F1 represents a new identity formed by the reference R4.

In the example shown in Figure 10.8, one component has a reference from a Prior EIS together with a new reference, and the other component has only a new reference. In general there can be four situations that occur:

1. If the component contains only references from one Prior EIS, it means there are no new references that share a match key value with the references in the prior

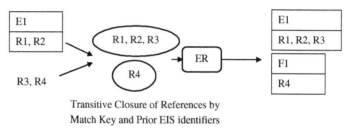

Transitive Closure of References by
Match Key and Prior EIS identifiers

FIGURE 10.9

Correct update of the simple scenario of Figure 10.6.

EIS. The result is that the prior EIS will not be modified by the update process. It will pass through unchanged and retain its original identifier.

2. If the component contains references from one prior EIS along with new references, then there is the potential that the Prior EIS will be updated. However, this is only a potential update because sharing a match key only means a match is possible, not guaranteed. Whether a match actually occurs will not be known until the component goes into the ER process where pairs of references are tested by the match rule. If none of the new references in the component match one of the references from the Prior EIS, then the new references will form one or more new EIS in the output.

3. If the component contains only new input references, then the references will not update any Prior EIS. Instead they will form one or more new EIS in the output that will be assigned new identifiers.

4. It is possible a component could include references from more than one Prior EIS. This would happen if one of the new references shares a match key with references in two or more Prior EIS. If the new reference that shares a match key turns out to actually match the references in the Prior EIS, then by transitive closure of equivalence, the EIS should be merged into a single EIS. The exception to this is when the EIS have been previously split by an assertion. EIS formed by a split assertion process are cross-referenced to prevent them from merging during an automated update process.

THE LARGE COMPONENT AND BIG ENTITY PROBLEMS

Although identity capture and identity update workflows, described in Figures 10.2 and 10.5 respectively, can be operationalized using preresolution transitive closure, they will only work well when the match keys are similar to, or the same as, the matching rule. The problem is not with logic of the system, but in interaction between the software and the data, the root of many data process problems (Zhou, Talburt, & Nelson, 2011). In the case of the preresolution transitive closure algorithm, the problem is the components (blocks) can become very large and overwhelm the capacity of the system even in a large-scale, distributed processing environment.

An example of how components can grow very large was described in Chapter 9 in the section "Dynamic Blocking versus Preresolution Blocking." In the CDI example only two match keys were defined — a first name match key and a last name match key. The transitive closure of these two match keys will likely grow into one component that includes every reference, a result that defeats the purpose of blocking. As described in Chapter 8, in the section "Cluster-to-Cluster Classification," reference equivalence is transitive, but reference matching is not transitive. The clusters formed by the ER process are the transitive closure of the reference-to-reference links made by the matching rules under the assumption that matching references are equivalent references.

However, two references that agree on a match key value are only potential matches and, consequently, are only potentially equivalent. As chains of references connected by common match key values continue to grow in the transitive closure process, the references at the extreme ends of the chain are less likely to match. Again using the first and last name match key example, "James Doe" and "Mary Doe" connect by last name, "Mary Doe" and "Mary Smith" connect by first name. However, "James Doe" and "Mary Doe" at the ends of the chain are not good match candidates even though they will be placed into the same component by the transitive closure of the two match keys. Given a set of match key generators, it is hard to predict how they will interact without actually starting the transitive closure process and observing the growth of the components.

To solve the problem of large components, the transitive closure process and the matching process must somehow be blended together to constrain the growth of the chains that create the large components. There are many different strategies for controlling this growth (Kardes, Konidena, Agarwal, Huff, & Sun, 2013; Kolb, Thor, & Rahm, 2011; Papadakis, Ioannou, Niederée, Palpanas, & Nedjl, 2012). Two described here are postresolution transitive closure and incremental transitive closure.

POSTRESOLUTION TRANSITIVE CLOSURE

The strategy of postresolution transitive closure is to translate each match key into an entity identifier and then perform the transitive closure on the entity identifiers. The process is illustrated in Figure 10.10.

In this process the same set of references (Ref) is resolved multiple times, one time for each match key (M-Kx). Each of these single match-key flows corresponds to Figure 10.1 where blocking takes place using only one match key. However, the ER process uses a full set of matching rules (or at least all of the matching rules that align with the match key), so the clusters formed at the end of each resolution step

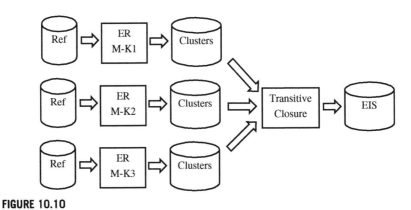

FIGURE 10.10

Postresolution transitive closure.

comprise only equivalent references. In the transitive closure process, the chaining takes place on the entity identifiers assigned to each reference rather than on the match key. Because a shared identifier represents equivalence instead of a possible match, the components formed in the closure process are actually the EIS that would be formed using all of the match keys and matching rules in one ER step. Therefore, the components in the postresolution transitive closure are constrained to be no larger than the largest entity that can be formed by the matching rules.

The advantage of postresolution transitive closure is the maximum size block for each match key is known in advance, and the growth of the components in the final transitive closure is constrained to only chain equivalent references. The disadvantage of this approach is if N is the number of match keys, then the full set of input references must run N times, and the input to the final transitive closure is N times the size of the original set of input references.

INCREMENTAL TRANSITIVE CLOSURE

Another strategy is similar to the update process shown in Figure 10.4. Here the idea is to blend each match key into the transitive closure process with the equivalences found by previously processed match keys. The process is illustrated in Figure 10.11.

The incremental transitive closure process starts in the same way as postresolution transitive closure where the ER process uses only the first match key generator. In the second step, the entity identifier assigned to each reference by the ER process is appended as an additional attribute to each of the original references. In addition, the next match key generator is applied, so each reference has two match keys — the entity identifier from the previous ER process and the match key from the next match key generator. The transitive closure operates on these two keys followed by the full

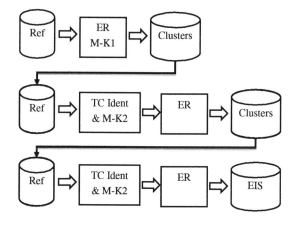

FIGURE 10.11

Incremental transitive closure.

ER process that assigns a new set of entity identifiers. This process continues until all of the match keys have been processed.

The advantage of the incremental process is both the transitive closure process and the ER process can be highly optimized. In the transitive closure process, the bootstrap phase can take advantage of the previous matching. For example, if a group of references sharing the next match key also has the same identifier from the previous ER process, then the group does not need to go through the closure process because the match key is not adding any incremental value. It is not bringing together any references that have not already been determined as equivalent. Similarly in the ER process, any references already determined to be equivalent in a previous ER process (i.e. share the same entity identifier) do not need to be matched again. Matching only needs to take place between references that have different entity identifiers while sharing the same match key.

THE BIG ENTITY PROBLEM

Aside from the problem of large components (blocks), there can also be a problem when some entities cluster a large number of references, so-called big entities. Sometimes a big entity is just a big entity because it really does comprise many references, but sometimes it is caused by data quality issues.

In the former this is sometimes caused by a client system repeatedly sending an entire set of references to the hub rather than only new references. For example, in student tracking the enrollment system may send the records of all students enrolled every day. Although a few of these may be new or changes, the vast majority are the same from day to day. This can be a problem for MDM systems that store every reference. For these cases the system implements logic for recognizing and handling duplicate records of previous inputs such as the duplicate record filter shown in Figure 4.4 in the section "Dedicated MDM Systems" in Chapter 4.

The data quality issues that cause big entities are often related to default values. Instead of leaving fields blank, many data entry systems are written to either automatically provide a default value or default values are entered by the operator because an entry is required by the software. For example, the entry of "LNU" for last name unknown or "999-99-9999" for a missing social security number. The problem is that when these fields are used as identity attributes in the ER process they can sometimes cause big entities to be formed. Again, the answer is usually a special filter that recognizes and handles default values in the matching process.

IDENTITY CAPTURE AND UPDATE FOR ATTRIBUTE-BASED RESOLUTION

Everything described to this point has assumed the ER systems are using record-based architecture, i.e. record-based projection and record-based EIS as described in Chapter 8. In the case of attribute-based resolution, the purely sequential work-flows given so far will not always work correctly. The reason is that, when an EIS is updated to include a new reference, the introduction of the new information may cause the updated EIS to match other references that it did not match prior to the update. This creates a problem for the preresolution transitive closure method. For example, in workflows such as those shown in Figures 10.2 and 10.5, the transitive closure operations are based on shared match keys and, for update, on shared EIS identifiers. However, the match keys used in the closure are generated from the new references and Prior EIS before starting the ER process. In a record-based ER architecture this is not a problem. As long as the match key generators are in alignment with the base matching rule, each connected component will contain all of the new references and Prior EIS that potentially match.

However, in the case of an attribute-based architecture, if a reference updates (i.e. is merged into) an EIS during the resolution process, the updated EIS can potentially generate new match key values that would not have existed before the update. These new, postresolution match key values may connect the updated EIS with other input references or other EIS not included in the component during the transitive closure process because the closure process took place before the EIS was updated.

One solution for the attribute-based resolution problem is to simply iterate the preresolution update workflow as shown in Figure 10.12. This workflow already assumes EIS from previous processes are (or can be) included as part of the input. If any prior EIS are included in the input, then index values are generated for these EIS by the IXG processes before starting the transitive index closure step.

In the case of attribute-based resolution, the first step is the same as for record-based resolution. The set of new references and any prior EIS are the inputs that

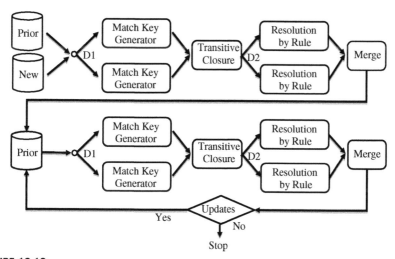

FIGURE 10.12

Iterative update process for attribute-based ER systems.

produce the updated EIS. However, if any EIS were updated during the initial phase, it is necessary to rerun the output EIS as input to a second, iterative step.

In the iterative step, all of the match key values are generated for the EIS followed by the transitive closure process and the resolution process. If during the resolution process some of the EIS are updated, the EIS must be processed again. This is repeated until there are no updates. The same process as shown in Figure 10.12 also works for attribute-based identity capture. The only difference is the input to the first step is only the set of new references, and there is no set of prior EIS.

CONCLUDING REMARKS

MDM for Big Data is difficult but possible using distributed computing. The two biggest problems to solve for distributed MDM are transitive closure and update. If an ER process only requires a single blocking key, then the distributed processing flow is quite simple. The key blocks of a single key partition the references, and the partition segments form natural key-value blocks that can be allocated to distributed processors. However, if more than one blocking key is used, there must be a transitive closure process. The transitive closure can occur at different points in the ER process – prior to matching (preresolution), after matching (postresolution) or intertwined with the matching process (incremental). The choice of strategy will be dictated by the nature of the data. The transitive closure process finds the components of the graph formed from reference nodes connected by edges of shared match key values. One advantage of pretransitive closure is the components of the match key graph represent the final set of clusters when the ER match rules are the same as the match key generation rules (null rules). Otherwise, the match key components must undergo a final resolution at each node using the full and complete set of matching rules. The greatest disadvantage to preresolution transitive closure is that for certain match key combinations it can create very large components too large to process. When this happens, a different strategy for transitive closure must be used.

In order to implement the full CSRUD MDM Life Cycle, the basic process capture process must be modified to allow for update. Update requires that both new references and old (previously clustered) references be input into the preresolution transitive closure process. Moreover, to preserve previous clustering decisions and maintain persistent entity identifiers, the old references must also carry along their previously assigned entity identifiers. This serves two purposes. The first is to retain and reuse the previous identifier whenever possible. The second is to preserve linking decisions from previous update processes. The previously assigned identifiers are input into the transitive closure process and treated by the transitive closure process the same as if they were generated match keys. In the case where the ER process is using an attribute-based project for cluster matching, the entire transitive closure/ER process must be repeated until no new clusters are formed.

ISO Data Quality Standards for Master Data

BACKGROUND

In 2009, the International Organization for Standardization (ISO) approved a set of standards for data quality as it relates to the exchange of master data between organizations and systems. These are primarily defined in the ISO 8000-110, -120, -130, -140, and the ISO 22745-10, -30, and -40 standards. Although these standards were originally inspired by the business of replacement parts cataloging, the standards potentially have a much broader application. The ISO 8000 standards are high-level requirements that do not prescribe any specific syntax or semantics. On the other hand, the ISO 22745 standards are for a specific implementation of the ISO 8000 standards in extensible markup language (XML) and are aimed primarily at parts cataloging and industrial suppliers.

The Electronic Commerce Code Management Association (ECCMA) formed in 1999 has largely guided the development of the ISO 8000 standards. The American National Standards Institute (ANSI) is the U.S. representative to ISO, and ECCMA is the ANSI accredited administrator of the U.S. Technical Advisory Group (TAG) to the ISO Technical Committee (TC) 184 and its subcommittees SC4 and SC5 that deal with industrial data and data interoperability, respectively. Under the leadership of Peter Benson, ECCMA continues to be active in developing new data quality standards for master data and providing ISO 8000 training and certification. This chapter will focus primarily on the ISO 8000-110 standard because it describes the overall framework and guidelines to which specific implementations of the ISO 8000 standard such as ISO 22745 must comply (ANSI, 2009).

DATA QUALITY VERSUS INFORMATION QUALITY

Before getting too deeply into the ISO 8000 standard, it might be helpful to review the basic principles of information and data quality. Even though there is almost universal acceptance that data and information are separate concepts, the same cannot be said for the terms *data quality* and *information quality*. Many noted experts use *data quality* and *information quality* interchangeably with the general definition of "fitness for use (purpose)" (Juran, 1989).

The discussion of the ISO 8000 standard is an occasion where it can be helpful to separate the concepts of data quality and information quality. In 2010, the International Association for Information and Data Quality (IAIDQ) undertook an extensive survey of information professionals to elicit their opinions on the knowledge and skills required to be successful as an information quality professional (Yonke, Walenta, & Talburt, 2012). The survey was part of the development process for the Information Quality Certified Professional (IQCP[sm]) credential (IAIDQ, 2014). The knowledge and skill descriptions gathered from the survey were analyzed and subsequently summarized into six categories, referred to as the IAIDQ Domains of Information Quality. The domains are

1. Information Quality Value and Business Impact
2. Information Quality Strategy and Governance
3. Information Quality Environment and Culture
4. Information Quality Measurement and Improvement
5. Sustaining Information Quality
6. Information Architecture Quality

An important principle emerging from the study was that information quality is primarily about helping organizations maximize the value of their information assets. The survey results provided strong support for the principle that information quality is a business function rather than an information technology responsibility. The first three domains that cover value, business impact, strategy, governance, environment, and culture are primarily business and management issues.

Even though successful MDM depends upon understanding many technical issues, many of which are presented in this book, its adoption is, or should be, a business-driven decision. Furthermore, MDM is generally viewed as a key component of data governance programs, which are themselves seen as essential for organizations to be competitive in an information-based economy.

Only the last three IAIDQ domains deal with measurement, improvement, monitoring, and data architecture, the activities comprising what can be generally defined as data quality. As ISO defines quality as meeting requirements, data quality can be defined as the degree to which data conform to data specifications (data requirements). Information quality includes data quality, but in the larger context it also addresses the business issue of creating value from information and how to manage information as product. Information quality requires information producers to understand the needs of information consumers. Once those are understood, they can be translated into the data specifications that underpin and define data quality.

Some have likened the difference between data and information quality to the classic engineering dilemma: Am I building the thing right? Or am I building the right thing? Building an information product the right way is about conforming to the data specifications for the product, which is the definition of data quality. Building the right thing is creating an information product that provides value to its users, the definition of information quality.

To be successful, data quality and information quality must work hand-in-hand. An organization should constantly align its data quality activities with its information quality activities. Data cleansing, assessment, and monitoring (DQ) should only be undertaken as a solution to a business need (IQ). Conversely, data quality assessments (DQ) can often uncover data problems whose solutions directly impact increased cost, lost revenue, operational risk, compliance default, and many other business issues (IQ).

RELEVANCE TO MDM

The ISO 8000 standards are relevant to MDM for several reasons. The most obvious is the standard is specifically for master data. In particular, the accuracy of ER that supports MDM has a strong dependence on understanding of reference identity attributes and the alignment of identity attributes across different sources.

But beyond that, there is general agreement that data standards are important for data quality but are hard to establish (Redman, 1996). The problem of establishing standards for data is probably best solved first through master data, because there is broad agreement about the things that require master data, at least at the industry level.

As organizations move to exploit Big Data, the need for metadata that describes data in a source becomes even more acute as data are created at an amazing rate of speed. Instead of simply automating manual processes, organizations are now creating new ways of collecting data highly dependent on instrumentation. Without information about provenance, completeness, accuracy, and other data characteristics, it is nearly impossible to understand what the data even represents.

GOALS AND SCOPE OF THE ISO 8000-110 STANDARD

Despite widespread adoption of the ISO 8000-110 standard in certain industries, it is not well understood in many information quality and MDM circles. Even though it is a generally applicable data quality standard for master data, its application has been mainly limited to replacement parts cataloging for the military and petroleum industry. For example, the North Atlantic Treaty Organization (NATO) now requires all parts suppliers to comply with the ISO 22745 version of the ISO 8000-110 standard.

UNAMBIGUOUS AND PORTABLE DATA

The ISO 8000-110 standard has two major goals. The first is to remove as much ambiguity as possible from the exchange of master data. The second is to make master data portable from system-to-system.

The goal of being unambiguous is addressed in the standard through extensive use of semantic encoding. Semantic encoding is the replacement of natural language terms and descriptions with unique identifiers that reference clear and unambiguous data dictionary entries. The standard requires the referenced data dictionary to be easily accessible by both the transmitting and receiving parties.

THE SCOPE OF ISO 8000-110

It is important to understand what the ISO 8000-110 standard covers, and also what it does not cover. At a high level, the ISO 8000-110 is a standard for representing data definitions and specifications for

- Master data in the form of characteristic data that are
- Exchanged between organizations and systems, and that
- Conform to the data specifications that can be validated by computer software.

The latter point about conformance to data requirements puts the ISO 8000-110 standard squarely in the realm of data quality. To place ISO 8000 into the vocabulary of this book, characteristics (also called properties) correspond to the identity attributes of the entities under management. Master data in the form of characteristic data are essentially the entity references described in Chapter 1.

Logically they comprise a set of attribute-value pairs where the attribute name is a characteristic or property of the entity, and the value is a specific instance of the characteristic or property for a particular entity. In a physical implementation the attribute-value pairs for an entity could be represented as a row in a spreadsheet, a record in a file, or XML document. For example, a characteristic of an electric motor might be its operating voltage with a value of 110 volts/AC. Other characteristics might be power consumption in watts or its type of mounting.

Perhaps the most common misunderstanding about the ISO 8000 standards is that they somehow establish certain levels of data quality such as 80% completeness or 95% accuracy for particular master data domains and characteristics. This is not at all the case. Instead, ISO 8000 describes a standard for embedding references to data definitions and data specifications into the master data exchanged between two organizations in such a way that the organizations can automatically validate that the referenced specifications have been met.

The automatic verification of conformance to specifications is an important aspect and innovation of the standard. Although several ISO standards address quality, such as the ISO 9000 family of standards for quality management systems, ISO 8000 specifically requires that conformance to the specifications must be verifiable by a computer (software) rather than by manual audits.

Another important point is the standard applies only to master data in transit between organizations and systems. The standard does not apply to data at rest inside of a system, nor does it provide a way to talk about an MDM system as being ISO 8000-100 compliant.

MOTIVATIONAL EXAMPLE

Consider the following example of how a master data exchange standard could be helpful. Suppose ABC Bank has developed a new financial product it wants to market to its existing customers. However, ABC also wants to target different customers in different ways depending on the customer's characteristics, i.e. through market segmentation. One important characteristic for segmenting its customers is their level of income. ABC has a customer MDM system, but income level is not one of the identity attributes of the MDM IKB nor is it a business attribute maintained by any of the internal clients of the ABC MDM system. In order to segment its customers, ABC needs to acquire this information from third-party data brokers.

ABC approaches two data brokers, DB1 and DB2, about providing income information. ABC sends both DB1 and DB2 a file of its customers' names and addresses. Both brokers match the ABC file against their MDM systems to append income information to ABC's file. When ABC receives the appended files from DB1 and DB2, it finds that both brokers also provided a separate document describing the formats and definitions of the items in the returned data.

When the marketing team examines the returned files, they have to decode the results. For example, when they look at the record for customer John Doe living at 123 Oak St, they find that broker DB1 has appended a code value of "C" for income level. Looking this up in the documentation provided by DB1 they find that "C" corresponds to an income level between $40,000 and $60,000.

The marketing team finds broker DB2 also recognized the same customer, John Doe, in its system and appended the income code "L4". The documentation from DB2 indicates that "L4" corresponds to an income level between $75,000 and $100,000.

After the analysis of the data returned from the two brokers, the marketing team now has two problems. The first problem is that the two brokers are using different income increments for their income brackets. DB1 reports in increments of $20,000, and DB2 in increments of $25,000. The difference creates a problem of how to assign a single income level code to each ABC customer. It turns out there are many cases where DB1 had income information, but DB2 did not, and conversely, cases where DB2 had information, but DB1 did not. If in these cases they simply use the broker's codes, then the income fields contain two different sets of codes. This is a data quality problem known as an overloaded field. At the same time, because the brackets are of different sizes, it is not clear how to translate the two different sets of data broker codes into a single set of meaningful codes for ABC.

A second, more troubling, problem is the case of John Doe where both brokers reported income, but the levels are entirely different. When the marketing team investigates further, they find DB2 levels are consistently higher than those reported by DB1. In an attempt to determine which broker might have more accurate reporting, the marketing team called both brokers to better understand their data collection process. It was during these conversations that ABC uncovered yet another issue. DB1 explained they were collecting individual income, but DB2 was collecting and reporting household income. In other words, the value reported by DB1 was their estimate of the income level for just John Doe himself. The value reported by DB2 not only included John Doe's income, but also his spouse's income, and possibly other family members. Even though both were reporting "income," each broker had a different definition of what that means.

In the context of ISO 8000-110, the master data are the customers of ABC Bank. The characteristic data are name, address, and income level. DB1 and DB2 are both using different semantics (definitions) for income level. In addition, both brokers also use different data syntax specifications, i.e. different bracket sizes and different bracket codes.

What ISO 8000-110 provides as a response to this problem might be a service level agreement (SLA) for data brokers supplying this information to ABC Bank. The ABC SLA might require that it will only buy income data from brokers willing to meet the following conditions and specifications:

1. The income level must represent "individual" income as defined by ABC.
2. The income level codes must be the letters "A", "B", "C", "D", and "E".
3. The income level brackets must be in $25,000 increments starting with $0, with the "E" level representing the bracket $100,000 and above.
4. All of the required specifications are published in an online data dictionary available to the data providers.
5. The transmitted file must include metadata encoded in a data specification language understood by both ABC and the data provider, which will allow ABC to automatically validate conformance to these specifications.

FOUR MAJOR COMPONENTS OF THE ISO 8000-110 STANDARD

The ISO 8000-110 standard has four major parts (ANSI, 2009). These are

Part 1 General Requirements
Part 2 Message Syntax Requirements
Part 3 Semantic Encoding Requirements
Part 4 Conformance to Data Specification

PART 1: GENERAL REQUIREMENTS

According to the ISO 8000-110 standard, a master data message must meet six general requirements.

Part 1.a The master data message shall unambiguously state all information necessary for the receiver to determine its meaning
Part 1.b A formal syntax must be specified using a formal notation
Part 1.c Any data specification required by the message shall be in a computer-interpretable language
Part 1.d The message must explicitly indicate both the data specifications it fulfills and the formal syntax (or syntaxes) to which it complies
Part 1.e It must be possible to check the correctness of the master data message against both its formal syntax and its data specifications
Part 1.f The references within the master data message to data dictionary entries must be in the form of unambiguous identifiers conforming to an internationally recognized scheme.

PART 2: SYNTAX OF THE MESSAGE

The requirements for master data message syntax are:

- The message shall contain in its header a reference to the formal syntax to which it complies.
- The reference shall be an unambiguous identifier for the specific version of the formal syntax used to encode the message.
- The formal syntax shall be available to all interested parties.

The first point is somewhat of a conundrum. The standard says the header of the message must point to the definition of the syntax in which the message is encoded. However, the receiver cannot really locate and understand the part of the message that comprises the header without already knowing the syntax of the message. The reason for this is likely the inspiration for the syntax standard in XML. All XML documents should start with the element

```
<?xml version="1.0"?>
```

declaring itself as an XML document.

There are some other things about message syntax worth noting. First of all, a compliant message can refer to more than one syntax. Again, this likely goes back to XML because there are many data standards defined as restrictions of XML. In other words, the first or underlying syntax can be XML. Then a second level of syntax is added by restricting the document to only use certain element names that have a predefined meaning.

Some examples where this has been done are the Global Justice XML Data Model (GJXML) for the exchange of information among law enforcement agencies and the eXtensible Business Reporting Language (XBRL) adopted by the Securities and Exchange Commission for financial reporting. Both syntaxes provide a common vocabulary through predefined XML tags (elements) and attributes. Most notably, the ISO 22745 standard, which is an ISO 8000 compliant standard, has a syntax that is a restriction of the XML syntax.

Even though XML and many of its restrictions such as XBRL are open and free, free access is not required by the standard. Nothing prevents an organization from developing its own syntax and charging a fee for its use. However, the message syntax must be formally defined in a formal notation (General Requirement Part1.b.), so it is computer readable.

Another point is that the syntax requirement does not preclude encryption of the message because encryption itself is not a syntax. The encryption of master data messages just adds a second layer of translation. Once a message has been created in the ISO 8000 compliant syntax, it can then be encrypted for transmission. The receiver must first decrypt the message, and then interpret the content according to the ISO 8000 compliant syntax.

From a practical standpoint, the formal syntax can be almost any commonly used computer-readable document or dataset format such as XML, comma separated values (CSV) files, spreadsheets, files in fixed-length field record format, ISO 22745-40 conformant messages, and ISO 9735 (EDIFACT) conformant messages.

PART 3: SEMANTIC ENCODING

The semantic encoding requirement is just an elaboration of the General Requirement Part 1.f. (The reference within the master data message to data dictionary entries must be in the form of unambiguous identifiers conforming to an internationally recognized scheme). Because the master data message must be in the form of characteristic data, its basic format of the master data message is a collection of property value pairs.

(property1, value1), (property2, value2), ..., (propertyN, valueN)

In order to meet the semantic encoding requirement, each property must be represented as an unambiguous identifier that references a data dictionary entry. This means that a typical message in the form

Message: (Name, "John Doe"), (Income, "A"), ...

is not compliant. However, a message of the form

Message: (ICTIP.Property.ABC.101, "John Doe"),
(ICTIP.Property.ABC.105, "A"), ...

can be compliant.

First of all, the properties are represented as valid, uniform resource identifiers (URI). This complies with the part of General Requirement Part 1.f requiring identifiers to conform to an internationally recognized scheme. The only question remaining is whether these identifiers reference data dictionary entries.

Minimally, a data dictionary entry must have three parts: a unique identifier, a term (name), and a clear definition. Therefore, for the second set of tuples in the above example to be compliant, there must exist a data dictionary entry in the form

Identifier   ICTIP.Property.ABC.105
Term   Individual_Income_Bracket
Definition   Range of individual income given in increments of $25,000 starting at $0 and coded with single letters "A", "B", "C", "D", and "E" where "A" for [0–25,000], "B" for [25,001–50,000], "C" for [50,001–75,000], "D" for [75,001–100,000], and "E" for [100,000 and above].

One weak point of the standard is that it only specifies the properties be "clear and well-defined," a quite subjective statement. However, this weakness can be offset somewhat by the data specification part of the requirement discussed next.

The standard does note that, in order to understand the meaning of a property value, its data type should always be given. The standard allows for the data type of a property to be given in several ways, including:

- Explicitly in the property value, e.g. quotation marks to indicate string values.
- In the data dictionary definition of the property as in the foregoing example.
- Reference to a data dictionary entry for data type.
- Reference to a data specification entry, which includes a data type specification.

Another requirement is the data dictionary must be accessible to the receiver of the message. Here again the standard allows for flexibility in compliance including:

- Providing a downloadable version of the entire dictionary from the Internet (downloadable free of charge).
- Making the data dictionary interactively accessible through an API available through the Internet (usable free of charge), e.g. web services using SOAP.
- Inserting data dictionary entries needed in the message into the same dataset (message) as the property value. If this last option is used, the data dictionary entries must also be defined and supported by the message syntax.

The standard is also quite flexible as to the overall schema for the message itself. It does not specify what the message syntax should be, only that it must have one that is machine readable. Generally there are two approaches, a single-record schema and a multiple-record schema.

In a single-record scheme the actual instance of a master data reference can mirror its logical structure where the reference is a sequence of property-value pairs. Figure 11.1 shows the structure of a single-record message referencing an external data dictionary.

The problem with representing each instance of a master data reference as a set of property-value pairs is when there are multiple instances of master data references in the same message, and all of the references have the same properties, then the message will contain a large amount of redundant data. There is no need to repeat the property reference for each property value in every record.

Figure 11.2 shows a schema in which each property definition is referenced only one time, and each instance comprises only the set of property values listed in the same order as the property definition references.

PART 4: CONFORMANCE TO DATA SPECIFICATIONS

The conformance to data specifications has three requirements:

1. Each master data message shall contain in its header a reference to the data specification or specifications to which the master data message complies.
2. Each reference shall be in the form of an unambiguous identifier for the specific version of the data specification used to encode the master data message.

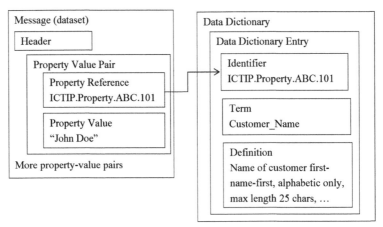

FIGURE 11.1

Single-record message structure.

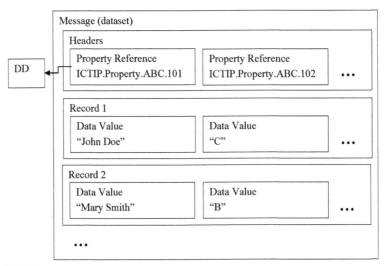

FIGURE 11.2

Multiple-record schema.

3. All referenced data specifications shall be available to all interested parties. If the master data is offered to the public, then all referenced data specifications shall be publicly available. The data specifications should be available at a reasonable cost.

Notice the similarity between this requirement and the semantic encoding requirement. In the semantic encoding requirement, the identifier points to a data dictionary entry that has the three parts — identifier, term, and definition. In the

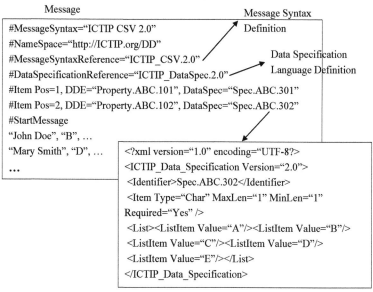

FIGURE 11.3

Message referencing a data specification.

conformance to data specification, the identifier points to a data specification. The main difference is that the definition of the property in the data dictionary is for human interpretation, but a data specification is for machine interpretation.

A data specification is basically a formalization of the data dictionary definition so as to make it actionable. Take as an example the data dictionary entry for Individual_Income_Bracket given earlier. Note the property definition laid out several specifications for this value. For example, it stated the values must be single alphabetic characters "A" through "E" with specific semantics. However, the data dictionary entry is for human reference; its purpose is to assure the sender and receiver have a common understanding of the data elements being transmitted. On the other hand, an ISO 8000 data specification is a set of machine interpretable instructions that will allow the receiver to verify by software whether data values are actually in compliance with the specification.

Take, as an example, the message and supporting references shown in Figure 11.3. The syntax of the message is that the text lines beginning with the "#" character comprise the header (metadata) section of the message. The first line identifies the message syntax. The second line gives the address of a web service where items referenced in the message can be found. The third line is a reference to the location where the complete and formal definition of the message syntax can be found. (Note that neither ICTIP_CSV.2.0 nor ICTIP_DataSpec.2.0 are actual formally defined syntaxes, although they could be. The sections of the message shown in the example are only intended to illustrate the concepts.)

Similarly, the fourth line is a reference to the location where the complete and formal definition of the data specification language can be found. The overall structure of the message follows the multiple-record scheme where each record in the message has two properties defined by the next two "Item" lines. Line five references Property.ABC.101, which is the Customer_Name data dictionary entry. The sixth line references the Individual_Income_Bracket data dictionary entry.

In the message schema shown in Figure 11.3, a property can have more than one identifier. The first identifier is the required reference to a data dictionary entry that defines the property. The second identifier is a reference to a data specification. For example, the Individual_Income_Bracket property references the data specification with the identifier "Spec.ABC.302". The content of the data specification is shown in the inset.

The data specification language used in this example is a (made-up) restricted set of XML elements. Although the formal semantics of the language are not shown here, they can be inferred from the names of the structure and names of the tags. The first part of the specification is given by the <Item> tag. It defines the data type as character, gives the requirement that the value must be present in every record, and the requirement that its length must be exactly one character. The second part of the specification is given by the <List> tag. The <List> tag encloses a set of <ListItem> tags that define the allowable property values "A", "B", "C", "D", and "E".

As long as the receiver has an interpreter for the data specification language, any incoming message with property value specifications written in that language can be verified for compliance with the specification. In this example, the receiver's software could verify all values of the second property (individual income bracket) are present and the value is one of the five character values in the list.

One interesting aspect of the ISO 8000 standard is data specifications are not required. The standard only requires the message contains a reference to the definition of a data specification language "if" data specifications are given. If the message is sent without data specifications other than the property definitions, then the message can still be ISO 8000-110 compliant. This means there are two levels of ISO 8000 compliance, simple and strong.

SIMPLE AND STRONG COMPLIANCE WITH ISO 8000-110

In order for an organization's master data messages to be in compliance with the ISO 8000-110 standard, certain things are mandatory. The primary requirement is the existence of a freely available data dictionary in which every property used in the message is defined. Furthermore, the identifiers must be unique and follow an international standard. The data dictionary entries must have at least an identifier, a term, and a clear definition.

Next, the organization must either define or adopt a formal syntax for its messages. Several existing standards, for example ISO 22745, ISO 13584, and EDI-FACT, define complete message syntaxes. Of these, ISO 22745 is the most flexible, and it is probably the best candidate for introducing ISO 8000 compliance into other MDM domains besides parts cataloging.

Compliance with the syntax and semantic encoding parts of the ISO 8000-110 standard is sufficient for overall compliance because the data specifications are optional. A data specification syntax and language only need to be referenced in the message if the message includes data specifications. Simple compliance to ISO 8000-110 does not include data specifications.

However, simple compliance fails to realize the full power of the standard which lies in the automated verification of the message against data specifications. In order to have strong compliance the organization must either define or adopt a formal data specification language, and insert data specifications in its master data messages.

ISO 22745 INDUSTRIAL SYSTEMS AND INTEGRATION

The ISO 22745 standard defines a specific implementation of ISO 8000-110 that includes both a message syntax and a data specification syntax based on a restriction of XML. ISO 22745 was primarily designed to support parts cataloging. It has been adopted by the North Atlantic Treaty Organization (NATO) for its supply chain management. There are also some commercial software solutions that implement the ISO 22745 standard including the PiLog® Data Quality Solution (PiLog, 2014).

Different parts of the ISO 22745 standard define the components necessary to meet the ISO 8000-110 standard. These include

- ISO 22745-10:2010(E) — Open Technical Dictionary (OTD) to meet data dictionary requirements of ISO 8000-110.
- ISO 22745-30:2009(E) — Identification Guide (IG) to meet the machine readable data specification language of ISO 8000.
- ISO 22745-40:2010(E) — Master data representation to meet the message syntax of ISO 8000.

The documentation of these standards is much lengthier and much more detailed than for the basic ISO 8000 framework. This is because these standards must formally define the data dictionary syntax, the message syntax, and the data specification syntax and logic.

BEYOND ISO 8000-110

After the initial development of the ISO 8000-110 standard, several smaller parts were added. The new parts of the standard try to address data quality dimensions difficult to put into a data specification language. Take, as an example, the property Individual_Income_Bracket, defined earlier. It is easy to see how a machine-readable data specification could be designed that would verify that the values for this property are only the characters "A" through "E" such as the specification instructions illustrated in Figure 11.3.

However, it is less clear how to verify that when the value "A" is used, the actual income of the customer is between $0 and $25,000, as required by the definition. This would require in the field verification and represent a measure of accuracy. Accuracy cannot be verified by applying a rule to the property value. Accuracy requires verification against the primary source, or against other records verified against the primary source, so-called "golden records." In short, data specifications are a powerful way to perform data validation, but they will not work for all data requirements.

PART 120: PROVENANCE

In its broadest sense, data provenance is the history of a data item from the time of its creation to the present. Provenance is a term commonly used in the art world, something art and auction galleries must verify, especially for high-value, historical works. Here provenance is being able to account for and scrupulously document all of the owners from the original artist to the present day without any gaps. The same concept is used in the court system where the chain of custody must be established for any physical evidence before it can be introduced at trial.

The ISO 8000-120 standard does not go quite that far. It basically looks at the most recent owner of the data. At the data element level, the standard requires the specification of two things:

1. When the data was extracted from the database.
2. The owner of the database.

PART 130: ACCURACY

As stated earlier, accuracy is a measure of how closely data represent the state of the real world at any given time. Usually, but not always, it means the current state of the world. For example, accuracy for customer address is usually understood to be the current address of the customer. However, previous addresses can be historically correct, i.e. correct at the time, but are no longer current. Because it relies on verification, rather than rule validation, accuracy is perhaps the most difficult of all the data quality dimensions to measure.

The ISO 8000 approach to accuracy is as follows. At the data elements level:

- The organization claiming the accuracy must be identified.
- The accuracy can either be covered by a warranty or be asserted.
  - If covered by warranty, the place where the warranty statement and terms can be found must be provided
  - If the accuracy is asserted, the location where a description of the assertion that explains why the data are believed to accurate must be provided.

PART 140: COMPLETENESS

Completeness is a data quality measure of the amount of data provided in proportion to the amount of data possible. Completeness can be measured at several levels. The two most common are at the population or data set level and the depth of completeness at the record level. For example, in a customer MDM system, population completeness would be the proportion of all customers of the company who are actually represented in the system and under management. On the other hand, at the depth or record level the question might be for the 20 attributes collected for each customer and what proportion of these values are actually present.

It is important to note here that a missing value is not necessarily a null value. Certainly a null value is a missing value, but a value can also be missing because it is an empty string, a blank value, or a placeholder value.

The ISO 8000 approach to completeness is simply to require that the organization claiming completeness must be identified.

CONCLUDING REMARKS

Whether ISO 8000 compliance produces value for an organization will depend on several factors. One of these factors is the position of the organization with respect to being primarily a data consumer or a data provider. The ISO 8000 was born from a consumer perspective, i.e. the need for a data consumer to have a systematic way of requisitioning equivalent replacement parts from multiple suppliers.

The lack of clear understanding about the syntax, semantics, and specifications of datasets exchanged between data providers and data consumers is a common problem in many industries and one of the primary motivations for MDM in the first place. Many organizations receive data from numerous sources and spend inordinate amounts of time and effort to rationalize the sources into the same format and semantics. If the data are references to real-world entities, then there is the further process of entity resolution.

Just as in the example of the ABC Bank at the beginning of this chapter, publishing data definitions and specifications, requiring data suppliers to conform to those definitions and specifications, and being able to verify their compliance automatically, could result in enormous cost savings and increased productivity. Common standards for these functions also helps to solve the problem of how to structure service level agreements that govern data quality requirements for data acquired from third parties (Caballero et al., 2014).

One consideration in adopting the ISO standards is how much initial time and effort it will take to create the definitions and specifications. A second is whether the organization has enough influence or authority to require that their suppliers conform to their data quality specifications.

From the data producer viewpoint, compliance to ISO 8000 can make the data products of an organization easier to use and understand. This could in turn create a competitive advantage and increased market share. Consumers of the information will know how to interpret the data and understand exactly what is in it.

Some Commonly Used ER Comparators

EXACT MATCH AND STANDARDIZATION

The most fundamental and most commonly used similarity is an exact match between two values. Exact match requires both values to be the same according to their data type, i.e. the same numeric value, the same date, or the same string.

In the case of string values, exact match is a demanding requirement. Two strings will only be exactly the same if they comprise exactly the same characters (by internal character code) in exactly the same order. For example, while "JOHN" and "JOHN" are exact string matches, the strings "JOHN" and "John" are not. The character code for an upper case "O" is different from the character code for a lower case "o". The same is true for the letters "H" and "N" as well.

Similarly, the strings "JOHN R. DOE" and "JOHN R DOE" are not an exact match because the first string contains a period (".") and the second does not. However, in both cases most people would consider these a match in the sense that they essentially represent the same name value. For this reason, when string values are compared they generally are subject to some alteration or standardization so that two strings representing the same underlying value will also be the same string value. The two examples given here are two of the most common standardizations used for string values, i.e. standardizing letter case and removing punctuation.

WHERE TO STANDARDIZE

There are two schools of thought on standardization of values. The first and most common is that standardization should be done in a separate process prior to the ER matching process. The other is that the comparison operators themselves should compensate for the differences. There are pros and cons to each approach. Preprocess standardization has the advantage that each value is transformed one time rather than having to be transformed each time it is used in a match operation. Preprocess standardization also often makes it easier to apply more complex transformations than having to build these into the code of the comparator logic.

However, there are two disadvantages to preprocess standardization. The first is that it creates a dependency between preprocess and the ensuing ER process. For the same set of input references, the ER process may deliver different results when there are changes to the standardization. This makes it difficult to understand the true action of the matching rules without first understanding preprocess standardization. Often this information is in two different places and may even be administered by different groups. If the standardization is built into the matching rules, then it is easier to manage the dependency between standardization and matching.

A second reason why it may be better to standardize in the comparator is a fundamental rule of data management — always keep the original data. For example, if the EIS is built from standardized data, then it is more difficult to know the true states of the original references from which the EIS was constructed.

OVERCOMING VARIATION IN STRING VALUES

So regardless of where standardization takes place, in preprocess or in the comparator logic, the goal is to overcome variations between two representations of the same underlying value. This is primarily a problem with values represented as string or character data types. Seven of the most common types of variation are:

1. Format variation — the characters that represent the value are the same, but they are couched in different formats. For example, two telephone numbers with exactly the same 10-digit sequence, but represented as "(012) 345-6789" versus "012.345.6789". This also includes standardizing letter casing and spacing.
2. Damaged value — even after removing format variation, the values are slightly different strings due to some type of input or process error that has removed, changed, inserted, or transposed characters. For example, "Johnson" versus "Jhonson", a common typing error.
3. Alias value — these are strings that can be entirely different, but semantically they mean the same thing. This is common with names such as "Robert" and "Bob" but also common in addresses with the use of abbreviations such as "Av" for "Avenue" or "MLK" for "Martin Luther King".
4. Phonetic variation — these are strings that when pronounced as words have a similar sound. Phonetic variations often occur when data are transcribed from speech such as on orders taken by telephone. For example, "Christy" versus "Kristi".
5. Alternate value — these are cases where there can be more than one valid value to represent an attribute. They often occur as the result of a name or address change or different usages in different contexts. For example, "Jane Doe" becomes "Jane Smith" after marriage.
6. Misfielding — this variation occurs when valid values are misclassified by attribute name. Common examples are name reversals where the first name value has been recorded in the last name field, and the last name value in the first name field. Similar misfielding often occurs with home telephone number versus work telephone number.
7. Missing value — there is no meaningful value present. They may be missing because the value is null, empty, or blank. However, a missing value can also

occur when a placeholder value is used to overcome data entry restrictions. For example, if telephone number is a required entry, but was not known when the data were recorded, the person entering the information may simply enter a value like "999-999-9999" in order to proceed to the next screen. Even though missing values cannot be easily overcome, it is important to know which attributes have missing values and to what degree the values are missing. Placeholder values can be harder to detect and can do more to lower matching accuracy than blank values. The reason is because they can cause a match between identity attributes when in fact they should not match and lead to false positive links.

SCANNING COMPARATORS

Scanning comparators are used to address format variations. Scanning comparators examine a string character-by-character looking for particular characters that should be changed or removed. For example, a comparator like ExactIgnoreCase will search for and replace each lower-case letter in a string with its corresponding upper-case character before comparing the two strings. By using the ExactIgnoreCase comparator the example strings "JOHN" and "John" will match.

Sometimes more sophisticated scanning comparators are used that can perform several types of operations in the same scan of the string. For example, the Char-Scan(A, B, C) comparator that takes three arguments where

A   Indicates the type of characters to retain, but omitting all other characters, e.g. letters, digits, letters & digits, etc.
B   Indicates the maximum number of characters to keep
C   Indicates when retaining letters whether lower-case letters should be converted to the corresponding upper-case character, or to keep them in their original case

For example, CharScan(Letters, All, ToUpper) would overcome the variation between the strings "John R. Doe" and "JOHN R DOE" by ignoring the blanks and the period while also changing the lower-case letters to upper-case. The final comparison would be between "JOHNRDOE" and "JOHNRDOE", resulting in an exact match.

It is important to note the transformations performed by the comparator do not change the original values of the string. They only create proxy strings, sometimes called hash values, for comparison purposes. The hashed values are discarded after the final comparison is made.

APPROXIMATE STRING MATCH COMPARATORS

To get beyond format variation and overcome damaged values, more sophisticated comparators are required. There is a large family of approximate string matching (ASM) comparators that judge the similarity between two strings in terms of the number or order of shared characters.

TRANSPOSE

One of the simplest ASM comparators is Transpose. The Transpose comparator returns a match signal whenever two strings differ by the transposition (reversal) of two adjacent characters. The transposition of two characters is a common keyboard entry error. For example, the strings "Jhon" and "John" will be considered a match by the Transpose comparator.

One could argue that if two strings are identical, the Transpose should also consider them a match as well. However, this is generally not the case. Most comparators that look for special conditions such as transposition generally do not match strings where the condition is not present. This is particularly true for systems using Boolean rules. The reason is that it allows the rule designer to isolate particular match conditions to specific rules.

Take, as an example, a situation where an exact match on the values of two attributes A and B is sufficient to link the references. However, it may be observed some false negatives are created by this rule because some values of A that should match vary by transposition. In order to convert these cases to true positives a second rule is added that requires a transposition match on the A attribute values match while still requiring an exact match on the values of B. However, because the transposition is a "softer" match it could possibly cause a false positive if, by chance, two different values of A that should not match differ by a transposition not the result of a typing error. To compensate, the second rule may be augmented by requiring some level of match on a third attribute C. The two rules allow the rule designer to separate these two issues, one where both A and B are an exact match, and the other where B is exact and A is a transposition match.

INITIAL MATCH

Another useful ASM for name matching is the Initial match. Like the transposition it only creates a match in specific circumstances. Generally the condition for an Initial match is there are two strings where one string comprises a single character and the other string comprises two or more characters. If the single character in the first string is the same as the first character of the second string, then the two strings are considered an Initial match.

Again, like transposition it does not signal match in other situations, such as when two names start with the same character or when both strings are a single character. For example, the strings "J" and "John" would match by Initial, but "Jon" and "John" would not.

LEVENSHTEIN EDIT COMPARATOR

Perhaps one of the most famous and used ASM comparators is based on the Levenshtein edit distance (Levenshtein, 1966). The Levenshtein edit distance between two strings is the minimum number of basic character operations required to transform one string into the other. Typically, the allowable operations are inserting a character, deleting a character, and replacing (substituting) a character, although some versions also allow transposing two adjacent characters. For example, the string "ALISA" and "ALYSSA" are separated by an edit distance of 2 because it requires at least two transformations to transform one string into the other. For example, starting with "ALISA", one transformation is replacing "I" with "Y" giving "ALYSA". The second transformation is to insert an "S" giving "ALYSSA".

By its definition the Levenshtein edit distance between two strings cannot exceed the length of the longest string. If L(A, B) represents the Levenshtein edit distance between two strings A and B, then the normalized edit distance NL can be calculated as (Christen, 2006):

$$NL(A, \ B) = 1 - \left(\frac{L(A, \ B)}{\max\{L_A, \ L_B\}} \right)$$

MAXIMUM Q-GRAM

Another family of ASM algorithms focuses on the ordering of the characters. These are called **q-Gram** or **n-Gram** algorithms. A q-Gram is a fixed sequence of characters of length q. For example, "ARM" is a 3-gram. The simplest q-Gram comparator is the Maximum q-Gram comparator. It is simply the length of the longest substring (q-Gram) shared by both strings. It is also normalized by dividing by the length of the longest string.

For example, the Maximum q-Gram similarity between "CRANSTON" and "RANSOM" is 0.5. The longest shared substring is "RANS" with length 4. The longer string "CRANSTON" has length 8, hence the Maximum q-Gram similarity is 4/8 or 0.50.

q-GRAM TETRAHEDRAL RATIO

The principle of q-Gram similarity between two strings can be extended in several ways. One way is to count the number of characters in all shared q-Grams. The more q-Grams they share, the more similar the strings. Consider the two strings "JULIE" and "JULES". These two strings share four 1-Grams, the single letters "J", "U", "L", and "E". They also share two 2-Grams of "JU" and "UL" and one 3-Gram of "JUL". Whereas the Maximum q-Gram only counts the longest, in this case 3, the q-Gram Tetrahedral Ratio (qTR) algorithm (Holland & Talburt, 2010b) scores the number of character as shared q-Grams against the total number possible. The total number of characters contained in all q-Grams (substrings) of a string of length N is the tetrahedral number of N given by:

$$T_N = \frac{N \cdot (N + 1) \cdot (N + 2)}{6}$$

In the example above, the string "JULIE" of length 5 has 15 possible substrings containing a total of 35 characters, i.e. $T_N = 35$. As noted above, "JULIE" shares 7 of these q-Grams with "JULES" with a total of 10 characters, so the q-Gram Tetrahedral Ratio of "JULIE" with respect to "JULES" gives

$$qTR = \frac{10}{35} = 0.286$$

In the case where the strings being compared are of different lengths, then the calculation of qTR will depend upon which string is selected to determine the tetrahedral number in the denominator of the ratio. To address these cases and make the qTR measure symmetric, an adjusted qTR measure is defined as the weighted average of the two directional measures (Holland & Talburt, 2010b). If N represents the length of the first string, M the length of the second, and Q the number of q-Grams shared by the two strings, then the adjusted qTR is given by

$$qTR_{adj} = Q \cdot \left(\frac{M \cdot T_N + N \cdot T_M}{T_N \cdot T_M \cdot (M + N)} \right)$$

JARO STRING COMPARATOR

Another q-Gram variant is the Jaro String Comparator (Jaro, 1989). It considers the number of characters in common between two strings and the number of character transpositions. If A and B represent two strings with at least one character in common, then the Jaro similarity is given by

$$J(A, B) = W_1 \cdot \frac{C}{L_A} + W_2 \cdot \frac{C}{L_B} + W_3 \cdot \frac{(C - T)}{C}$$

where W_1, W_2, W_3 are the weights assigned to the first string, second string, and transpositions, respectively, and where $W_1 + W_2 + W_3 = 1$, where C is the common character count, T is the number of transpositions, and L_A and L_B are the lengths of the two strings. For example, the strings "SHAKLER" and "SHAKEL" have 6 characters in common and one transposition of "LE" to "EL". Assuming three equal weights of $\{1/3\}$ each, the Jaro Similarity between these strings would be

$$J(SHAKLER, SHAKEL) = \frac{1}{3} \cdot \frac{6}{7} + \frac{1}{3} \cdot \frac{6}{6} + \frac{1}{3} \cdot \frac{(6 - 1)}{6} = 0.897$$

Some implementations of the algorithm not only require sharing the same sequence of q characters, but also require that the shared sequences both start at the same or almost the same position in the strings. These types of q-Grams are called **positional q-Grams**.

JARO-WINKLER COMPARATOR

The Jaro-Winkler Comparator (Winkler, 1999) is an example of a positional q-Gram algorithm. The Jaro-Winkler comparator is a modification of the Jaro Comparator that gives additional weight to the agreements on the first four characters of the two strings. If N represents the number of the first four characters that agree, then the Jaro-Winker similarity is calculated as

$$W(A, B) = J(A, B) + 0.1 \cdot N \cdot (1 - J(A, B))$$

In the example of "SHAKLER" and "SHAKEL" the value N is 4. The Jaro-Winkler similarity of these two strings is calculated by

$$W(SHAKLER, SHAKEL) = 0.897 + 0.1 \cdot 4 \cdot (1 - 0.897) = 0.938$$

The Transpose, Initial, Levenshtein, Maximum Length q-Gram, Tetrahedral Ratio, Jaro, and Jaro-Winkler are only a few examples of the many ASM algorithms that are used in ER matching processes. A quick search of the Internet using the keywords "approximate string matching" will reveal many others along with details of their implementation.

TOKEN AND MULTIVALUED COMPARATORS

Most of the ASM comparators are based on comparing a single string value to another string value. However, there are many cases where a string represents multiple values — for example, a name field given as "John R. Doe". Rather than representing a single value, this string contains several values: a first name value, a middle name value, and a last name value. The substrings of "John R. Doe" separated by spaces or punctuation are called tokens. In the example there are three tokens: "John", "R" and "Doe".

JACCARD COEFFICIENT

The Jaccard Coefficient is perhaps the most canonical similarity measure. In its most general form, it compares the similarity of two sets P and Q with the following formula:

$$Jaccard(P, Q) = \frac{|P \cap Q|}{|P \cup Q|}$$

The Jaccard Coefficient can be applied at two levels. For multivalued fields, such as an address or complete name, P and Q can be sets of tokens. For example, the Jaccard Coefficient for values "Dr Sean Doe" and "John Sean Doe" is calculated by first tokenizing the two fields.

$$Jaccard(\text{Dr Ted Doe, John Ted Doe}) = \frac{|\{\text{Dr, Ted, Doe}\} \cap \{\text{John, Ted, Doe}\}|}{|\{\text{Dr, Ted, Doe}\} \cup \{\text{John, Ted, Doe}\}|}$$
$$= \frac{2}{4} = 0.5$$

The Jaccard Coefficient can also be applied at the character level. For example,

$$Jaccard(\text{John, Josh}) = \frac{|\{J, o, h, n\} \cap \{J, o, s, h\}|}{|\{J, o, h, n\} \cup \{J, o, s, h\}|} = \frac{3}{5} = 0.6$$

The advantage of the Jaccard Coefficient for token comparison is it is not sensitive to word order because it considers only whether a token exists in a string, not at which position (Naumann & Herschel, 2010).

tf-idf COSINE SIMILARITY

The term frequency-inverse document frequency (tf-idf) and the cosine similarity are often used in information retrieval and duplicate detection.

Given a finite domain denoted as D, the d distinct terms that appear in any string in D are called d dimensions. The vectors made out of the terms in D have d dimensions. Consider the example taken from Naumann & Herschel (2010).

In Table A.1, the number of distinct terms is 19. Therefore, it is a 19-dimensional domain. Each entry is a candidate. Assuming a term t appears in the value v of an object description of a candidate c, its term frequency is denoted as $tf(t, c)$. For example, $tf(\text{"Insurance"}, c4) = 1.0$.

The inverse document frequency of a token t occurring in the object description of a candidate c represented as $idf(t, c)$ is defined as

$$idf(t,c) = \frac{\text{Total Number of Candidates}}{\text{The Number of Candidates Containing term } t}$$

For example in Table A.1, the total number of candidates is 10 and there are 6 candidates containing the term "Insurance", therefore $idf(\text{"Insurance"}, c4) = 10/6 = 1.67$.

The *tf-idf* score combines both the term frequency and the inverse document frequency into a single score, using the following formula:

$$tf - idf(t,c) = \log(tf(t,c) + 1) \cdot \log(idf(t,c))$$

Table A.1 Sample Table Listing Insurance Companies

CID	Name
c1	Allstate
c2	American Automobile Association
c3	American National Insurance Company
c4	Farmers Insurance
c5	GEICO
c6	John Hancock Insurance
c7	Liberty Insurance
c8	Mutual of America Life Insurance
c9	Safeway Insurance Group
c10	Westfield

Thus

$$tf - idf(\text{Insurance}, c4) = 0.07$$

$$tf - idf(\text{Farmers}, c4) = 0.30$$

$$tf - idf(\text{Liberty}, c7) = 0.30$$

The other part of *tf-idf* cosine similarity is the final computation of cosine similarity. In general, given two *n*-dimensional vectors *V* and *W*, the cosine similarity is the cosine of the angle α between the two vectors as

$$\text{Cosine Similarity}(V, \ W) = \cos(\alpha) = \frac{V \cdot W}{\|V\| \cdot \|W\|}$$

where

$$V \cdot W = \sum_{j=1}^{n} v_j \cdot w_j$$

$$\|V\| = \text{Length of vector } V = [v_1, v_2, v_3, \ldots] = \sqrt{v_1^2 + v_2^2 + v_3^2 + \ldots}$$

Going back to the example of Table A.1, there are 19 distinct terms across the 10 candidates. If the 19 terms are given fixed order from 1 to 19, then each candidate *C* can be considered a 19-dimensional vector V_C where

$$V_C = [v_1, v_2, \ v_3, \ldots, v_{19}]$$

$$v_j = \begin{bmatrix} 0 & \text{if } C \text{ does not contain term } t_j \\ tf - idf(t_j, C) & \text{if } C \text{ contains term } t_j \end{bmatrix}$$

For example, for candidate C4 in Table A.1, its vector would be

$$V_{C4} = [0, 0, 0, 0, 0, 0.07, 0, 0.30, 0, 0, 0, 0, 0, 0, 0, 0, 0, 0, 0]$$

where "Insurance" is the 6th term and "Farmers" is the 8th term. Therefore, using the Cosine Similarity,

$$\text{Cosine Similarity}(V_{C4}, V_{C7}) = \frac{0.07^2}{\left(\sqrt{0.07^2 + 0.30^2}\right)^2} = 0.05$$

ALIGNMENT COMPARATOR FOR MULTI-VALUED ATTRIBUTES

Originally developed for comparing author lists of publications (Mazzucchi-Augel & Ceballos, 2014), the Alignment Comparator for Multi-valued Attributes (ACMA) can also be adapted to the more general problem of comparing unstructured fields (Mazzucchi-Augel, 2014).

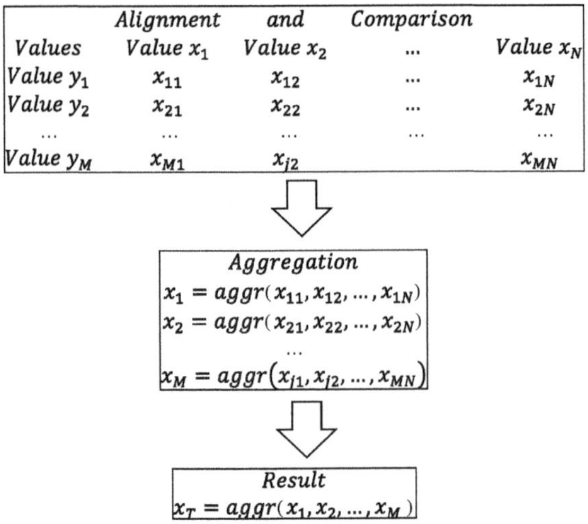

	Alignment	*and*	*Comparison*	
Values	*Value x_1*	*Value x_2*	...	*Value x_N*
Value y_1	x_{11}	x_{12}	...	x_{1N}
Value y_2	x_{21}	x_{22}	...	x_{2N}
...	...	...	...	...
Value y_M	x_{M1}	x_{j2}		x_{MN}

$$\Downarrow$$

Aggregation
$$x_1 = aggr(x_{11}, x_{12}, ..., x_{1N})$$
$$x_2 = aggr(x_{21}, x_{22}, ..., x_{2N})$$
$$...$$
$$x_M = aggr(x_{j1}, x_{j2}, ..., x_{MN})$$

$$\Downarrow$$

Result
$$x_T = aggr(x_1, x_2, ..., x_M)$$

FIGURE A.1

ACMA comparator framework.

The general framework for ACMA is shown in Figure A.1.

Given two multivalued fields where the first field contains M values and the second field contains N values, the starting point for ACMA is an $M \times N$ matrix where each row is labeled by one value of the first multivalued field and each column is labeled by one value of the second multivalued field. Each cell of the $M \times N$ matrix is populated with the rating (a number in the interval [0, 1]) that represents the similarity between the corresponding row and column values.

In the first step, the similarity ratings in each row are aggregated into a single similarity rating. In the second step, the aggregated row similarity ratings are aggregated into a final similarity rating. The framework is flexible and can be customized at every step. Customization points include the method for determining the similarity rating between two values, the method of row aggregation, and the method of final aggregation.

For value similarity at the cell level, a single similarity function can be used such as the normalized Levenshtein Edit Distance. Comparators are typically applied after some standardization of the values has been applied, such as removal of punctuation, upper casing, and standard spacing. Instead of one comparator, the framework allows for several comparators to be used to calculate one cell rating. For example, Jaro-Winkler and Maximum q-Gram, which each produce a similarity rating. Reducing multiple ratings to a single cell rating provides another degree of freedom as to how these ratings will be combined — for example, maximum rating, average, or root mean square (RMS) of the ratings.

The simplest form of aggregation is to simply compute the average of all of the similarity ratings, i.e.

$$x_T = \frac{\sum_{i=1}^{M}\sum_{j=1}^{N} x_{ij}}{M \cdot N}$$

Table A.2 Average Row-Column Maxima by Row Order Traversal

Authors	Khan, M.J.	Maroof, S.A.	Uzair, M.	Khan, M.T.
Uzair, M.	0.48	0.42	1.00	
Maroof, S.A.	0.36	1.00		
Khan, M.J.	1.00			
Khan, M.Y.				0.88

An alternate strategy that often works better when $M \neq N$ is to calculate the overall rating as the average of the row-column maxima. This is an iterative process starting with the largest cell rating, then the next largest cell rating not in the same row or column of the first rating, then the next largest cell rating not in the same row or column of either of the previous two ratings, and so on. If $M \geq N$, then the iteration will produce N cell ratings. Again, the final rating can be calculated as the maximum rating, the average of the N ratings, or the RMS of ratings.

Table A.2 shows a variation of the row-column maxima algorithm comparing author names. To minimize the number of comparisons, the algorithm uses a row-order traversal of the matrix. The algorithm proceeds as follows. Start by assigning the shorter of the two lists of values as row labels. Starting with the first row, calculate the similarity rating for each cell in the row in order. If a rating exceeds a predefined match threshold (e.g. 0.80), stop the comparisons in the row and select that value as the row maximum. Remove the column of the row maximum from further consideration. Go to the next row and follow the same procedure, but do not make any comparisons in columns previously removed from consideration.

In Table A.2, three comparisons were made before reaching the 0.80 threshold. This removes Row 1 and Column 3 from further consideration. In Row 2, the process stops at Column 2, and in Row 3 it stops at Column 1. This leaves Column 4 as the only comparison to be made in Row 4. The final rating for the entire matrix is 0.97, the average of row-column maxima of 1.0, 1.0, 1.0, and 0.88.

ALIAS COMPARATORS

Approximate semantic matching is when the similarity between strings is based upon their linguistic meaning rather than their character structure. For example, in the English language the name "JIM" is well-known and well-understood as an alternate name (nickname) for the name "JAMES". Most probabilistic matching schemes for names incorporate some type of nickname or alias table to handle these situations. The problem is the mapping of names to nicknames is not one-to-one. For example, the name "HARRY" could be a nickname for the name "HENRY", the name "HAROLD", or perhaps not a nickname at all, i.e. the birth name was given as "HARRY".

Semantic similarity is even more problematic when dealing with business names. For example, the determination that "TOWING AND RECOVERY" represents the same business activity as "WRECKER SERVICE" is difficult to automate. The methods and techniques for making these discoveries fall into the area of research called **latent semantic analysis** (Deaton, Doan, Schweiger, 2010; Landauer, Foltz, & Laham, 1998).

PHONETIC COMPARATORS
SOUNDEX COMPARATOR

One of the first derived match codes schemes is called the Soundex algorithm. It was first patented in 1918 (Odell & Russell, 1918) and was used in the 1930s as a manual process to match records in the Social Security Administration (Herzog et al., 2007). The name Soundex comes from the combination of the words "Sound" and "Indexing" because it attempts to recognize both the syntactic and phonetic similarity between two names. As with most approximate matching, there are many variations resulting from the adaptation of the algorithm to different applications. The algorithm presented here is from Herzog et al. (2007) using the name "Checker":

1. Capitalize all letters and drop punctuation → CHECKER
2. Remove the letters A, E, I, O, U, H, W, and Y after the first letter → CCKR
3. Keep first letter but replace the other letters by digits according to the coding {B, F, P, V} replace with 1, {C, G, J, K, Q, S, X, Z} replace with 2, {D, T} replace with 3, {L} replace with 4, {M, N} replace with 5, and {R} replace with 6 → C226
4. Replace consecutive sequences of the same digit with a single digit if the letters they represent were originally next to each other in the name or separated by H or W → C26 (because the 22 comes from letters CK that were next to each other)
5. If the result is longer than 4 characters total, drop digits at the end to make it 4 characters long. If the result is less than 4 characters, add zeros at the end to make it 4 characters long → C260

Using this same algorithm the name "John" produces the Soundex match code value J500. By using these match codes as proxies for the attribute values, the name "John Checker" would be matches to any other names that produce the same match codes such as "Jon Cecker".

References

Abu-Halimeh, A., Pullen, D., Tudoreanu, M.E., 2013. Perception of value-added through a visual join operation. 2013 International Conference on Information Quality. November 7–9, 2013, Little Rock, AR, pp. 326–337.

ANSI, 2009. Data quality part 110: Master data: Exchange of characteristic data: Syntax, semantic encoding, and conformance to data specification. International Standard ISO 8000-11:2009(E) First edition 2009-11-15. Downloaded from ansi.org on January 3, 2012.

Baxter, R., Christen, P., Churches, T., 2003. A comparison of fast blocking methods for record linkage. First Workshop on Data Cleaning, Record Linkage, and Object Consolidation. KDD-2003, Washington, DC, August 24–27, 2013.

Benjelloun, O., Garcia-Molina, H., Menestrina, D., Su, Q., Whang, S.E., Widom, J., 2009. Swoosh: A generic approach to entity resolution. The VLDB Journal 18 (1), 255–276.

Benjelloun, O., Garcia-Molina, H., Su, Q., Widom, J., 2005. Swoosh: A Generic Approach to Entity Resolution. Stanford InfoLab Technical Report. dbpubs.stanford.edu/pub/2005-5.

Berson, A., Dubov, L., 2011. Master data management and data governance. McGraw Hill, New York, NY.

Bianco, G.D., Galante, R., Heuser, C.A., 2011. A fast approach for parallel deduplication on multicore processors. SAC'11, March 21–25, 2011, TaiChung, Taiwan.

Borgman, C., Siegfried, S., 1992. Getty's Synoname™ and its cousins: A survey of applications of personal name-matching algorithms. Journal of the American Society for Information Science 43 (7), 459–476.

Caballero, I., Parody, L., Bermejo, I., Lopez, T.G., Gasca, R., Piattini, M., 2014. Service level agreement for data quality governed by ISO 8000-1X0. The 19th International Conference on Information and Data Quality (ICIQ-2014). Xi'an, China, August 1–3, 2014, pp. 114–127.

Center for Identity, 2014. Identity threat assessment and prediction (ITAP). Available at: http://identity.utexas.edu/research/model.

Cervo, D., Allen, M., 2011. Master data management in practice: Achieving true customer MDM. Wiley.

Chen, C., Hanna, J., Talburt, J.R., Brochhausen, M., Hogan, W.R., 2013a. A demonstration of entity identity information management applied to demographic data in a referent tracking system. International Conference on Biomedical Ontology (ICBO 2013). Montreal, Canada, July 7–12, 2013, pp. 136–137.

Chen, C., Mohammed, M., Talburt, J.R., 2013b. Visualization tools for results of entity resolution. The 2013 International Conference on Information and Knowledge Engineering (IKE'13). Las Vegas, Nevada, July 22–25, 2013, CSREA Press, pp. 87–91.

Chiang, C., Talburt, J., Wu, N., Pierce, E., Heien, C., Gulley, E., Moore, J., 2008. A case study in partial parsing unstructured text. Fifth International Conference on Information Technology: New Generations. Las Vegas, NV, IEEE Press, pp. 447–452.

Christen, P., 2006. A comparison of personal name matching: techniques and practical issues. Sixth IEEE International Conference on Data Mining Workshops, pp. 290–294.

Christen, P., 2008. Febrl − A freely available record linkage system with a graphical user interface. Proceedings of the Australian Workshop on Health Data and Knowledge

Management (HDKM). Conferences in Research and Practice in Information Technology (CRPIT), Wollongong, Australia, January 2008, vol. 80.

Christen, P., 2012. Data matching: Concepts and techniques for record linkage, entity resolution, and duplicate detection. Springer.

Deaton, R., Doan, T., Schweiger, T., 2010. Semantic data matching: Principles and performance. In: Chan, Y., Talburt, J., Talley, T. (Eds.), Data Engineering: Mining, Information and Intelligence. Springer, pp. 17–38.

Decker, W., Liu, F., Talburt, J.R., Wang, P., Wu, N., 2013. A case study on data quality, privacy, and entity resolution. In: Yeoh, W., Talburt, J.R., Zhou, Y. (Eds.), Information Quality and Governance for Business Intelligence. IGI Global, pp. 66–87.

Doan, A., Halevy, A., Ives, Z., 2012. Principles of data integration. Morgan Kaufmann.

Dreibelbis, A., Eberhard, H., Milman, I., Oberhofer, M., van Run, P., Wolfson, D., 2008. Enterprise master data management: An SOA approach to managing core information. IBM Press.

Dyché, J., Levy, E., 2006. Customer data integration: Reaching a single version of the truth. Wiley, New York.

English, L., 1999. Improving data warehouse and business information quality: Methods for reducing costs and increasing profits. Wiley, New York.

Fellegi, I., Sunter, A., 1969. A theory for record linkage. Journal of the American Statistical Association 64 (328), 1183–1210.

Gibson, N., Talburt, J., 2010. Visualizing student growth: Applications of student growth models. Ninth Annual Conference on Applied Research in Information Technology. University of Central Arkansas, Conway, AR, April 9, 2010, pp. 9–13. research.acxiom.com/publications.

Hashemi, R., Talburt, J., Wang, R., 2006. Significance test for the Talburt-Wang Similarity Index. In: Talburt, J., Pierce, E., Wu, N., Campbell, T. (Eds.), 11th International Conference on Information Quality. MIT IQ Publishing, Cambridge, MA, pp. 125–132.

Heien, C., Wu, N., Talburt, J., 2010. Methods to Measure Importance of Data Attributes to Consumers of Information Products. AMCIS 2010 Proceedings. Paper 582. http://aisel.aisnet.org/amcis2010/582.

Herzog, T.N., Scheuren, F.J., Winkler, W.E., 2007. Data quality and record linkage techniques. Springer, New York.

Holland, G., Talburt, J., 2008. A framework for evaluating information source interactions. In: Hu, C., Berleant, D. (Eds.), 2008 Conference on Applied Research in Information Technology. University of Central Arkansas, Conway, AR, pp. 13–19. http://research.acxiom.com/publications.html.

Holland, G., Talburt, J., 2010a. An entity-based integration framework for modeling and evaluating data enhancement products. Journal of Computing Sciences in Colleges 24 (5), 65–73.

Holland, G., Talburt, J., 2010b. q-Gram Tetrahedral Ratio (qTR) for approximate pattern matching. Ninth Annual Conference on Applied Research in Information Technology. University of Central Arkansas, Conway, AR, April 9, 2010, pp. 14–17. research.acxiom.com/publications.

Holmes, D., McCabe, C., 2002. Improving precision and recall for Soundex retrieval. In Proc. of the IEEE International Conference on Information Technology – Coding and Computing. Las Vegas, NV.

Huang, K., Lee, Y.W., Wang, R.Y., 1999. Quality Information and Knowledge Management. Prentice Hall.

International Association for Information and Data Quality (IAIDQ), 2014. IQCP^SM — Information Quality Certified Professional. Available from: http://iaidq.org/iqcp/iqcp.shtml.

Isele, R., Jentzsch, A., Bizer, C., 2011. Efficient multidimensional blocking for link discovery without losing recall. Fourteenth International Workshop on the Web and Databases. WebDB-2011, June 12, 2011, Athens, Greece.

Jaro, M.A., 1989. Advances in record-linkage methodology as applied to matching the 1985 census of Tampa, Florida. Journal of the American Statistical Association 84 (406), 414–420.

Jonas, J., 2007. To know semantic reconciliation is to love semantic reconciliation. Downloaded from: http://jeffjonas.typepad.com/jeff_jonas/2007/04/to_know_semanti.html on December 25, 2014.

Josang, A., Pope, S., 2005. User Centric Identity Management. In: Proceedings of AusCERT Conference.

Jugulum, R., 2014. Competing with high-quality data: Concepts, tools, and techniques for building a successful approach to data quality. Wiley.

Juran, J.M., 1989. Juran on leadership for quality. The Free Press.

Kardes, H., Konidena, D., Agarwal, S., Huff, M., Sun, A., 2013. Graph-based approaches for organizational entity resolution in MapReduce. Proceedings of the TextGraphs-8 Workshop. October 18, 2013, Seattle, WA, pp. 70–78.

Kirsten, T., Kolb, L., Hartung, M., Gross, A., Kopche, H., Rahm, E., 2010. Data partitioning for parallel entity matching. Proceedings of the VLDB Endowment, Vol. 3. No. 2.

Kobayashi, F., Talburt, J.R., 2013. Probabilistic Scoring Methods to Assist Entity Resolution Systems Using Boolean Rules. The 2013 International Conference on Information and Knowledge Engineering (IKE'13). Las Vegas, Nevada, July 22–25, 2013, CSREA Press, pp. 101–107.

Kobayashi, F., Talburt, J.R., 2014a. Decoupling Identity Resolution from the Maintenance of Identity Information. 11th Information and Knowledge Engineering Conference. July 21–24, 2014, Las Vegas, NV, pp. 349–354.

Kobayashi, F., Talburt, J.R., 2014b. Improving the Quality of Entity Resolution for School Enrollment Data through Affinity Scores. 19th MIT International Conference on Information Quality. August 1–3, 2014, Xi'an, China.

Kobayashi, F., Nelson, E.D., Talburt, J.R., 2011. Design consideration for identity resolution in batch and interactive architectures. International Conference on Information Quality (ICIQ 2011). Adelaide, Australia, 2011.

Kolb, L., Thor, A., Rahm, E., 2011. Block-based load balancing for entity resolution with MapReduce. CIKM'11, October 24–28, 2011, Glasgow, Scotland, pp. 2397–2400.

Kotter, J.P., 1996. Leading change. Harvard Business Review Press.

Landauer, T.K., Foltz, P.W., Laham, D., 1998. Introduction to latent semantic analysis. Discourse Processes 25, 259–284.

Lawley, E., 2010. Building a health data hub. March 29, 2010. Nashville Post (online version, downloaded July 24, 2010).

Lee, Y., Madnick, S., Wang, R., Wang, F., Zhang, H., 2014. A cubic framework for the Chief Data Officer: Succeeding in a world of big data. MIS Quarterly Executive. March 2014 (13:1).

Lee, Y., Pierce, E., Talburt, J., Wang, R., Zhu, H., 2007. A curriculum for a master of science in information quality. The Journal of Information Systems Education 18 (2), 233–242.

Lee, Y.W., Pipino, L.L., Funk, J.D., Wang, R.Y., 2006. Journey to Data Quality. MIT Press, Cambridge, MA.

Levenshtein, V., 1966. Binary Codes capable of correcting deletions, insertions and reversals. Soviet Physics Doklady 10 (8), 707–710.

Loshin, D., 2009. Master data management. Knowledge Integrity, Inc.

Mahata, D., Talburt, J.R., 2014. A framework for collecting and managing entity identity information from social media. 19th MIT International Conference on Information Quality. August 1–3, 2014, Xi'an, China, pp. 216–233.

Maydanchik, A., 2007. Data Quality Assessment. Technics Publications.

Mazzucchi-Augel, P.N., Ceballos, H.G., 2014. An alignment comparator for entity resolution with multi-valued attributes. 13th Mexican International Conference on Artificial Intelligence (MICAI), 8857 (2), pp. 272–284. November 2014.

Mazzucchi-Augel, P.N., 2014. An aggregation and alignment operator to solve the entity matching problem. Master's thesis, Instituto Tecnológico y de Esudios Superiores de Monterrey. Mexico, December 2014.

McGilvray, D., 2008. Executing Data Quality Projects: Ten Steps to Quality Data and Trusted Information. Morgan Kaufmann.

Menestrina, D., Whang, S.E., Garcia-Molina, H., 2010. Evaluating entity resolution results. Proceedings of the VLDB Endowment Vol. 3, No. 1.

Naumann, F., Herschel, M., 2010. An introduction to duplicate detection. Synthesis Lectures on Data Management. Morgan and Claypool Publishers.

Nelson, E., Talburt, J., 2008. Improving the quality of law enforcement information through entity resolution. In: Hu, C., Berleant, D. (Eds.), 2008 Conference on Applied Research in Information Technology. University of Central Arkansas, Conway, AR, pp. 113–118. http://research.acxiom.com/publications.html.

Nelson, E., Talburt, J., 2011. Entity resolution for longitudinal studies in education using OYSTER. Proceedings: 2011 Information and Knowledge Engineering Conference (IKE 2011). Las Vegas, NV, July 18–20, 2011, pp. 286–290.

Oberhofer, M., Hechler, E., Milman, I., Schumacher, S., Wolfson, D., 2014. Beyond Big Data: Using social MDM to drive deep customer insight. IBM Press.

Odell, M., Russell, R., 1918. U.S. patent number 1,261,167. U.S. Patent Office, Washington, DC.

Osesina, I., Talburt, J., 2012. A data-intensive approach to named entity recognition combining contextual and intrinsic indicators. International Journal of Business Intelligence Research 3 (1), 55–71.

Papadakis, G., Ioannou, E., Niederée, C., Palpanas, T., Nedjl, W., 2012. WSDM'12. February 8–12, 2012, Seattle, WA, pp. 53–62.

Penning, M., Talburt, J.R., 2012. Information quality assessment and improvement of student information in the university environment. The 2012 International Conference on Information and Knowledge Engineering (IKE'12). Las Vegas, Nevada, July 16–29, 2012, pp. 351–357.

Philips, L., 2000. The double-metaphone search algorithm. C/C++ User's Journal, 18(6).

PiLog, 2014. Master data quality solutions. Website available at: http://www.pilog.in/.

Power, D., Hunt, J., 2013. The 8 worst practices in master data management and how to avoid them. White paper downloaded from: http://www.informationbuilders.com on December 22, 2014.

Power, D., Lyngsø, 2013. Multidomain MDM — Why it's a superior solution. Inside Analysis online newsletter on Downloaded from: http://insideanalysis.com/2013/08/multidomain-mdm/ on December 22, 2014.

Provost, F., Fawcett, T., 2013. Data science for business: What you need to know about data mining and data-analytic thinking. O'Reilly.

Pullen, D., 2012. Developing and refining matching rules for entity resolution. 2012 International Conference on Information and Knowledge Engineering (IKE'12) 2012. Las Vegas, NV, pp. 345–350.

Pullen, D., Wang, P., Talburt, J.R., Wu, N., 2013a. A false positive review indicator for entity resolution systems using Boolean rules. The 18th International Conference on Information Quality (ICIQ-2013). University of Arkansas at Little Rock, November 7–9, 2013, pp. 26–36.

Pullen, D., Wang, P., Wu, N., Talburt, J.R., 2013b. Mitigating data quality impairment on entity resolution errors in student enrollment data. 2013 Information and Knowledge Engineering Conference. July 21–24, 2013, Las Vegas, NV, pp. 96–100.

Rand, W.M., 1971. Objective criteria for the evaluation of clustering methods. Journal of the American Statistical Association 66, 846–850.

Redman, T.C., 1996. Data quality for the information age. Artech House.

Redman, T.C., 1998. The impact of poor data quality on the typical enterprise. Communications of the ACM 41 (2), 79–82.

Redman, T.C., 2008. Data driven: Profiting from your most important business asset. Harvard Business Press, Boston, MA.

Schumacher, S., 2010. The need for accuracy in today's data world. Database Trends and Applications (online newsletter). Downloaded from: http://www.dbta.com on December 28, 2014.

Sebastian-Coleman, L., 2013. Measuring data quality for ongoing improvement. Morgan Kaufmann.

Sedgewick, R., Wayne, K., 2011. Algorithms, Fourth Edition. Addison Wesley.

Shannon, C.E., 1948. A mathematical theory of communication. Bell System Technical Journal.

Soares, S., 2013a. Big Data governance: An emerging imperative. MC Press Online.

Soares, S., 2013b. IBM InfoSphere: A platform for Big Data governance and process data governance. MC Press Online.

Soares, S., 2014. Data governance tools: Evaluation criteria, Big Data governance, and alignment with enterprise data management. MC Press Online.

Sørensen, H.L., 2011. The Liliendahl 101 on MDM. Downloaded from: http://liliendahl.com/mdm-notes on December 22, 2014.

Sørensen, H.L., 2012. Beyond True Positives in Deduplication. Blog Post. Downloaded from: http://liliendahl.com/2012/11/20/beyond-true-positives-in-deduplication on December 22, 2014.

Syed, H., Talburt, J.R., Liu, F., Pullen, D., Wu, N., 2012. Developing and refining matching rules for entity resolution. The 2012 International Conference on Information and Knowledge Engineering (IKE'12). Las Vegas, Nevada, July 16–29, 2012, pp. 345–350.

Taguchi, G., Chowdhury, S., Wu, Y., 2005. Taguchi's Quality Engineering Handbook. In: Part III: Quality Loss Function. Wiley-Interscience, NJ, 2005, pp. 171 –98.

Talburt, J., Hashemi, R., 2008. A formal framework for defining entity-based, data source integration. In: Arabnia, H., Hashemi, R. (Eds.), 2008 International Conference on Information and Knowledge Engineering. CSREA Press, Las Vegas, NV, pp. 394–398.

Talburt, J., Nelson, E., 2009. CoDoSA: A light-weight, XML framework for integrating unstructured textual information. 15th Americas Conference on Information Systems. San Francisco, CA, AIS Electronic Library (aisel.asnet.org), Paper 489.

Talburt, J., Zhou, Y., 2012. OYSTER: An open source entity resolution system supporting identity information management. ID360 – The Global Forum on Identity. Austin, TX, April 23–24, 2012, Best Paper Award, pp. 69–86.

Talburt, J., Zhou, Y., 2013. A practical guide to entity resolution with OYSTER. In: Sadiq, Shazia (Ed.), Handbook on Research and Practice in Data Quality. Springer, pp. 235–270.

Talburt, J., Kuo, E., Wang, R., Hess, K., 2004. An algebraic approach to data quality metrics for customer recognition. In: Chengular-Smith, S., Raschid, L., Long, J., Seko, C. (Eds.), 9th International Conference on Information Quality. MIT IQ Publishing, Cambridge, MA, pp. 234–247.

Talburt, J., Morgan, C., Talley, T., Archer, K., 2005. Using commercial data integration technologies to improve the quality of anonymous entity resolution in the public sector. In: Naumann, F., Gertz, M., Madnick, S. (Eds.), 10th International Conference on Information Quality. MIT IQ Publishing, Cambridge, MA, pp. 133–142.

Talburt, J., Wang, R., Hess, K., Kuo, E., 2007. An algebraic approach to data quality metrics for entity resolution over large datasets. In: Al-Hakim, L. (Ed.), Information quality management: Theory and applications. Idea Group Publishing, Hershey, PA, pp. 1–22.

Talburt, J., Zhou, Y., Shivaiah, S., 2009. SOG: A synthetic occupancy generator to support entity resolution instruction and research. 2009 International Conference on Information Quality. Potsdam, Germany, November 2009, pp. 91–105.

Talburt, J.R., 2011. Entity resolution and information quality. Morgan Kaufmann.

Talburt, J.R., 2013. Overview: The criticality of entity resolution in data and information quality. The ACM Journal of Data and Information Quality (JDIQ), Vol. 4, No. 2, pp. 6:1–2.

Wang, P., Pullen, D., Talburt, J.R., Wu, N., 2014a. Iterative approach to weight calculation in probabilistic entity resolution. 2014 International Conference on Information Quality. August 1–3, 2014, Xi'an, China.

Wang, P., Pullen, D., Talburt, J.R., Wu, N., 2014b. Probabilistic matching compared to deterministic matching for student enrollment records. 2014 International Conference on Information Technology: New Generation. April 7–9, 2014, Las Vegas, NV, pp. 355–359.

Wang, R.Y., 1998. A product perspective on total data quality management. Communications of the ACM 41 (2), 58–65.

Wang, R.Y., Strong, D.M., 1996. Beyond accuracy: What data quality means to consumers. Journal of Management Information Systems 12 (4), 5–34.

Winkler, W.E., 1988. Using the EM algorithm for weight computation in the Fellegi–Sunter model of record linkage. Journal of the American Statistical Association, Proceedings of the Section on Survey Research Methods 667–671.

Winkler, W.E., 1989a. Methods for adjusting for lack of independence in an application of the Fellegi-Sunter Model of record linkage. Survey Methodology 15, 101–117.

Winkler, W.E., 1989b. Near automatic weight computation in the Fellegi-Sunter Model of record linkage. Proceedings of the Fifth Census Bureau Annual Research Conference, pp. 145–155.

Winkler, W.E., 1999. The state of record linkage and current research problems. Statistics of Income Division, Internal Revenue Service Publication R99/04.

Wu, N., Talburt, J., Heien, C., Pippenger, N., Chiang, C., Pierce, E., et al., 2007. A method for entity identification in open source documents with partially redacted attributes. The Journal of Computing Sciences in Colleges 22 (5), 138–144.

Yancey, W., 2007. BigMatch: A program extracting possible matches from a large file. In: Research Report Series (Computing #2007-1). Statistical Research Division, U.S. Census Bureau, Washington, DC.

Yonke, C.L., Walenta, C., Talburt, J.R., 2012. The job of the information/data quality professional. Industry Report from the International Association for Information and Data Quality. Retrieved from: http://iaidq.org/publications/yonke-2011-02.shtml.

Zhou, Y., Talburt, J.R., 2011a. Entity identity information management. International Conference on Information Quality 2011. Adelaide, Australia, November 18–20, 2011, electronic proceedings at: http://iciq2011.unisa.edu.au/doc/ICIQ2011_Proceeding_Nov.zip.

Zhou, Y., Talburt, J., 2011b. Staging a Realistic Entity Resolution Challenge for Students. Journal of Computing Sciences in Colleges 26 (5), 88–95.

Zhou, Y., Talburt, J., 2011c. The role of asserted resolution in entity identity information management. Proceedings: 2011 Information and Knowledge Engineering Conference (IKE 2011). Las Vegas, NV, July 18–20, 2011, pp. 291–296.

Zhou, Y., Talburt, J.R., 2014. Strategies for large-scale entity resolution based on inverted index data partitioning. In: Talburt, J., Yeoh, W., Zhou, Y. (Eds.), Information Quality and Governance for Business Intelligence. IGI Global, pp. 329–151.

Zhou, Y., Kooshesh, A., Talburt, J., 2012. Optimizing the accuracy of entity-based data integration of multiple data sources using genetic programming methods. International Journal of Business Intelligence Research 3 (1), 72–82.

Zhou, Y., Nelson, E.D., Kobayashi, F., Talburt, J.R., 2013. A graduate-level course on entity resolution and information quality: A step toward ER education. Journal of Data and Information Quality (JDIQ). Special Issue on Entity Resolution, Vol. 4, No. 2, March 2013, Article No. 10.

Zhou, Y., Talburt, J., Nelson, E., 2011. The interaction of data, data structures, and software in entity resolution systems. Software Quality Professional 13 (4), 32–41.

Zhou, Y., Talburt, J., Su, Y., Yin, L., 2010. OYSTER: A tool for entity resolution in health information exchange. 5th International Conference on the Cooperation and Promotion of Information Resources in Science and Technology (COINFO'10). Beijing, China, November 27–29, 2010, pp. 356–362.

Index

Note: Page numbers followed by "b", "f" and "t" indicate boxes, figures and tables respectively.

A

Accuracy loss, causes of, 148–149
Accuracy measurement, 42
Alias comparators, 217–218
Alignment Comparator for Multi-valued
       Attributes (ACMA), 215–217, 216f
Ambiguous representation, 24, 24f
American National Standards
       Institute (ANSI), 191
Application programming interface (API), 93
  families, 95–96
  GetIdentifier(), 94f
  GetIdentifierList(), 96f
  GetKeywords(), 95f
  identity resolution, 94
Approximate string match (ASM), 47
  algorithms, 47
  comparators, 209
    initial match, 210
    Jaro String Comparator, 212
    Jaro-Winkler Comparator, 212–213
    Levenshtein edit comparator, 210–211
    Maximum q-Gram, 211
    qTR algorithm, 211–212
    transpose, 210
Asserted resolution, 71
  confirmation assertions, 74–77
  correction assertions, 71–74
Assertion management, 78. *See also* Structure-
      split assertion
  assertion cart, 80
  grouping identifiers, 80
  initial login screen, 79f
  IVS, 79
    home page, 79f
    operating modes, 80
  login identifier, 78
Attribute-based projection, 124–125, 124t
  One-Pass algorithm using, 134b–140b
  R-Swoosh algorithm using, 140b–145b
Attribute-based resolution. *See also* Batch identity
     resolution
  identity capture and update for, 188–190
  iterative update process for ER system, 189f
Attribute-level matching, 46. *See also* Match key
  character strings, 47
  comparator, 46

ER and MDM comparators, 47
  Soundex algorithm, 47
  variation in string values, 47
Attribute(s), 19–20. *See also* Identity attributes
  entropy, 36
  level weights, 110–111
  uniqueness, 35
  weight, 35–37
Automated update process, 66, 67f. *See also*
     Manual update process
  clerical review indicators, 67
    analysis of cases, 68–69
    entity resolution and record linking, 67–68
    ER assessment, 68
    ER outcome analysis and root cause
      analysis, 68
    quality assurance validation processes, 68
  cluster-level review indicators, 69–70
  IKB, 67
  new entity references, 66
  pair-level review indicators, 69

B

Batch identity resolution, 89–90, 90f. *See also*
     Attribute-based resolution
  client system, 90
  managed entity identifiers, 91–92
  unmanaged entity identifiers, 91–92
Benchmarking, 38–39
Best record version, 55, 55f
Big Data, 13, 193
  challenges, 15
  MDM and, 15–16
  value-added proposition, 14
Big entities, 188
  problems, 188
Blocking, 147
  causes of accuracy loss, 148–149
  dynamic *vs.* preresolution, 153–155
  ER system, 147
  match key, 150
    and match rule alignment, 151–152
    problem of similarity functions, 152–153
    for scoring rules, 158–160
  precision, 155–156
  as prematching, 149–150
  recall, 155–156

Boolean rules, 47–48, 48f, 69, 107, 120–121.
    See also Hybrid rules; Scoring rules
  match key blocking for, 157–158
Bootstrap phase, 168–170
Bring-Your-Own-Identifier (BYOI), 53–54
"Brute force" method, 126

C
Capture, Store, Resolution, Update, Dispose
    model (CSRUD model), 28, 161. *See also*
    Big Data; CSRUD Life Cycle
  attribute-based resolution, 188–190
  capture phase and IKB, 179–180
  distributed resolution, 165–167
  large component, 185
    big entity problems, 188
    incremental transitive closure, 187–188, 187f
    postresolution transitive closure, 186–187,
      186f
  large-scale ER
    for MDM, 161–163
    with single match key blocking, 161–163
  multiple-index resolution, 165–167
  persistent entity identifiers, 181–182
    capture based on match keys transitive
      closure, 183f
    Prior EIS, 185
    simple update scenario, 182f, 184f
    transitive closure of references, 183
  record-based resolution, 165–167
  single index generator, 162f
  transitive closure problem, 163–165
  update problem identification, 180–181
Capture phase, 31, 31f
  attribute
    entropy, 36
    uniqueness, 35
    weight, 36–37
  benchmarking, 38–39
  building foundation, 32–33
  data matching strategies, 46–50
  data preparation, 33–34
  ER results assessment, 37–46
  identity attributes selection, 34–37
  IKB, 31–32
  input references, 32
  intersection matrix, 39, 40t, 42
    equivalent pairs, 41
    equivalent references, 41
    fundamental law of ER, 41
    linked pairs, 42
    partition classes, 40–41

    partition of set, 39
    references with sets of links, 40t
    true and false positives and negatives, 41
    True Link, 40
  problem sets, 39
  proposed measures, 44–45
    Cluster Comparison method, 45–46
    pairwise method, 45
  review indicators, 32
  truth sets, 38
  TWi, 43–44
    characteristics, 44
    True link and ER link, 44, 45t
    truth set evaluation, 44
    utility, 44
  understanding data, 33
  unique identifier, 31
Capture phase, 179–180
Capture process implementation, 50
CDEs. *See* Critical data elements
CDI. *See* Customer data integration
CDO. *See* Chief data officer
Central registry, 58–59
"Certified records". *See* "Golden records"
Chief data officer (CDO), 9, 116
Chief information officer (CIO), 116
Churn rate, 6–7
CIO. *See* Chief information officer
Clerical review indicators, 67
  analysis of cases, 68–69
  entity resolution and record
    linking, 67–68
  ER
    assessment, 68
    outcome analysis and root cause
      analysis, 68
    quality assurance validation processes, 68
Closed universe models, 99–100
Cluster Comparison method, 45–46
Cluster-level matching, 50
Cluster-level review indicators, 69–70
Cluster-to-cluster classification, 122, 126
  attribute-based projection, 124–125, 124t
  record-based projection, 123
  reference-to-cluster
    classification, 124–125
    match scenario, 123f
  transitive closure, 125–126
  unique reference assumption, 125–126
CoDoSA. *See* Compressed Document Set
    Architecture
Comma-separated values (CSV), 163, 197–198

Common Object Request Broker Architecture (CORBA), 94
Comparator, 46
Compressed Document Set Architecture (CoDoSA), 163
Confidence scores, 96
  depth and degree of match, 97—99
  match context, 99—100
  model, 100—102
Confirmation assertions, 74
  reference-to-reference assertion, 76, 77f
  reference-to-structure assertion, 77, 77f
  true negative assertion, 75—76, 76f
  true positive assertion, 74—75, 75f
Conformance to data specifications, 199—200
  ISO 8000 standard, 202
  message and supporting references, 201
  message referencing data specification, 201f
  multiple-record schema, 200f
  single-record message structure, 200f
  XML elements, 202
CORBA. *See* Common Object Request Broker Architecture
Correction assertions, 71
  reference-transfer assertion, 74, 74f
  structure-split assertion, 72, 73f
    levels of grouping, 73
    synchronization of identifiers, 73
    transactions, 73
  structure-to-structure assertion, 71, 72f
    EIS, 72
    set of assertion transactions, 72
Critical data elements (CDEs), 34
CRM. *See* Customer relationship management
CRUD model, 27
CSRUD Life Cycle, 119. *See also* Automated update process
  automated update configuration, 180—181
  update problem identification, 180—181
CSRUD model. *See* Capture, Store, Resolution, Update, Dispose model
CSV. *See* Comma-separated values
Customer data integration (CDI), 8, 55
Customer recognition, 89
Customer relationship management (CRM), 6—7, 55
Customer satisfaction, 6—8

D

Data
  preparation, 33—34
  quality, 191—193

science, 14
scientists, 15
Data governance program (DG program), 9—10
  adoption, 10
  control, 10
  data stewardship model, 10
  DBA, 9—10
Data matching strategies, 46
  attribute-level matching, 46
    character strings, 47
    comparator, 46
    ER and MDM comparators, 47
    Soundex algorithm, 47
    variation in string values, 47
  Boolean rules, 47—48, 48f
  capture process implementation, 50
  cluster-level matching, 50
  hybrid rules, 49—50
  MDM, 46
  reference-level matching, 47
  scoring rule, 48—49, 49f
Data stewardship, 65
  asserted resolution, 71—77
  automated update process, 66—70
  CSRUD life cycle, 65
  EIS visualization tools, 77—83
  entity identifiers management, 84—87
  manual update process, 66, 70—71
  model, 10
  rate of change, 66
  root cause of information quality issues, 65
Data warehousing (DW), 6—7
Database administrator (DBA), 9—10
Dedicated MDM systems, 55—58
Deduplication phase, 169, 171—177
Depth and degree of match, 97—99
Deterministic matching, 119—121
DG program. *See* Data governance program
Distributed resolution, 165
  references and match keys as graph, 166—167
  transitive closure as graph problem, 165—166
DW. *See* Data warehousing
Dynamic blocking, 153—155

E

E-R database model. *See* Entity-relation database model
ECCMA. *See* Electronic Commerce Code Management Association
EIIM. *See* Entity identity information management
EIS. *See* Entity identity structure

Electronic Commerce Code Management
 Association (ECCMA), 191
Entity identifiers management, 84
 models for, 85
  pull model, 85—87
  push model, 87
 problem of association information latency,
  84—85
Entity identity information management (EIIM),
 3—4, 10—11, 21—22, 27, 53, 115. *See also*
 Stanford Entity Resolution Framework
 (SERF)
 configurations, 119
 EIS, 4—6
 ER and data structures, 4
 false negative error, 22
 false positive error, 22
 and Fellegi-Sunter, 115—116
 goal of, 22
 identity information, 4
 life cycle management models, 27
  CSRUD model, 28
  Loshin model, 27—28
  POSMAD model, 27
 "matching" records, 6
 "merge-purge" operation, 5
 OYSTER open source ER system, 6
 SERF, 116
 strategies, 53—54
 time aspect, 5
Entity identity integrity, 22—23, 23f
 ambiguous representation, 24, 24f
 culture and expectation, 25
 discovery, 26
 false negative, 25
 incomplete state, 25, 26f
 master data table, 22—23
 MDM
  registry entries, 25—26
  system, 24
 meaningless state, 25, 25f
 primary key value, 23
 proper representation, 23—24, 23f
 surjective function, 24
Entity identity structure (EIS), 4—6,
 21—22, 31, 53, 116
 attribute-based, 56, 56f
  duplicate record filter, 57
  exemplar record, 56
 BYOI, 53—54
 dedicated MDM systems, 55—58
 EIIM strategies, 53—54

ER algorithms and, 58
 IKB, 58—60
 O&D MDM, 54
 record-based, 56, 57f, 58
  with duplicate record filter, 57f
  with exemplar record, 58f
  issue with, 57
  with record filter and exemplar record, 58f
 storing *vs.* sharing, 59—60
 survivor record strategy, 55
  best record version, 55, 55f
  exemplar record, 55f, 56
  rules, 56
  versions, 55
 visualization tools, 77—78
  assertion management, 78—80
  negative resolution review mode, 81—82, 83f
  positive resolution review mode, 83, 85f
  search mode, 80—81, 81f
Entity resolution (ER), 3—4, 18, 53, 119, 165
 appropriate algorithm selection, 126—145
 checklist, 119
  deterministic, 119—121
  weights calculation, 121—122
 cluster-to-cluster classification, 122—126
 comparators
  alias comparators, 217—218
  ASM comparators, 209—213
  multivalued comparators, 213—217
  phonetic comparators, 218
  token comparators, 213—217
 consistency, 115
 with consistent classification, 5f
 de-duplication applications, 3—4
 exact match and standardization, 207
  overcoming variation in string values,
   208—209
  scanning comparators, 209
  standardizing, 207—208
 fundamental law, 19
 information quality, 4
 key data cleansing process, 3
 using Null Rule, 177—179
 One-Pass algorithm, 128—145
 outcomes measurements, 42
  accuracy measurement, 42
  F-Measure, 43
  false negative rate, 43
  false positive rate, 43
 R-Swoosh algorithm, 137b—142b
 results assessment, 37—46
 set of references, 114—115

Entity-relation database model (E-R database model), 11
Entity/entities, 17–18
  of entities, 12
  entity-based data integration, 6–8
  reference, 18
    resolution problem, 19
ER. *See* Entity resolution
Exemplar record, 55f, 56
eXtensible Business Reporting Language (XBRL), 197
Extensible markup language (XML), 191
External reference architecture, 60–61, 61f

F
F-Measure, 43
False negatives (FN), 43
  errors, 22, 148
  rate, 43
False positives (FP), 43
  errors, 22, 148
  rate, 43
Fellegi-Sunter Theory of Record Linking, 67–68, 105
  context and constraints of record linkage, 105–106
  EIIM and, 115–116
  fundamental Fellegi-Sunter theorem, 108–110
  matching rule, 106–107
  scoring rule, 110–111
    attribute level weights and, 110–111
    frequency-based weights and, 112
FN. *See* False negatives
Format variation, 208
FP. *See* False positives
Frequency-based weights, 112
"Fuzzy" match, 46, 49

G
Garbage-in-garbage-out rule (GIGO rule), 92
Global Justice XML Data Model (GJXML), 197
"Golden records", 1, 203–204
Google™, 14

H
Hadoop File System (HDFS), 91, 161, 179
Hadoop implementation, 175–177
Hadoop Map/Reduce framework, 161–162
Hash keys, 151
Hashing algorithms, 151
Hierarchical MDM, 12

Hybrid rules, 49–50. *See also* Boolean rules; Scoring rules

I
IAIDQ. *See* International Association for Information and Data Quality
IAIDQ Domains of Information Quality, 192
Identification Guide (IG), 203
Identity, internal *vs.* external view, 19–20. *See also* Entity identity information management (EIIM)
  issues, 20
  merge-purge process, 21
  occupancy history, 20, 20f
  occupancy records, 21
Identity attributes, 17, 19–20
  internal view of identity, 20
  selection, 34
    measures, 35
    primary identity attributes, 34–35
    supporting identity attributes, 35
Identity knowledge base (IKB), 31, 58–60, 66, 179–180
Identity resolution, 89
  access modes, 89
    batch identity resolution, 89–92, 90f
    interactive identity resolution, 92–93, 93f
  API, 94–96
  confidence scores, 96–102
Identity Visualization System (IVS), 78, 79f
IG. *See* Identification Guide
IKB. *See* Identity knowledge base
Incomplete state, 25, 26f
Incremental transitive closure, 187–188, 187f
Information quality, 191–193
Information Quality Certified Professional (IQCP), 4, 192
Information retrieval (IR), 155
Informed linking. *See* Asserted resolution
Interactive identity resolution, 92–93, 93f. *See also* Batch identity resolution
International Association for Information and Data Quality (IAIDQ), 192
International Organization for Standardization (ISO), 191. *See also* ISO 8000–110 standard
  data quality *vs.* information quality, 191–193
  relevance to MDM, 193
Intersection matrix, 39, 40t, 42
  equivalent pairs, 41
  equivalent references, 41
  fundamental law of ER, 41

Intersection matrix (*Continued*)
  linked pairs, 42
  partition classes, 40–41
  partition of set, 39
  references with sets of links, 40t
  true and false positives and negatives, 41
  True Link, 40
Inverted indexing, 150
IQCP. *See* Information Quality Certified
      Professional
IR. *See* Information retrieval
ISO. *See* International Organization for
      Standardization
ISO 8000–110 standard, 191
  adding new parts, 203
    accuracy, 204
    completeness, 204–205
    provenance, 204
  components, 196
    conformance to data specifications,
      199–202
    general requirements, 196
    message referencing a data
      specification, 201f
    multiple-record schema, 200f
    semantic encoding, 198–199
    single-record message structure, 200f
    syntax of message, 197–198
  goals, 193
  ISO 22745 standard industrial systems and
      integration, 203
  motivational example, 194–196
  scope, 193–194
  simple and strong compliance with, 202–203
  unambiguous and portable data, 193
Iteration phase, 169–171
IVS. *See* Identity Visualization System

J

Jaccard coefficient, 213–214
Jaro String Comparator, 212
Jaro-Winkler Comparator, 212–213

K

Key-value pairs, decoding, 163
Knowledge-based
      linking. *See* Asserted resolution

L

"Large entity" problem, 150
Large-scale ER
  for MDM, 161–163

with single match key blocking, 161
  decoding key-value pairs, 163
  Hadoop Map/Reduce framework, 162
  single index generator, 162f
Latent semantic analysis, 218
Left-to-right (LR), 158
Levenshtein edit comparator, 210–211
Levenshtein Edit Distance comparator, 47
Link append process, 91
Loshin model, 27–28
LR. *See* Left-to-right

M

Managed entity identifiers, 91–92
Manual update process, 66, 70–71. *See also*
      Automated update process
Master data, 1
Master data management (MDM), 1–4. *See also*
      Reference data management (RDM)
  architectures, 60
    external reference architecture, 60–61, 61f
    reconciliation engine, 63
    registry architecture, 61–63
    transaction hub architecture, 63–64
  business case for, 6
    better security, 10–11
    better service, 8
    cost reduction of poor data quality, 9
    customer satisfaction and entity-based data
      integration, 6–8
    success measurement, 11
  components, 3f
  DG program, 9–10
    adoption, 10
    control, 10
    data stewardship model, 10
    DBA, 9–10
  dimensions, 11
    hierarchical MDM, 12
    multi-channel MDM, 13
    multi-cultural MDM, 13
    multi-domain MDM, 11–12
  policies, 2
  relevance to, 193
  system using background and foreground
      operations, 59f
Match context, 99
  closed universe models, 99–100
  confidence score model, 100–102
  open universe models, 99–100
Match key, 151. *See also* Attribute-level matching
  blocking, 150

for Boolean rules, 157—158
and match rule alignment, 151—152
preresolution blocking with multiple, 154—155
problem of similarity functions, 152—153
for scoring rules, 158—160
generators, 151
indexing, 150
Match threshold, 111
Matching rule, 106—107
"Matching" records, 6
Maximum q-Gram, 211
MDM. *See* Master data management
Meaningless state, 25, 25f
Merge-purge
operation, 5
process, 21, 26
Metadata, 2
Multi-channel MDM, 13
Multi-cultural MDM, 13
Multiple-index resolution, 165
references and match keys as graph, 166—167
transitive closure as graph problem, 165—166
Multivalued comparators, 213—217

N

n-Gram algorithms, 211
N-squared problem, 15—16
Natural language processing (NLP), 14
Negative resolution review mode, 81—82, 83f
North Atlantic Treaty Organization (NATO), 193, 203
Null Rule, ER using, 177—178

O

Occupancy history, 20, 20f
Once-and-Done MDM (O&D MDM), 54
One-Pass algorithm, 128
using attribute-based projection, 134b—136b
input reordered, 137b—140b
using record-based projection, 128b—131b
input reordered, 131b—133b
Open Technical Dictionary (OTD), 203
Open universe models, 99—100
OYSTER open source ER system, 6, 7f

P

Pair-level review indicators, 69
Pairwise method, 45
Party domain, 11
Pattern ratio, 108
Period entities, 11—12
Persistent identifiers, 26—27, 84

Phonetic comparators, 218
Phonetic encoding algorithms, 151
Phonetic variation, 208
Place domain, 11—12
Point-of-sale (POS), 92—93
Positive resolution review mode, 83, 85f
POSMAD model, 27
Postresolution transitive closure, 186—187, 186f
Precision, 43, 127
Prematching, blocking as, 149—150
Preprocess standardization, 207—208
Preresolution blocking, 153—155
Primary identity attributes, 34—35
Probabilistic matching, 37, 119—121
Problem sets, 39
Product domain, 11—12
Proper representation, 23—24, 23f
Pull model, 85—87
Push model, 87

Q

q-Gram algorithms, 211
q-Gram Tetrahedral Ratio algorithm
(qTR algorithm), 211—212

R

R-Swoosh algorithm, 115, 137b—140b
using attribute-based projection, 140b—142b
input reordered, 142b—145b
Radio frequency tag identification (RFID), 54
RDM. *See* Reference data management
Recall, 43, 126
Reconciliation engine, 63
Record linking, 105—106
Record-based projection, 123, 165
One-Pass algorithm using, 125b—133b
references and match keys as graph, 166—167
transitive closure as graph problem, 165—166
Reference
codes, 2
data, 2
Reference data management (RDM), 1
Reference-level matching, 47
Reference-to-cluster classification, 124—125
Reference-to-reference assertion, 76, 77f
Reference-to-structure assertion, 77, 77f
Reference-transfer assertion, 74, 74f
Registry architecture, 61
hub organization, 62—63
IKB and systems, 62
reference, 61—62
schema, 61f

Registry architecture (*Continued*)
  semantic encoding, 62
  trusted broker architecture, 62
Representational State Transfer (REST), 94
RESTful APIs, 94
Return-on-investment (ROI), 11
Review indicators, 32
Review threshold, 111
RFID. *See* Radio frequency tag identification
ROI. *See* Return-on-investment
Root mean square (RMS), 216

S

SaaS. *See* Software-as-a-service
Scanning comparators, 209
Scoring rules, 48–49, 49f, 69, 110–111, 122.
        See also Boolean rules; Hybrid rules
  attribute level weights and, 110–111
  frequency-based weights and, 112
  match key blocking for, 158–160
Search mode, 80–81, 81f
Semantic encoding, 62, 193, 198–199
SERF. *See* Stanford Entity Resolution Framework
Service level agreement (SLA), 89–90, 196
Shannon's Schematic for Communication, 18
SLA. *See* Service level agreement
Social security number (SSN), 34–35, 158
Soft rules, 67–68
Software-as-a-service (SaaS), 10
SOR. *See* Systems of record
Soundex algorithm, 47, 218
Soundex comparator, 218
SQL. *See* Structure query language
SSN. *See* Social security number
Standard blocking, 150
Stanford Entity Resolution Framework (SERF),
        112–113, 116, 137b–140b. *See also* Entity
        identity information management (EIIM)
  abstraction of match, 113–114
  consistent ER, 115
  merge operations, 113–114
  R-Swoosh algorithm, 115
  set of references ER, 114–115
Structure query language (SQL), 179
Structure-split assertion, 72, 73f. *See also* Asser-
        tion management
  levels of grouping, 73
  synchronization of identifiers, 73
  transactions, 73
Structure-to-structure assertion, 71, 72f
  EIS, 72
  set of assertion transactions, 72

Supporting identity attributes, 35
Surjective function, 24
Surrogate identity, 18
Survivor record strategy, 55
  best record version, 55, 55f
  exemplar record, 55f, 56
  rules, 56
  versions, 55
Syntax of message, 197–198
System hub. *See* Central registry
Systems of record (SOR), 1

T

TAG. *See* U.S. Technical Advisory Group
Taguchi's Loss Function, 9
Talburt-Wang Index (TWi), 43–44
  characteristics, 44
  True link and ER link, 44, 45t
  truth set evaluation, 44
  utility, 44
Technical Committee (TC), 191
term frequency-inverse document frequency
        (tf-idf), 214
  cosine similarity, 214–215
Theoretical foundations
  EIIM, 115–116
  Fellegi-Sunter Theory Of Record Linkage,
        105–112
  SERF, 112–115
Token comparators, 213–217
Transaction hub architecture, 63–64
Transitive closure, 125–126
  as graph problem, 165–166
  incremental, 187–188, 187f
  iterative, nonrecursive algorithm for, 167–168
    bootstrap phase, 168–170, 173t
    deduplication phase, 169, 171–177, 174t
    distributed processing, 168
    Hadoop implementation example, 175–177
    iteration phase, 169–171
    key-value pairs, 168–169
    postresolution, 186–187, 186f
    problem, 163
      ER process, 165
      match key generators, 164
      match key values, 164t
True Link, 40
True negative assertion, 75–76, 76f
True positive assertion, 74–75, 75f
Trusted broker architecture, 62
Truth sets, 38
TWi. *See* Talburt-Wang Index

U

U.S. Technical Advisory Group (TAG), 191
Uniform resource identifiers (URI), 198
Unique reference assumption, 18, 125–126
Universal Product Code (UPC), 19–20
Unmanaged entity identifiers, 91–92

V

Variation in string values, 208–209
Very large database system (VLDBS), 59–60

W

Weak rules, 67–69

X

XBRL. *See* eXtensible Business Reporting
    Language
XML. *See* Extensible markup
    language

Edwards Brothers Malloy
Ann Arbor MI. USA
April 24, 2015